A Short History of
Medieval Philosophy

A Short History of
Medieval Philosophy

BY JULIUS R. WEINBERG

PRINCETON, NEW JERSEY
PRINCETON UNIVERSITY PRESS

Published by Princeton University Press,
Princeton, New Jersey
In the United Kingdom: Princeton University Press,
Chichester, West Sussex
Copyright © 1964 by Princeton University Press

L. C. Card: 63-18652

ISBN 0-691-01956-8 (paperback edn.)

ISBN 0-691-07135-7 (hardcover edn.)

First PRINCETON PAPERBACK Edition, 1967

Fifth Printing, 1974

Fifth Hardcover Printing, 1974

Twelfth printing, 1991

Printed in the United States of America

To Mark and Marilyn

PREFACE

To the great works of Ueberweg, Gilson, and others I am deeply indebted: I could not have written this sketch of medieval philosophy without constant dependence on these more extensive treatments. I am also personally indebted to a number of scholars with whom I have discussed special questions. Particular acknowledgment is due to Professor Harry Wolfson and to Professor Marshall Clagett. I felt obliged to include chapters on Islamic and Jewish philosophy, but I make no claim to any expertness in these areas, indeed, honesty obliges me to make the confession Gibbon made when he wrote of the rise of Islam.*

The present book is addressed primarily to students of philosophy who are not specialists in medieval thought, but I hope it will be of some interest to the general educated reader. There are many authors who deserve a fuller treatment than I have given them and some who would have been discussed had I been able to compose a more extensive work. The bibliographies of Ueberweg and Gilson will guide the interested reader into those aspects of medieval philosophy which I have failed to treat adequately.

To the American Council of Learned Societies

* Edward Gibbon, *Decline and Fall of the Roman Empire*, ch. 50: "As in this and the following chapter I shall display much Arabic learning, I must profess my total ignorance of the Oriental tongues, and my gratitude to the learned interpreters, who have transfused their science into the Latin, French, and English languages." To this the present author would have to add his indebtedness to the scholars of Germany, Spain, and other nations.

and to the Institute for Research in Humanities of the University of Wisconsin, my grateful thanks for the help which they afforded me.

JULIUS WEINBERG

Madison, Wisconsin, June 1963

CONTENTS

CONTENTS

A Short History of
Medieval Philosophy

CHAPTER I · INTRODUCTION

HE THREE great religious systems of the Western world—Judaism, Christianity, and Islam—have employed philosophy as a handmaid of theology. The degree of servitude has varied with time and differences in these religious traditions, but there is no doubt in principle that philosophical investigations were confined within a set of more or less determinate theological commitments. Sometimes, indeed, philosophical arguments and methods were even used in attempts to destroy philosophy, and in any case the free exercise of thought was hampered by the existence of some sort of religious control of the activities of men. Under these circumstances, it might be asked whether any philosophy, properly so called, could exist. If we take as a standard the kind of philosophizing with which we have been familiar since the Enlightenment, we might be tempted to deny that philosophy existed under such control of thought and action as we know existed in the first fifteen centuries of the Christian era. But all these reflections suffer from a completely unhistorical view of the circumstances in which men act and think. Moreover, to single out the Middle Ages as unique in respect of the control of thought is to be victimized by the propaganda against medieval thought which began in the sixteenth century as a reaction of humanists and reformers against the older ways of thought and action.

In this sketch of medieval philosophy I hope to show, more by illustration than by explicit argument, that philosophy did exist in the period from the first to the fifteenth century, not merely in spite of, but also because of the religious traditions in which it developed. This is not to deny that religious doctrines and practices, supported by vast and powerful ecclesiastical organizations, greatly restricted the exercise of inquiry.

The very subjects investigated were to a large extent determined by the religious aspirations of the peoples and the times. Yet philosophical investigations into the nature of the world, of knowledge, and of human actions and welfare, in the sense laid down by the Greek philosophers, continued to such an extent that it is no exaggeration to say that the philosophical terminology of modern times, as well as many varieties of systematic solutions of problems, were forged during the medieval period.

We must, however, set forth some peculiarities of medieval thought in Christendom, Islam, and Judaism which differentiate it from the thought of our own time. I have already mentioned the existence of an official control of the subjects and manner of investigation by ecclesiastical authorities, but the main point can be made in another way. Philosophy is an attempt to render intelligible and consistent a body of purported fact. In the Middle Ages there were three such distinguishable bodies of fact: the principles of logic as they were understood at any given period; experience (i.e., the data of observation of the world and of man, including, of course, the data of introspection); and revelation (comprising, in the first instance, a body of sacred writings such as the Bible or the Koran, and, in the second, the decisions of ecclesiastical authorities insofar as they were thought to have divine sanction and inspiration).[1] When these main sources of human knowledge and belief were in apparent conflict with one another, it was felt necessary either to reject a part of reason and experience in favor of revealed doctrine or to bring about a reconciliation between them. Rarely, if ever, was revelation sacrificed in the interests of reason or experience. But almost as rarely

[1] Cf. Carra de Vaux, *Les Penseurs de l'Islam* Paris 1921-1926, Tome 4, p. 181ff., who quotes a catechism dating from the twelfth century by al-Nasafi, a Muslim of the Hanefite persuasion: "Science in general has as a basis truth and the reality of things. Hence friends of truth admit the existence of all true and real things. One succeeds in knowing them by three different principles: Sound senses, Trustworthy tradition, and Reason."

was there an arbitrary rejection of reason or experience. The common method was so to interpret the pronouncements of experience, reason, and revelation as to bring them into mutual harmony. And it was the method of *interpretation* which made philosophy both possible and necessary.

That a scriptural passage admitted of several interpretations was already established by the doctrine that recorded events have an allegorical or moral meaning in addition to the literal meaning of the words describing them. For example, events in the Old Testament foreshadow events in the New Testament. That even the *literal* meaning is sometimes couched in *figurative* language was also insisted upon, not only by medieval Christians but also by the Hellenizing Jews of pre-Christian times (for example, in the paraphrases of Genesis, the Targums of Onkelos and Jonathan). Thus, while no attempt was made to explain away all miracles by purely naturalistic interpretations, the crudely anthropomorphic and anthropopathic descriptions of God and His actions were elucidated as merely figurative language. The apparent conflict between the Greek philosophical explanations of origins and processes of nature and those encountered in sacred texts were likewise explained in terms of the people for whom the revelations of sacred writings were first intended. Genesis, for instance, was first revealed to an intellectually uncultured people who did not expect, and who could not have understood, a scientific cosmology. All these devices, then, were employed to make possible a harmony between Greek rationalism and religious revelation.

Moreover, the acceptance of reason and experience along with revelation made philosophy necessary. It was felt important to appeal to the reason and experience of as yet uncommitted peoples in order to obtain their acceptance of a new religious faith, and it was also necessary to defend the faith against the attack and derision of its intellectual opponents. Above all, it was deemed necessary to make the body of theological doctrines internally consistent, and even, whenever possible, intellectually compelling. Aquinas stated the whole matter succinctly in this way: ". . . in Sacred Teaching we can use philosophy in a three-fold way.

"First, we can use it to demonstrate the preambles of faith, which are necessary in the science of faith as being the things that are proved of God by natural arguments, e.g., that God exists, that God is one, or similar propositions concerning God or creatures that faith proposes as having been proved in philosophy.

"Second, we can use philosophy to make known through certain likenesses what belongs to faith, as Augustine in his book *On the Trinity* uses many likenesses drawn from the teachings of the philosophers to explain the Trinity.

"Third, we can use philosophy to oppose what is said against faith, either by showing that these things are false or by showing that they are not necessary."[2] We can find similar, if not exactly parallel, passages in Averroes and Maimonides.

This viewpoint, however, was not universal. There were from the beginning many different attitudes of religious leaders toward the problem of rendering religion and philosophy consistent. Among Christians, Jews, and Muslims we find outspoken enemies of thought. It will be enough to illustrate this with reference to early Christian writers. In addition to St. Paul's hostile remarks about the wisdom of this world, we have the well-known attack on philosophy by Tertullian. "It is this philosophy which is the subject matter of this world's wisdom, that rash interpreter of the divine nature and order. In fact, heresies are themselves prompted by philosophy. It is the source of 'aeons,' and I know not what infinite 'forms' and the 'trinity of man' in the system of Valentinus. He was a Platonist. It is the source of Marcion's 'better God,' 'better,' because of his tranquillity. Marcion came from the Stoics.

---

[2] In Boethius, *De Trinitate*, q. 2, a. 3, trans. Anton C. Pegis, *On the Truth of the Catholic Faith, Summa Contra Gentiles*, New York 1955, I, 25-26.

Again, when it is said that the soul perishes, that opinion is taken from the Epicureans. The denial of the restoration of the flesh is taken over from the universal teaching of the philosophers; the equation of matter with God is the doctrine of Zeno; and when any assertion is made about a God of fire, then Heraclitus comes in. Heretics and philosophers handle the same subject-matter; both treat of the same topics— Whence came evil? And why? Whence came man? And how? And a question lately posed by Valentinus—Whence came God? Answer: From *enthymesis* and *ectroma*! Wretched Aristotle! who taught them dialectic, that art of building up and demolishing, so protean in statement, so far-fetched in conjecture, so unyielding in controversy, so productive in disputes; self-stultifying, since it is ever handling questions but never settling anything. . . . What is there in common between Athens and Jerusalem? What between the Academy and the Church? What between heretics and Christians? . . . Away with all projects for a 'Stoic,' a 'Platonic' or a 'dialectic' Christianity! After Christ Jesus we desire no subtle theories, no acute inquiries after the gospel . . ."[3]

On the other hand we have the views of Clement of Alexandria and Justin Martyr who can be said definitely to favor the use of Greek philosophy in the interests of religion. For, since there is a "Light that lighteth *every* man that cometh into the world" a natural revelation to non-Christian thinkers is far from impossible. And the thoughts of such men can be used to the advantage of religion.

"But lest any, to turn men from our teaching, should attack us with the unreasonable argument that we say that Christ was born one hundred and fifty years ago in the time of Cyrenius, and that he taught what we affirm he taught thereafter in the time of Pontius Pilate, if, I say, they should find fault with us for treating as irresponsible all men born

[3] Tertullian, *De Praescriptione Haereticorum*, vii (quoted from *Documents of the Christian Church*, New York 1947, pp. 9-10.)

7

before him, let us solve this difficulty by anticipation. [2] We are taught that Christ is the first-born of God, and we have shown above that He is the reason (Word) of whom the whole human race partake, [4] and those who live according to reason are Christians, even though they are accounted atheists. Such were Socrates and Heraclitus among the Greeks, and those like them. . . ."[4]

"Thus philosophy was necessary to the Greeks for right-eousness, until the coming of the Lord. And now it assists towards true religion as a kind of preparatory training for those who arrive at faith by way of demonstration. For 'Thy foot shall not stumble' if thou attribute to Providence all good, whether it belong to the Greeks or to us. For God is the source of all good things; of some primarily, as of the old and new Testaments; of others by consequence, as of philosophy. But it may be, indeed, that philosophy was given to the Greeks immediately and primarily, until the Lord should call the Greeks. For philosophy was a 'schoolmaster' to bring the Greek mind to Christ, as the Law brought the Hebrews. Thus philosophy was a preparation, paving the way towards perfection in Christ."[5]

The attitude of Augustine toward Greek philosophy and pagan learning in general is complex, and the following passage presents only one aspect of it. In the eighth book of *On Christian Doctrine* he stated: "As the Egyptians had vessels and ornaments of gold and silver and clothing which that people departing from Egypt appropriated to itself as to a better use, so the doctrines of the gentiles contain liberal disciplines better suited to the use of Truth and contain more useful moral precepts; and some points are found in these philosophers concerning even the worship of God himself; which gold, as it were, and silver of theirs, the Christian should take from them for good use in preaching the gospel!"

[4] Justin, *Apology*, I. xlvi. 1-4 (*Documents of the Christian Church*, p. 8.)
[5] Clement of Alexandria, *Stromateis*, I. v. 28 (*Documents of the Christian Church*, p. 10.)

This passage was frequently quoted as a justification for turning pagan philosophy to Christian uses, and it represents one stage in the development toward a more general acceptance of the methods and some of the results of Greek thought in the interest of religion.

The extreme hostility to philosophy will be encountered often among Christian, Muslim, and Jewish writers. But the view which seemed to gain general acceptance among the theologians and philosophers of the Middle Ages was what may be called the humanistic view that truth can be discovered in many places and is to be appropriated wherever encountered.

It must be admitted that scientific curiosity such as was encountered in antiquity in the persons of Democritus, Aristotle, and the Hellenistic scientists is almost absent from the Fathers of the Christian Church, and not much in evidence among the Jews of the early periods (the Talmudists and even later).[6] Yet from the ninth century onward, Muslim and Jewish writers on scientific subjects are numerous, and serious science is cultivated among Christians from the twelfth century until the end of the Middle Ages. In general, the attitude toward pagan philosophy and science softened as the centuries rolled on, until there are genuine and systematic scientific and philosophic studies in all the great religious groups of the Western world.

I I

It is now necessary to sketch some of the major systems of antiquity which determined the philosophical views of medieval thinkers. For our purposes it will be well to devote some time to Plato, Aristotle, and the Neoplatonists. I cannot hope to do more here than indicate some of the main themes in the philosophies which had the most influence on medieval thought. In the Christian West, at least, this influence was

---

[6] Cf. Marshall Clagett, *Greek Science in Antiquity*, New York 1955, Part II.

determined by the sources available; hence, it is necessary at the outset to say something about these sources.

The writing of Plato which was used by the Latin West was, primarily, the *Timaeus*, in an incomplete translation with commentary made by Chalcidius, at the end of the third or the beginning of the fourth century. This translation and commentary show Neoplatonic influence so that, from the beginning, the Plato whom the medievals knew had undergone a transformation which made him more suitable for Christian uses. Later, in the twelfth century, the *Meno* and *Phaedo* were translated by Henricus Aristippus. Platonic doctrines, also deeply tinged with Neoplatonism, were known to medieval philosophers through Macrobius'[7] *Commentary on Cicero's Dream of Scipio*, and the system which underlies Boethius' *Consolation of Philosophy* is also Platonic and Neoplatonic.

The Latin West, from the early Middle Ages to the early part of the twelfth century, knew little of Aristotle's own writings, but *De Interpretatione* (Aristotle's Treatise on Propositions) in the translations of Victorinus and Boethius was available in the twelfth century. It was at this time also that translations from Greek were made of Aristotle's *Physics*, *Metaphysics*, and other writings, but it was not until the thirteenth century that reasonably satisfactory translations of most of Aristotle's works were available. Commentaries on Aristotle by Porphyry (*Introduction to Aristotle's Categories*) and Boethius (*On Aristotle's De Interpretatione*) were known before the twelfth century, and during the twelfth and thirteenth centuries the commentaries of Themistius, Simplicius, and others were made available in Latin translations.

The philosophy of Plotinus and Proclus was available in a number of works. In addition to Macrobius and Boethius, already mentioned, the works of the so-called Dionysius the Areopagite (translated by Scotus Eriugena in the ninth cen-

[7] Macrobius flourished around A.D. 400.

tury), an epitome of Plotinus called *Theologia Aristotelis*, and a work based on Proclus, *Liber de Causis*, all served to imprint an almost indelible stamp on medieval thought in the Christian West. These last two works came to the West as translations from Arabic and had, therefore, already left their mark on Islamic philosophy.

The cosmological doctrines which Plato sets forth in the *Timaeus* must now be considered. The physical world is in constant change. Things arise and perish. Whatever comes into existence necessarily requires a cause; without a cause it could not attain existence. Moreover, whatever characteristics the world of change exhibits are in need of some explanation beyond themselves. These characteristics themselves are only fluctuating approximations to ideal limits or variations on perfect themes which are only suggested by them; hence, both the existence and the character of physical reality call for causes beyond themselves. Accordingly, Plato supposes that a divine Architect fashioned the world out of some kind of preexisting eternal material[8] looking to a realm of perfect patterns or forms for guidance. His motive for creating was simply that, being without envy, He did not wish to withhold from other beings the existence He enjoyed. The model by which He was guided was the Ideal or Intelligible Living Thing which contained the patterns of all kinds of existence in itself. And the necessity of a preexisting stuff, Plato argued, was simply that change required a medium in which to occur. The Architect was described in other dialogues (e.g., *Laws* and *Philebus*) in language which implies that He is a Soul or Mind. Thus there are three primitive constituents or causes of the physical world, Soul or Mind, Forms or Ideal Patterns, and the Medium wherein change occurs. Soul or Mind is the self-originating cause of motion, the structures of change are

---

[8] "Material" is not entirely correct: what Plato meant by "that in which becoming occurs" is far from clear, but its likeness to matter in the Aristotelian sense has often been remarked.

determined by the fact that Mind or Intelligence is guided by Ideal Patterns, and the locus of change is the Place, Receptacle, or Nurse (Plato uses all these expressions).

The Ideal Patterns are eternal structures hierarchically arranged. (Although it is impossible to discover in Plato's dialogues a single, consistent scheme of arrangement, the *Timaeus* represents the natural forms as one Intelligible Living Thing containing all the subsidiary forms of living things.) These Ideal Patterns are *not* thoughts or concepts in the mind of the Architect, but owing to Neoplatonic influences, later interpreters understood Plato to mean that these Patterns were thoughts in the Divine Mind. The Ideal Patterns are distinct from Mind or Soul, human or divine, although they are available to minds. They are not completely realized in the physical world but, with one exception, are only imperfectly reflected in the forms of physical things. The exception is Soul or Mind. The Architect is represented as creating the Soul of the world as well as the souls of the animate creatures within the world by mixing the changeless reality of the Ideal Pattern with the changeable reality of the physical domain. Soul thus completely realizes the Ideal and at the same time contains the element of change and motion. Its reality is thus an intermediate one between forms and physical or bodily things. The physical universe is thus a living being having the form of a sphere within which are contained the bodies of the celestial and terrestrial objects and the souls of gods, men, and animals.

The *Phaedo* and *Meno* provide us with further details of the relation between Ideal Patterns or Forms and bodily existence as well as the manner in which knowledge of these Forms is obtained by human beings. Since the physical world is in constant flux, everything in it is always in process of becoming and never really achieves stable and permanent being. Such a fluctuating world affects the senses of men but from the resulting sense experience no sure knowledge can be obtained. Yet, since human beings have knowledge of exact and stable forms in the concepts of mathematics and morals, another source of this knowledge must be discovered. Plato found this in the doctrine of Reminiscence. Experience of the physical world and of the social relations of men as well as discussions about them cause us to recall knowledge that is, as it were, stored up in us. This suggests that the human soul existed before the body in some supramundane realm where the mind was not darkened and obscured by its incarceration in a body. Knowledge of the Forms, then, is not an abstraction from sensory experience but a recollection of what we unconsciously have within us from a previous existence, which recollection is evoked by observation of the physical world in which the Forms are copied or imitated. The soul, then, must be distinct from the body, and the consideration that the soul is as inseparable from the principle of life as oddness is inseparable from the number three leads Plato to affirm the postexistence or survival of the soul after the body dissolves again into its elements. The distinction of soul from body, and the doctrine of knowledge as reminiscence are distinctive and permanently influential features of Plato's thought.

Modern commentators (as well as most, though not all, ancient ones) have interpreted Plato's story of creation as taking place temporally as simply a pictorial way of explaining what is, in fact, nontemporal. The Architect is, according to this view, a quasi-mystical figure, used to show the essential dependence of the ever changing physical world on an eternal and intelligent cause of becoming. The order in the physical world and its relatively permanent structure and relatively uniform behavior are caused by Mind directing from beyond the physical system. But Aristotle and some of the medieval philosophers interpreted Plato as literally holding to a creation in time of an ordered universe out of a preexisting chaos. It was this interpretation that endeared Plato to many Christian thinkers. There is enough resemblance between the Platonic Deity who "being without jealousy, desired that all things should come as near as possible to being like himself"[9] and the "God who so loved the world that He sent His only-begotten son" to render Platonism amiable to Christian philosophers.

In fact, it was on such an interpretation that Philo of Alexandria attempted to rationalize the Mosaic account of creation. The Stoics began the tradition of religious philosophy by attempting to adjust their speculations about the nature of things to the views and attitudes of popular religion, but the particular form and the methods of Philo set a pattern which was to be followed throughout the Middle Ages in the three great religions of the West. Philo is of especial importance because it was Plato's thought which he modified and adjusted to the intellectual and religious needs of Hellenistic Judaism.

Aristotle was to play an equally important rôle in shaping and developing religious philosophy in the Middle Ages. He departed radically from Plato on a number of points which constituted centers of medieval controversy. While there are counterparts in Aristotle's thought for almost every element of Plato's system, the differences are crucial. Aristotle begins by rejecting the separation of Form and the physical world (although there is one exception to this to which I shall presently allude). Structure and matter are two mutually complementary parts of each physical object, and are related as the actual and the potential. Matter has the potentiality to assume forms and never exists without the forms of the elements.[10] A combination of matter and form of a suitable kind has the further potentiality or capacity of assuming another form. This is brought about by something already

[9] F. M. Cornford, *Plato's Cosmology*, New York and London 1937, p. 33.
[10] *Hot* and *cold*, *moist* and *dry* are qualitative forms which are the fundamental contraries. Their possible combinations are hot-dry, hot-moist, cold-moist, and cold-dry. Primary matter, combined with these pairs constitutes the basic elements, viz., fire, air, water, and earth.

14

possessing the form in question. That is to say, every matter potentially capable of being further developed by assuming a form is made to do so only by something actually possessing that form. There are some exceptions to this generalization. One is the spontaneous generation of some of the lower animals. The cause always resembles its effect, and conversely an effect arises only from the action of something which already possesses the structure which the effect is to exhibit.

This fundamental principle of causality is defended on two grounds. First of all, Aristotle (together with all his predecessors among the Greek philosophers) accepted the maxim "Ex nihilo nihil fit," nothing comes from nothing, in its full force. A preexisting material substratum underlies physical change: alteration of quality, change of size, movement in place, and the very generation and corruption of things, all require a matter. But it is also true that the forms which matter is to assume must be derived from beings already possessing those forms. In fact, Aristotle distinguishes two actualities in organic beings: form is the first actuality and operation is the second actuality. The latter, the operations and powers of anything, are consequent on the former. In the second place, Aristotle's thought is dominated by several patterns of explanation, several analogies, in terms of which natural processes become intelligible for him. One of the most important of these is the analogy of the artist producing some artefact from some material. The form which the artist induces in the material on which he works must already preexist in his mind. Nature, Aristotle is fond of repeating, works like an artist. The world of nature is thus immanently teleological. Designs are being constantly and repeatedly realized in nature by the actions of causes upon their effects.

This teleology is, admittedly, of an unusual kind. Although Aristotle sometimes wrote of God making something, such expressions are extremely rare. His most characteristic expressions leave no place for a creating or designing deity. The fixity of natural kinds and the eternal existence of the physical world are consequences of his principles of causality and of the inseparable union of form and matter. If matter never exists without some form or other, if forms are only the static and dynamic features of matter, and finally if a form is induced in a material only by action of some material agent already possessing such a form, there can be no creation and no first form of a given kind; hence, the world and the motions in it are eternal. Aristotle is therefore obliged to elucidate the teleology or directed development in the world in another way. Moreover, although there is no temporal beginning of things, the series of simultaneously acting causes must have a first uncaused member. For, because every effect requires a cause numerically distinct from itself,[11] and because an infinite regression of causes of a given effect would fail to produce such an effect, there must be a first uncaused cause, an unmoved mover. The unmoved mover cannot have any potentiality and must therefore be a form free from matter. It produces motion without undergoing motion. Aristotle conceives this to be possible only if the first cause moves the universe as an object of desire attracts things without undergoing any change in itself. This explains the goal-directed activities of the heavens and all the inhabitants of the earth. Each thing, so far as possible, attempts to become as much like the First Cause (or Prime Mover) as its nature permits. Animate beings thus act and reproduce and achieve an immortality (an eternity) for their kind, and all the other things in nature in characteristic ways imitate the Divine life. God (the Prime Mover) enjoys an eternal felicity by thinking of the most worthy object of thought, viz., His own thinking. Thus Aristotle's universe is a finite enclosed system of celestial and terrestrial substances, eternally moving and changing in

[11] The only exception to this, and it is not a genuine exception, is the case in which an agent brings about a change within itself. But in this case, as Aristotle explains, the agent must be considered as twofold, one part of which acts on the other.

accordance with their desire to imitate God, the Pure Form and Prime Mover.

Aristotle's theory of knowledge is determined by the rejection of the Platonic Forms considered as separate from the physical world. If the structures which determine the natures and activities of things are not separable from them, a science of the physical world is possible. Though there is contingency and occasional failure of organisms to develop to their full perfection and also some irregularity in the operation of agents due to impediments or other interferences, the general uniformity of natural developments and movements depends on the forms immanent in matter. Therefore, if animal and human psychological functions are adequate to the task, knowledge of the physical world and the uniformly acting natures constituting it is possible. Aristotle finds that the human form is so constituted that it can, when the sense-organs are suitably affected by external influences, retain perceptions mnemonically, and the remembrances of perceptions can be so unified that the forms of external things are stabilized in consciousness. The human intellect has a twofold aspect. As active, it can abstract the forms from their concrete particularizing attachments and thus conceive the forms of external objects without their material parts. The matter, as underlying substratum, is not directly intelligible since it cannot be duplicated in consciousness. It is known, Aristotle held, by a kind of analogy. That there must be such a substratum is proved (1) by the necessity of a subject when several predicates are connected together, i.e., one attribute is predicable of another only if both are attributes of the same thing, (2) by the need of something to persist throughout an alteration of quality or throughout some other sort of change. Since the human intellect can abstract the forms of things and retain such forms in itself as passive intellect, there is no need of a doctrine of Reminiscence and so no need of a doctrine of preexistence of the soul.

The soul itself in all living things is simply the form or first actuality of organic body. As such it does not survive the dissolution of the bodies of plants, animals, or men. But Aristotle's theory of human cognition has one survival of Platonism. The intellect as active, said Aristotle in a famous passage,[12] is unmixed with the body and unaffectible by bodily changes, and is alone eternal. Without it nothing thinks. This implies that the capacity to think depends on a part of the soul that somehow survives the body. Aristotle's language suggests that God, or at least some purely formal being with divine qualities, is the separable eternal part of the soul by which men think. Man achieves his characteristic perfection and ethical goal in the theoretical life, that is, in contemplating the nature of the world and its ultimate Cause. In this activity we are more closely imitating God for the short time available to men in life. But Aristotle nowhere clearly suggests that each man has his own personal active intellect which survives bodily death, although a few medieval commentators so interpreted him.

The ultimate knowledge which is to be gained from abstraction and induction is, according to Aristotle, a knowledge of the basic premisses of science. Following Plato's distinction between knowledge and opinion, Aristotle holds that the acquisition of true knowledge of principles and basic premisses is often the temporally latest stage in investigation. For what is prior in the order of nature or existence is posterior both in the order of change and the order of knowing. We start from what is more evident to us in perception and, if the scientific investigation is completed, we finally arrive at what is better known in itself. Perhaps we can explain the point by saying what is logically prior is, for us, psychologically the last stage in enquiry. Thus the process of discovery is regressive. We begin with the confused masses presented in sense-perception and, by analysis into their parts, finally arrive at

---

[12] *De Anima*, III, 5.

the constituent elements and causes of those masses of experience from which we began. The complete scientific structure is then set forth in demonstrative syllogisms which give the reasons for the facts revealed by sense-experience. Discovery, therefore, is achieved by experience, induction, and dialectic, while the reasoned exposition of the causes of things is set forth in *demonstrations*. Aristotle attaches a very special meaning to *demonstration*: A valid argument whose premisses are true, necessary, and better known than the conclusion. There can be little doubt that his ideal of all science was taken from mathematics which most closely conforms to such an ideal.

It is necessary to say a few words about the hierarchical arrangement of the universe as Aristotle conceives it. The world is a closed system of celestial bodies moving around the earth as a fixed center. The events in the celestial part of the closed system—the revolutions of the heavenly bodies—occur according to necessary and therefore exceptionless principles, but our knowledge of these events is inexact because they are too far away for us to know anything for certain about them. The events below the moon, i.e., on or in the immediate environment of the earth, are somewhat variable and occur with less than absolute regularity, but, since they are close at hand, our knowledge of them is more accurate. We can, therefore, understand the laws of development and behavior of substances on the earth from observing what is the case for the most part. There is, then, necessity in the events of the suprahuman part of the universe and a measure of contingency in the sublunar realm. To what extent this contingency implies any objective chance is not at all clear. In any case, Aristotle seems to think that some necessary truth about the properties of terrestrial substances can be obtained by man.

Aristotle accepted the scheme of homocentric spheres. At the center of the universe is the motionless earth surrounded by layers of water, air, and fire. The heavenly bodies exist in

spheres concentrically arranged around the earth and moving
with the motion of their spheres. The moon, sun, planets, and
fixed stars are made of a fifth element (different from air,
earth, fire, and water in that it undergoes no change save
locomotion). The outermost sphere contains the fixed stars.
Beyond the universe there is nothing, neither empty nor full
space, but within the universe, space is filled out with some
matter (i.e., no vacuum). The universe is thus a hierarchy
starting from the elements, whose natural motions carry them
downward—in the case of water and earth—and upward—in
the case of air and fire; next, the mixtures of these elements;
then organisms, both plant and animal. The movements of
the heavenly spheres are due to the spiritual substances which
are their movers, and these movements are ultimately caused
by the desire of these spiritual substances to be as much like
the Prime Mover as possible. I do not propose to go into the
very controversial problem about whether there is only one
Prime Mover or many. W. Jaeger argued that Aristotle's
later view favored a plurality of Prime Movers on the ground
that ch. 8 of Aristotle's *Metaphysics*, Book Lambda, is a later
addition. This may well be correct; however, most of the
medieval interpreters of Aristotle read him as favoring one
Prime Mover. Many variations on this scheme are to be
encountered in the Middle Ages, but the general contours of
this system of the universe were universally accepted by
medieval man.

Ultimately, then, the two philosophies which exerted the
most influence on medieval thought were those of Plato and
Aristotle. But, as I have already indicated, both Plato and
Aristotle were interpreted (until the twelfth century in Islam
and the thirteenth century in Christendom) in Neoplatonic
ways. What this means can be understood only by way of some
account of Neoplatonism. It will be enough to indicate the
general features of this system of thought. It was begun,
for our purposes, by Philo, the Hellenizing Jew, who

flourished around A.D. 39 and its most important representatives were Plotinus (about A.D. 205–270) and Proclus (A.D. 410–485). Beginnings of this movement can be detected in the so-called Wisdom Literature of Hellenistic Judaism (e.g., the Wisdom of Solomon and Ecclesiasticus which are part of the Old Testament Apocrypha and a part of the Canonical Scriptures of the Roman Catholic Canon). In these writings, Wisdom is quasi-personified and represented as the first creation of God, before the creation of the world, a kind of effulgence of the divine splendor (Ecclesiasticus 1: 24; Wisdom of Solomon, ch. 7). In Philo, the Stoic doctrine of the Divine Wisdom or Logos is similarly developed. The Logos is a sort of intermediary between God and the world, containing the Forms (Ideas). The Logos or Wisdom of God is thus produced from and by a God who is Himself ineffable. This Logos encompasses the Ideas (Philo, *De Opificio Mundi*, 1, 4) and is at once the ideal pattern of the created world and the power by which the world is produced. Thus the monotheism of Philo is rendered consistent with Plato's doctrines by placing the Forms in a kind of mind derived from the transcendent God who simply *is*, and is otherwise indescribable.

Plotinus developed these and other themes from Plato and Aristotle into the characteristic form of Neoplatonism. The ultimate reality from which all things come is variously described as One, Being, or the Good. These descriptions suggest that Plotinus conflated the three realms of Plato into one: Mind, the Hierarchy of Forms, and the Physical World will all be derived by a gradual series of *emanations* from a single principle. This Source of all existence is indescribable and can be grasped only by supraintellectual means. This reflects Plato's teaching in the *Republic* that the Form of the Good, the head of the hierarchy of Forms, can be grasped only by a flash of intuition, distinct in some way from the insights by which we achieve knowledge of lesser forms. The remainder of existence is derived from the One by a flowing forth or emanation. The emanation *must* take place, because the superabundance of the One must overflow. As the *Book of Causes* has it, all good diffuses itself. In this flux of all things out of the Primal Source, all possible degrees of existence are realized. The flux is, of necessity, a nontemporal process. Otherwise, the One would have to be affected by a cause other than Itself; hence, as in Aristotle and the Stoics, the universe is an eternal effect of God.

The first emanation is Mind (*nous*). It is the unity and aggregate of Forms. When it is radiated forth, its separation from its source produces a turning back or yearning for its source (*Epistrophé*). This yearning is encountered all the way down through the hierarchy of emanations, and is the Neoplatonic interpretation of the Eros motif of Plato's *Symposium* and *Phaedrus*. As Plato had declared that love of the physically beautiful leads us on to the love and knowledge of the Form of the Beautiful, so the Neoplatonists teach that love for the Source of existence leads everything back to its ultimate origin. This Eros motif in Neoplatonism also found support from Aristotle's views and from the Stoic monism.

From Mind emanates the World-Soul which contains active and seminal principles (the "Spermatic Reasons" of Stoicism). The souls of gods, men, and animals in turn, as well as the physical part of the universe emanate from Soul. Individual souls are only parts of the World-Soul and never lose complete connection therewith, although the ascent back into the World-Soul requires a combination of love and acquisition of knowledge. The various stages in human knowledge from sense perception of material things through the knowledge of Forms represent an actual retracing of the path by which the human soul has been derived from the One. The ultimate reunion of the individual soul with its Primal Source is accomplished in ecstasy or mystical experience.

Despite the monistic tendency of Plotinus' system, he remains essentially a dualist with respect to the relation of soul and body. Following Plato's definition of man as a soul using a body (*Alcibiades*, i, 129-131), Plotinus maintains that the soul is distinct from the body, is the principle of bodily unity and function, and is incorporeal. The incorporeality of the soul is further argued from the fact that perceiving and thinking require a unity of operation which the body (being extended and divisible) cannot have.[13] The distinction between body and soul also gives the soul the basic capacity of self-knowledge independent of the body. It is this point (among others) which Augustine will use to refute ancient Scepticism. But this radical distinction of soul and body does not mean that the spiritual world is free from matter. For whatever is generated, since it contains potentiality, contains matter. There is therefore an intelligible matter even in eternal things, the spiritual substances of the celestial world and the souls of animals and men.[14] This doctrine that matter and form are encountered throughout the hierarchy of existence, excepting the absolutely undifferentiated One, is called universal hylomorphism, and will be encountered throughout the Middle Ages. It is espoused by Jewish philosophers, such as Ibn Gabirol, by many Islamic philosophers, and it will be dear to many Christian authors, although some (e.g., Aquinas) will reject it.

There are many details of these philosophies which cannot be gone into here. But these systems were the most influential in the formation of medieval thought. Works of ancient and early medieval origin, many of them anonymous, exhibit variations on the systems of Plotinus and Proclus. Often these variations are intermixed with Stoic and Neopythagorean elements, but the main contours are there. It is true that the

[13] All this is developed in Plotinus, *Enneads*, IV, 7, §1–§9. The doctrine that the unity of consciousness implies an incorporeal soul was previously argued in Plato, *Theaetetus*, 184-186, and it is the first form of an argument which is to be used repeatedly by Plato's successors throughout the entire history of western thought. We find it, e.g., in Augustine, Avicenna, many of the scholastics, and in modern philosophy it occurs in Berkeley, Kant, the absolute Idealists, and even philosophers of the twentieth century such as McTaggart and Keeling.

[14] *Enneads*, II, 4.

commitments of the great religions require departures from, or truncation of, the views of these Greek philosophers. But the influence remains to the very end of medieval, and even into modern, times.

III

Although there are many elements of Christianity, Judaism, and Islam which are fundamentally inconsistent with the philosophy of Plato, Aristotle, and Plotinus (as well as other —e.g., Stoic—elements of antique thought), it is likewise true that many elements favored the use of ancient thought. The strict monotheism of Judaism and Islam could utilize Platonic, Aristotelian, and Neoplatonic ideas of divinity, and the Christian doctrine of the Divine Word was adjusted to features of Neoplatonism. The very language of the Jewish and Christian Scriptures is paralleled by that of the philosophers. Statements such as "The heavens declare the glory of God," and "The invisible things of Him are clearly seen being understood by the things that are made, even His eternal power and Godhood" (Paul, Romans 1: 20), "Lift up your eyes on high, and behold who has created these things" (Isaiah 40: 26), were used to justify causal arguments for the existence of God or to show that the discoveries of philosophers have already been anticipated by the Sacred Texts. Above all, the formulation of creeds (disregarding, for the moment, the fact that the importance and authority of a formally accepted body of dogma is more prominent in Christianity than in Judaism or Islam) is a kind of philosophical undertaking insofar as it represents an attempt to state in explicit form the fundamental elements of religion. In fact, in all such attempts, Christian, Jewish, and Muslim, the language and influence of philosophy can be detected.

It is advisable to set forth some of the early formulations of creed in Judaism and Christianity in order to see exactly what main doctrines religious philosophers were committed to, as well as the limits within which their speculation moved. In the case of the Jews, Philo was one of the first to attempt such a formulation. In his treatise on creation (*De Opificio Mundi*, 61), Philo suggests that the following principles are fundamental: (1) God exists; (2) God is *one*; (3) God created the world; (4) only one world was created (compare Plato's insistence on this in the *Timaeus*); (5) God is a Providence (also insisted upon by Plato in *Laws*, Book x); and (6) belief in God's providence as *accepted* and *understood* will bring happiness. But this formulation omits explicit mention of other beliefs which the majority of Jews from the earliest times regarded as indispensable. Chief among these were (1) the general doctrine of the prophetic revelation of the Divine Will to specially chosen individuals; (2) the freedom of men as the basis of responsibility; (3) the eternity of the Torah; (4) the doctrine of immortality with the accompanying doctrine of reward and punishment; (5) resurrection; and (6) the Messiah. What was absolutely fundamental was never formally decided by a body which had both theoretical and practical authority for all Jews. But such attempts as were later made, particularly that of Maimonides in the twelfth century in his *Thirteen Articles of Creed*, enjoyed widespread acceptance. In fact, it is a part of the official prayer book of orthodox Jews to the present day.

In Christendom the organization of the Church and its official recognition by secular rulers from the fourth century onward made possible the general imposition of a single creed, variously formulated. The Apostles' Creed contains the religious essentials with little of specifically philosophical import, but the Nicene Creed embodies the doctrine of the Logos as the instrument of creation, while the Athanasian Creed defines more precisely the doctrine of the Trinity and the Incarnation. Altogether the formal creeds of the Western and Eastern Churches commit the Christian to the doctrines that (1) one omnipotent God created the universe; (2) this one God is one substantially and of three persons: the Father, the Son begotten eternally of the Father, and the Holy Spirit proceeding from the Father and the Son (the Greek Orthodox formula omits the last clause); (3) the world was made from nothing by the instrumentality of the Son who is variously called Logos or Wisdom of the Father or Light; (4) the Son became incarnate in the God-man Jesus who suffered, died, was resurrected, and ascended into Heaven; (5) by God's Grace alone salvation was possible; and (6) those of the community of believers who are the recipients of this Grace will enjoy an eternity of blessedness in the vision of God in Heaven.

Philosophically, the most important ideas in this body of belief are the doctrines of the existence and triune nature of God, the creation of the world from nothing (a dogma which is first explicitly stated in Maccabees 2: 7), the Son (Logos) as the instrument of creation as well as the Illuminator of all men (John 1: 1-14), and Christ as the Redeemer of men, the Intermediary between God and man through the Church He established. And both the belief in creation as well as the doctrine of the Logos endeared certain elements of Platonism to Christian philosophers from the beginning.

The question of a creed in Islam is, for a number of reasons which it is not necessary to discuss here in any detail, very much more difficult to describe. Its main tenets may be characterized as follows: First of all, it is unqualifiedly monotheistic, and the formulations of monotheism are obviously directed against the Trinitarian doctrines of the Christians. (The various epithets of "Creator," "Judge," "Compassionate," etc. emphasize aspects of the Divine nature which figure in the philosophies of both orthodox theologians and the "philosophers" of Islam.)

The belief in angels, satans (especially the leader Iblis),[15]

---

[15] A corruption of "Diabolos."

and jinni is of considerable importance. Not only does the doctrine of angels play an important rôle in Muslim theology (Gabriel is the angel of revelation), but the doctrine is later combined, by the philosophers, with the Neoplatonic doctrine of Intelligences.

Mohammed is regarded as the last of the prophets or Apostles of God, and his Koran the last of the revealed books, the Torah, Psalms, Gospels having anticipated and foretold the final revelation. One of the most important doctrines concerning the Koran, a natural consequence of its divine source, is the doctrine that the Koran is Eternal.[16] It became a dogma at the end of the Umayyad Caliphate and, in some ways, is a parallel to the Judaic belief in the Eternity of Wisdom (in the Wisdom-Literature) and the Eternity of the Word in Christian dogma. Although the Koran occupies a place in the Muslim faith comparable to that of the Old Testament among Jews and that of the Old and New Testaments among Christians, one of its tenets—the doctrine of abrogation[17]—differentiates it from the Judaeo-Christian Scriptures. According to this doctrine, later revelations cancel or abrogate any earlier ones with which they are in conflict.

The belief in a Judgment and an after-life, which was described in some vivid and elaborate detail, was general in the Islamic world of the Middle Ages.[18] It is true that the philosophers and some of the mystics interpreted this lurid account allegorically, but the average Muslim of the period must have taken it quite literally.

The main sources of religious authority were the Koran, tradition, the Consensus of the Faithful, and decision about custom and law based on Analogy. The first two of these

[16] The Koranic basis for this doctrine is probably the following: *Suras*, X, 37/38-40/41; XLIII, 1-4/3; XXIX, 47/46-51/50.

[17] See the following: *Suras*, II, 106/100; LXXXVII, 6-7; XVI, 101/103; XIII, 39.

[18] See especially *Islam: Mohammad and his Religion*, ed. Arthur Jeffery, New York 1958, pp. 98-103.

have clear parallels in the development of religious authority among Jews and Christians, but the last two are peculiar to Islam. The main sources of truth were, as in the cases of the medieval Jews and Christians, perception, religious tradition, and reason.[19]

The Liberal Theologians (the Mutazilites) tended to reject all the anthropomorphisms in the Koran and the Tradition, some raised doubts about the eternity of the Koran, and, despite Koranic authority, many questioned the doctrine of Predestination.

The orthodox reacted strongly against such liberalizing tendencies, and insisted on the eternity of the Koran, the literal interpretation of anthropomorphic expressions applied to God, and defended Predestination as the only view consistent with the absoluteness of divine power. Indeed, the Asharites, among others, went so far as to deny causal efficacy to anything in the created world, and held that God is the sole real cause.

It is difficult to give a general characterization of the relations between religious authorities and philosophers in Islam. The Caliph (and later in some cases the Emir) claimed to be the principal arbiter of matters religious, and sometimes protected philosophers but more often ruthlessly stamped out any signs of deviation from what, at the particular time and place, was thought to be orthodox. Perhaps the main difference between Islam and the Christian worlds with respect to philosophy was this: whereas the medieval Latin Church assumed full control over philosophical speculation and afforded protection for those philosophers who were engaged in defending the accepted view of the Church, the philosopher in Islam was fortunate if he enjoyed the protection of a Caliph or was left alone.

After the attack on philosophy by Al-Ghazali in the eleventh century, independent philosophical speculation ceases outside

[19] See Carra de Vaux, *loc.cit.*

the Spanish Peninsula, and Averroes is the last great Muslim philosopher in Spain.

Persecution of avowed and overt heretics is generally recognized as a legitimate function of the heads of states, and even Averroes defends this practice.

CHAPTER II · ST. AUGUSTINE

O OTHER single Christian author played so important and decisive a rôle as did Augustine in formulating the main problems of Christian philosophy and in indicating their general solutions. The main sources of his teaching must be sought in the Scriptures and his interpretation of them, and this interpretation was guided by the main themes of Plato and the Neoplatonists. This is not to say, of course, that Augustine was either Platonist or Neoplatonist. This would have been impossible for a Christian, for some of the characteristic doctrines of these schools are radically incompatible with Christian belief, such as, to mention only a few examples, creation from a preexisting matter,[1] the preexistence of the soul, or the doctrine of emanation. But such ideas as could be modified and used in a Christian philosophy were mainly derived from Platonic and Neoplatonic sources.

Augustine was born in 354 in Numidia, of a pagan father and a Christian mother. His first interest in philosophy was aroused by a reading of Cicero's *Hortensius* (a work not now extant, supposed to have been inspired by Aristotle's exhortation to philosophy, the *Protreptricus*). From this work he learned to believe that the wisdom of life can be achieved, and he searched for this wisdom in the Scriptures. His search was at first disappointed, and he turned to the sect of Manichaeans.[2] After many years he turned to the New Academy.

[1] But see Marshall Clagett, *Greek Science in Antiquity*, New York 1955, p. 139.

[2] This sect, founded by Mani in A.D. 238, was a mixture of Gnostic, Christian, and Zoroastrian ideas. It was fundamentally dualistic: The good principle is, from the beginning of things, in conflict with the evil principle, as in the Zoroastrian religion, and the world results from the dual activity of these opposed elements of light and darkness. Man is a fragment of the principle of good and light (conceived materialistically), and the purpose of his life is to free the luminous element in himself from the prison of his material body.

This was a sceptical development within Platonism, chiefly represented by Carneades (214–129 B.C.) who held that nothing can be known with absolute certainty but that we can have several degrees of probable cognition which suffice for practical life and for the attainment of personal happiness. When Augustine was concerned with this sceptical philosophy he went from Rome to Milan where Neoplatonism engaged his interest. He came under the influence of St. Ambrose, and after a while decided to accept the Catholic faith, and was baptized by St. Ambrose at Easter 387. He returned to Africa in 388, was ordained a priest in 391, and became Bishop of Hippo in 395. From this time until his death he was involved in many theological controversies, and most of his works during this time were directed against various heresies. His main philosophical works were written between 386 and 390.[3]

In his Sermons (CL, 3, 4), Augustine asserted that all philosophers have sought the way to a happy life and that this search was the sole cause of philosophy. Although Aristotle and some of the "Presocratic" philosophers appear to have made the disinterested effort to satisfy scientific curiosity their main aim, the efforts of most ancient philosophy were guided by practical concerns, and this is especially true of the great post-Aristotelian schools. Stoics, Epicureans, and Sceptics alike were seeking happiness for the individual by way of a rule of life. Moreover, Stoics and later Neoplatonists sought a philosophy that was also a form of religion, and this amalgamation of religious and philosophical interests was characteristic of the intellectual interests of the Late Hellenistic and Roman periods. It was natural, therefore, for Augustine to think of philosophy as having primarily an ethical and religious purpose. And in the thought of Augustine this purpose reaches the highest point of concentration, for he asserted repeatedly that the only things he wishes to know are God and the soul (*De Ordine* II, 18, 47; *Soliloquies* II, 1, 1 and II, 2,

---

[3] *De Libero Arbitrio, De Beata Vita*, and *De Immortalitate Animae*.

7). The knowledge of the natural world of minerals, plants, animals, and the heavens is valuable only insofar as it helps in understanding the symbolic sense of Scriptures or reveals the traces and vestiges of its Maker (*On Christian Doctrine*, II, 11-32). And he is explicitly contemptuous of the scientific investigations of the Greek physical philosophers as being unnecessary to the work of the Church.[4] And although many patristic as well as pagan writers of the early centuries show a similar indifference or hostility to scientific subjects (so that Augustine is by no means unique), it is necessary to emphasize his attitude toward science conducted for its own sake. He is willing to use scientific discoveries and speculations when they contribute to his main ethical and religious purpose. He believes it a mistake to adhere to any physical theory tenaciously (so that, if it turns out to be a mistake, the faith will not be held up to derision by its opponents). And his lack of interest in the natural sciences is perhaps supported by his Platonic conviction that genuine truth and reality are not to be found in the realm of change and instability which is the natural world.

The data for the Christian philosopher, therefore, are presented by the content of Faith. The firm acceptance of Revealed Truth is the point of departure for human reason. "Believe in order that you may understand" (*On the Gospel of John*, Tract 29, 6 and Sermon CXVIII, 1) rather than "understand in order that you may believe" expresses his fundamental attitude that Faith precedes and understanding follows. But this does not exclude completely sound arguments depending on reason alone for some of the propositions initially believed. On the contrary, Augustine is convinced that reason can establish the need for belief and can elucidate and even establish some of what is initially believed. Augustine bequeathed this conviction to his Christian successors, and Anselm of Canter-

---

[4] On this see Clagett, *Greek Science in Antiquity*, pp. 130-145.

bury makes it the point of departure in his attempts to establish some of the doctrines of Faith by "necessary reasons."

Augustine begins his metaphysics of inner experience" (as Windelband called it), with a refutation of Academic Scepticism. These Sceptics had argued that all previous philosophers (especially the Stoics) who held to the certainty of knowledge based on sense experience were mistaken. For every datum of sense which is deceptive is exactly like the data which we regard as dependable. If some experiences delude us, it is because they are indistinguishable from those which are apparently trustworthy; in fact, illusion could not occur if this were not so. Since no datum of sensation is beyond suspicion, none can form the basis of absolutely certain knowledge. But Scepticism did not stop with the uncertainties of sensation. Reasoning itself fell under their critical scrutiny and they concluded that it, too, was as uncertain as sensation. The inferences from sensation to the existence of things not directly perceivable (the gods and Providence, for example) were, therefore, doubly suspect: the data were untrustworthy and principles of inference were themselves open to question.

Augustine undertook to refute this view by pointing out its internal inconsistencies and by showing that three sorts of propositions are invulnerable to the Sceptical attack: the existence of the self, the truths of mathematics, and the principles of moral conduct. Even if the sensations of a world in flux can give only belief or opinion, my inner experience of myself and the truths of number that I discover in thought resist criticism. The discovery of the certain existence of the self and its intellectual contents provides Augustine with a proof that there is a God and thus gives him the two main things of central religious concern.

If I am deceived, at any rate I exist, and I am at once certain of my own existence, and all that it contains. Thus I know that I am, that I live, and that I understand. All these things I discover when I realize the absurdity of denying my existence. The Sceptic can tell me that I am totally deceived in my sense experiences, but this would be impossible if I did not exist. If I know or believe I am deceived, it follows logically that I exist and know that I exist. And this at once establishes that I exist, that I live, and that I understand. This discovery not only leads to a knowledge of God but also informs me of the *nature* of the soul. The order of reasoning will be, first, the discovery of the self, then of God and His good works.[5]

In his book *On Free Will*, Augustine develops the general course of his argument. Each man can prove to himself that he exists, lives, and understands by the fact that he must do

[5] The resemblances here between Augustine and Descartes are striking, and Antoine Arnauld questioned Descartes about it. Whether Descartes was directly influenced in his famous "cogito ergo sum" by Augustine is very probable but not certain. But so many writers after Augustine used the argument that Descartes could have had a number of sources on which to draw. This is not the place to go into an investigation of the matter but a few facts may be indicated. Since the argument was also used by Avicenna (Ibn Sina) in the eleventh century and was followed by many medieval authors (see E. Gilson, *Les Sources greco-arabes de l'augustinisme avicennisant*, Archives d'histoire literaire et doctrinale du moyen âge, Paris 1929-1930, Tome 3), Gilson has conjectured that Avicenna might have been the indirect source of Descartes' argument. In any case, the argument itself can, I believe, be traced back as far at least as Plato's *Theaetetus*. It was used in the *Metaphysics of Herrenios* (cf. E. Heitz, *Sitzungsbericht der Berlin. Akademie der Wissenschaft*, 1889, pp. 1167ff.), and, above all, it is suggested in several passages of Plotinus (e.g., *Enneads*, IV, 8, 1; IV, 2, 2; V, 3). Now Plotinus' work was known both to Augustine and to the medieval Islamic writers. The latter read him in the so-called *Theology of Aristotle* which was an epitome of *Enneads* IV to VI. Thus the medieval philosopher had two sources for the argument and the metaphysics in which it finds a congenial place. For while the *cogito* argument occurs throughout the Middle Ages in philosophies which are predominantly Platonic or Neoplatonic in inspiration, it is noteworthy that it is not utilized by the relatively pure Aristotelians. For the latter, the discovery of the self is an indirect process which comes *after* the primary activity of consciousness which is the perception of the physical world.

It is worth remarking also that the Sceptics themselves suggest the *cogito* argument. According to Diogenes Laertius (IX, 77) "They [sc. the Sceptics] would say that they sought, not thoughts, since thoughts are evidently thought, but the things in which sensation plays a part" and again (*ibid.*, ch. 104) "[the Sceptics] do not deny that we see . . ." (trans. R. D. Hicks, New York 1925).

34

all these things even if he is deceived. He discovers, more-over, that his understanding implies life and existence, and then a hierarchy of excellence is revealed among things: to understand is superior to mere living as it, in turn, is superior to bare existence. Moreover, the nature of the soul is indicated by the fact of understanding, and, in the works *On the Magnitude of the Soul* and *On the Trinity*, Augustine uses this fact to determine the nature of the soul. Thus self-knowledge is the starting point of Augustine's metaphysics.

We know that we have five external senses and that some objects are perceived by more than one sense. Our reason shows that there is also an interior sense to which the reports of the external senses are referred. By means of this interior sense (which recalls Aristotle's doctrine of a common sense),[6] we perceive the data of the several external senses and also the action of these senses themselves. By means of it we know whether the external senses are or are not functioning. But evidently since animals also must have an interior sense, the interior sense is not *reason* although it is discovered by reason; hence, a hierarchy of powers of consciousness is revealed: exterior senses, the interior sense which *judges* the exterior senses, and reason which is, as it were, a standard or judge of all three.

Now if there is anything more excellent than human reason it will be some immutable standard or judge above reason. Bodies change, life itself is mutable, our human reason is plainly changeable, for human reason often falls short of truth and even when it grasps truth it does so incompletely. If reason, then, can find evidence that there is something eternal and unchangeable to which reason must defer in its discoveries, reason will perforce admit that there is a God. How can this be shown?

---

[6] In his *On the Soul*, Aristotle postulates a *common sense* in order to account for the assembling of the data of the several external senses, the perception of qualities common to several senses, etc.

Each man has his own senses, exterior and interior, and each man has his own reason. Some objects of sense are perceived by one man and not by another, but the objects of reason are common. Thus, when two or more men understand a truth of mathematics, it is the same truth which is understood, despite the fact that their several minds do not overlap or even, in an important sense, intercommunicate. But a truth of mathematics is something which does not change. That two times three is six is necessarily and unchangeably the case. Such an arithmetical fact is not grasped by sensation. In fact, *one* or *unity itself* cannot be grasped by sensation, for the objects of sensation are made up of innumerable parts and have at best a derived unity. Unity itself must, therefore, be understood through our reason, and this by some interior light. What is the case regarding mathematical knowledge is also true of wisdom (i.e., the principles according to which right conduct is judged). Thus each man discovers that we should live justly, that the incorruptible is better than the corruptible, and that the eternal is better than the temporal. These truths of wisdom, like the unchangeable rules of number, are available to all men and shared by all those who reason. Augustine even finds that these two sets of truth are combined in Scripture, for God is said in Scripture to have disposed all things in due proportions.

It has been shown, therefore, that there is an immutable truth, superior to human reason, which is a standard by which we judged things. We do not judge these eternal rules. Rather, by means of these rules other things are judged. Our minds undergo change, the rules of number and wisdom do not. This shows their superiority to our mind. And we achieve our freedom when we subordinate ourselves to the Truth. This Truth is discovered within us, and, in *Concerning the Teacher*, Augustine argues that It (to be identified with the Divine Wisdom) teaches us from within. Now, since it was admitted that if something superior to human reason could be found, either it or something superior to it would be God; hence, God's existence has been established.

The full force of this proof can be grasped only by considering *On Free Will* in connection with *Concerning the Teacher* and *On Music*. In these works Augustine attempts to show (1) that we can learn nothing of pure mathematics or morals from experience or human teachers, and (2) that in sensation the body does not affect the soul, and that the understanding of the contents of sensation require some apprehension of mathematical truth. Consequently the presence of mathematical truth in several different men proves in three ways that this truth has a superhuman source: (a) all truths share a common feature by virtue of which they are truths. This is derived from the Platonic view that resemblance must be accounted for by common Forms or Ideas; (b) truths must be founded in something, and *eternal* Truth must be founded in something which is itself eternal; (c) finally, the presence of the same truths in several different minds (which cannot teach each other) proves that a single eternal Source of eternal Truth must be postulated.

There is another argument for the existence of God which Augustine offers in *On Free Will*[7] which is superficially like the causal proofs of Plato, Aristotle, and the later medieval philosophers. Whatever is mutable is capable of being formed (i.e., given a mathematical arrangement of its several parts and functions). But nothing can give such form to itself, since nothing can give itself what it does not initially have. (This depends on the causal principle which Augustine accepts as an evident truth.)[8] Hence we must concede that all things which exist are produced and sustained by a Providence from which they have their forms. Body, life, and understanding are all included in this generalization, and hence owe their existence and nature to God. There is no doubt that this proof from the

---

[7] *On Free Will*, II, 17; and also *On the Immortality of the Soul*, ch. 8.
[8] *On Free Will*, II, 17.

contingent nature of finite things depends on the principle of causality and argues from the sensible evidence of the change of things in the world. But it must be understood in the context of a view in which the evidence of inner experience is superior to that of the outer senses, and in which the structure of external things can be understood only from the inner evidence of mathematical and moral truth.

Since God and the soul are Augustine's principal, if not exclusive, concerns, we must turn our attention to the question of their natures. Augustine here makes his contribution to the doctrine of negative theology which was to play such an important part in later thought. No knowledge of God exists in the soul save the knowledge of how the soul does not know Him.[9] All the descriptions we give of God fall short, since He is good but without quality, great without quantity, everywhere without occupying place, etc.[10] Yet we can say that God is that than which nothing better can be thought.[11] And since God's message to the children of Israel through Moses was "I am He who is" and "He who is, sent me [Moses] to you," we can say that God is Being in the only full sense of the word. God alone truly *is*, since all other beings are mutable and *are* only to a limited degree.[12] This determination of the divine nature as *Being* in the fullest sense was also to be a constant theme of medieval thought. It resulted from the conflation of the realm of Forms and the Architect of the Universe. For Plato had, in the *Sophist*, placed *Being* as the first Form, whereas in the *Republic* the Form of the Good is at the head of the hierarchy of Forms. The Neoplatonists had, in an effort to systematize Plato, identified the *One*, the *Good*, and *Being* and then made the union of these the causal origin of things; hence, it was open to their successors to choose one of these descriptions to characterize the ultimate origin of all

[9] *On Order*, II, 18, 47. [10] *On the Trinity*, V, 1.
[11] *On Christian Doctrine*, I, 7, 7.
[12] *On the City of God*, XII, 2. Cf. Exodus 3: 4.

things. Plotinus emphasized the One or the Good whereas Augustine emphasized *Being*.

God created the world from nothing[13] by a free act. No cause of God's free decree can be assigned,[14] but we can say that the world is good because God made it. Evil is a privation of goodness and of being, and the theory of evil as privation of being, derived from Neoplatonism, is the main device by which the divine ways can be justified to man. Augustine adopted and adapted the Platonic doctrine of Forms or Ideas. The Ideas now become patterns or exemplary forms somehow in the divine wisdom by which God created the world and illumines the human intellect. The world was created in time and its matter and form were created together. The seeds of all things, the *seminal reasons*, were created simultaneously so that all the future production on the earth was established in the first instant of creation, although these seeds developed at different times. The seeds are, as it were, the active counterparts of the Divine Ideas. This doctrine was later adopted by the school of Chartres in the twelfth century and continued into the thirteenth century among, for example, the Franciscans. St. Bonaventure defends the doctrine, and it constitutes, for him and others, a more rational account of development than the Aristotelian doctrine of potency and act. For the development of these seeds is simply the unfolding of what is in them from the beginning, whereas the actualization of potentialities will be a source of puzzlement because the doctrine of a potency which does not contain implicitly the form is more difficult, if not impossible, to understand.

God is understood by His rational creatures from the shadows, traces, and images that He leaves in His work. So Augustine finds both in physical nature and in man indications of the Trinity which produced all things. This doctrine, derived from the Platonic view of the physical world as a reflection of the Ideal world, is one of the foundations of the

---

[13] *Confessions*, XIII, 33; XI, 5.   [14] *On the City of God*, XI, 21.

medieval conceptions that the world and everything in it are symbols of the Creator. It supported the allegorical interpretation of the Scriptures. God, in fact, is represented as producing the Book of Nature and the Revealed Book in both of which the symbols have a mystical significance beyond their apparent meaning.

The human soul is known to be a rational substance made to rule a body,[15] but Augustine insists that man, a rational soul having a body, is *one* thing. That the soul is distinct from the body is shown by the fact that body is extended in three dimensions and soul is not extended. And we *know* that the soul is nonextended. For nothing is more present to the soul than itself. The mind does not have to seek for itself as if it were elsewhere. Now the mind *knows* that it understands and lives, but only *thinks*, and therefore can doubt, that it is air, fire, blood, etc. But whatever can be doubted concerning the nature of mind does not belong to its nature. For, in confronting my own mind in knowing *that* I exist, I am confronting my own substance.[16] What I discover in this self-knowledge is what the soul is; what I can only think or doubt is what does not belong to the soul.

The soul is thus a rational substance in which is discovered a trinity of capacities: memory, understanding, and will. Augustine's proof of these powers is very detailed, but one of the essential points in it is his argument that memory is required not only in understanding but also in recognizing the objects of sensation. Augustine exhibited a remarkable capacity for psychological insight in disentangling many of the elements involved in human cognition, and, although the student of ancient philosophy will find his antecedents, Augustine's reflections about the rôle of memory bear the stamp of one who has rethought the problems for himself. Memory, for Augustine, includes all that we know, even though we are not

[15] *On the Magnitude of the Soul* (chs. 13, 22); cf. Plato, *Alcibiades*, I, 130c, and Plotinus, *Enneads*, VI, 7, 5.
[16] *On the Trinity*, X, 16.

at the moment consciously thinking of it. In fact, in the hidden depths of our memory we find truth even when we think of it for the first time. And so memory is the fundamental source of all our truth.[17] For even the illumination of the mind by God can be said to be effected in our memory, if "memory" is so broadly interpreted.

The proof that illumination is necessary for true and sure knowledge is undertaken in *Concerning the Teacher*. There are eternal, necessary truths that are supersensible. More than one man knows some of these truths. But there are as many minds as men, no two minds overlap, and these truths can be derived neither from sensation of the world of flux nor from verbal or written communication between men. For sounds and marks are not ideas; hence, the causal origin of the same truth in many distinct minds constitutes a problem the solution of which requires an inner source of knowledge. The Platonic doctrine of Reminiscence was rejected because it required the non-Christian belief in the preexistence of the soul. Augustine did not accept the doctrine of innate ideas which was later adopted in the seventeenth century. His own solution is that the truth is taught to us by Christ, the Interior Teacher, who is always present to each man's soul, and who will always teach any man of good will who interrogates concerning the truth. Thus God is the causal origin of a body of mathematical and moral truth common to the minds of many men. Does this mean that, when we know, we are seeing the divine Ideas? Augustine appears not to think so. Illumination does not involve a direct vision of the divine Ideas. If it did, the vision of God, vouchsafed the blessed souls, would also be available to the wayfarer still in the earthly state. Somehow God impresses notions on the human mind without revealing Himself directly. Illumination is rather the enabling of men to perceive the rules of number and wisdom.[18] This doctrine is, in detail,

[17] *On the Trinity*, XV, 40.
[18] See *On the Trinity*, VII, 3, 4; *On Free Will*, II, 9, 10; *Soliloquies*, I, 8, n.15.

unclear for several reasons which were to be debated in the later Middle Ages. How a knowledge of the relations of Ideas can be had without directly knowing the Ideas, whether the illumination was general for all men, or a special grace conferred only upon the elect, and similar questions remained unanswered, although parties to the subsequent controversies could quote texts to support various interpretations.

The problem of sensory cognition was resolved by Augustine in a curious way. The discovery of the self revealed a hierarchy of being and of dignity in the world. The soul as something which understands is superior to what merely lives or merely exists (as physical object). Since the superior cannot be passive with respect to the inferior, the soul cannot suffer from the changes in the body. A causal action of body upon soul is, therefore, out of the question. Sensation is the active awareness, a sort of vital attention, which the soul has concerning changes in the body.[19]

But, although the soul is essentially active with respect to the body and thus suffers nothing from the action of the body, the soul is passive with respect to itself. For, in forming the images of bodies in itself, it acts upon itself. This action, by which the soul impresses its own awarenesses upon itself and thus preserves them in memory, is necessary for cognition. For in order to recognize an object or a process (such as the lines of verse in a hymn, Augustine's favorite example), my memory must preserve earlier parts of an experience and compare them with later parts. Perception thus involves recognition and, therefore, the mnemonic retention of earlier parts of sensation.

The experience of time would be quite impossible were it not for this capacity of retention. As Augustine developed

[19] *On the Magnitude of the Soul*, ch. 23. The doctrine seems to have been derived from Plotinus (*Enneads*, IV, 4, 19), who maintained that the soul itself is not affected when the body suffers pain but only *knows* that some part of the body is thus affected. Augustine's doctrine is most fully developed in *On Music*, Book VI.

the theory in the *Confessions*, "I am about to repeat a psalm that I know. Before I begin, my attention is extended to the whole; but when I have begun, as much of it as becomes past by my saying it is extended in my memory; and the life of this action of mine is extended both ways between my memory, on account of what I have repeated, and my expectation, on account of what I am about to repeat; yet my consideration is present with me, through which that which was future may be carried over so that it may become past. The more this is done and repeated, by so much (expectation being shortened) the memory is enlarged, until the whole expectation be exhausted, when that whole action being ended shall have passed into memory. And what takes place in the entire psalm, takes place also in each individual part of it, and in each individual syllable: this holds in the longer action, of which that psalm is perchance a portion; the same holds in the whole life of man, of which all the actions of man are parts; the same holds in the whole age of the sons of men, of which all the lives of men are parts."[20] Thus the recognition of an articulate sound or sequence of sounds requires this mnemonic retention which can be explained, according to Augustine, only by the fact that the soul preserves the order and, as it were, a living, moving memory of a past event. This it is which enables us to measure the length of an ongoing process, for we can compare what is now ensuing in consciousness with what is past only if the past is preserved and relived in memory.

Consistent with his Platonist views of knowledge, Augustine also insists that sensory cognition involves knowledge of perfect Forms somehow made present to us by the Interior Teacher. For we can have cognition of relatively equal intervals and relatively harmonious proportions of the data of sensation only if we are in possession of some perfect rules

[20] *Confessions*, XI, 28. *Basic Writings of St. Augustine*, ed. Whitney J. Oates, New York 1948, pp. 201-202.

of number and proportions, and these can come to us only from the Source of eternal rules.

St. Augustine's attitude toward our knowledge of the world of bodies and other minds is conditioned in part by the doctrine that the physical world is a flux the structure of which can be understood only in terms of the rules of numbers which transcend the flux, and in part by the fact that he is interested mainly in God and the soul, and not in the details of physical science. Thus we can only *believe* in the existence of physical objects. Such belief, however, is indispensable in practice and sceptical doubts about physical reality readily would lead us quickly into worse errors than would uncritical belief. The Christian, therefore, will believe in the evidence of his senses which the mind employs with the aid of the body; he will believe in the existence of minds and wills other than his own, and in the testimony of witnesses to events he himself has not seen.[21] Strictly speaking, of course, none of these things can be objects of knowledge.

The thought of Augustine is fundamentally Christian and his Platonism has been regarded the instrument by which he constructed a Christian philosophy. The doctrines of self-knowledge, of illumination, seminal reasons, and of the active character of sensation were to dominate the earlier attempts of the Scholastics of the thirteenth century. Not until the body of Aristotelian writings had been translated and thoroughly absorbed was there to be a serious rival to Augustine. That Islamic philosophers, especially Avicenna, borrowed from the same Platonic and Neoplatonic sources as Augustine made it easy for the early thirteenth-century writers in Christendom to suppose that a complete philosophy of nature was possible within an essentially Augustinian framework. But the time came when compromise was more difficult, and it is fair

[21] *On the City of God*, XIX, 18; *On the Belief of Things Which Are Not Seen*, ch. 1; *On the Trinity*, XV, 12.

to regard Aquinas as the principal representative of a radically different and more Aristotelian way of thinking. Yet even Aquinas accepts some of the themes of Augustine. In Western Christendom no other author had more sustained authority in philosophy and theology than did Augustine.

CHAPTER III · THE MYSTICAL ELEMENT IN MEDIEVAL THOUGHT: PSEUDO-DIONYSIUS AND JOHN SCOTUS ERIUGENA

NE OF THE characteristic forms of medieval thought and emotion is the cultivation of contemplative mysticism. Its remote source is Neoplatonism and it was communicated to the medieval Christian world mainly (though not exclusively) by the works attributed to Dionysius the Areopagite, companion to St. Paul. These works comprise some letters, *Celestial Hierarchy*, *Ecclesiastical Hierarchy*, *On Divine Names*, and *Mystical Theology*. There are references in these writings to a now lost treatise on *Foundation of Theology*. Since the earliest known reference to these writings is in the sixth century (532), and because they show marked influence of Proclus who died in 485, they must have been composed by some unknown person about the beginning of the sixth century. It is altogether remarkable that these works, representing as they do a Neoplatonic system of mystical theology combined with Christian doctrine, should have achieved such authority in medieval Christendom. While many of the great scholastics wrote commentaries on them (regarding them as inspired writings), the doctrines expressed and implied in these works are inconsistent with several of the fundamental dogmas of Christianity. There can be no doubt that the language is pantheistic, and implies that God permeates the world, or rather, that the world is an emanation or procession of God (the very word πρόοδος, from Proclus, is used to express the derivation of the world from God).

The fundamental thesis of Pseudo-Dionysius is the absolute incomprehensibility of God. We can approach the Divine nature by an *affirmative theology* which applies to God the names taken from Scripture, He is one, good, living, etc. But, as we realize that the Divine nature is incomprehensible in its indescribable remoteness from anything in the world, we are obliged to adopt a *negative theology* which denies all the predicates ascribed to God by affirmative theology. Thus we must hold that God is not any of these things and that the approach to God is by way of a learned ignorance; we know Him best by admitting our inescapable ignorance of His nature. We express this discovery and reconcile it with affirmative theology by a third way, symbolic or superlative theology in which God can be called Super-being, Super-goodness, Super-life, and the like. These words are justified because creation is good, contains life, and the like, and the terms "Super-good" and the like imply that since God is the source of the world which issues forth from Him and since the world as effect can contain only that which exists in its cause, God must be superlatively everything that is in the created universe. The universe is a symbolic manifestation of God and falls short of its Source without, however, being separated from It.

The universe proceeds from God as a hierarchy (as in Neoplatonism) ranging through the several ranks of angels, man, the realm of organic creatures, and finally the inorganic constituents of the world. Corresponding to the celestial hierarchy, there is on the earth an ecclesiastical hierarchy of the Sacraments (especially baptism, Eucharist, and anointment), those who administer them (bishops, priests, and deacons), and finally the "therapeutists" (monks and hermits), the laity, and preconverts and penitents. This procession of all things from the Super-substance is due to Its excess of Goodness[1] The several stages in the hierarchy are manifestations or theophanies of the inaccessible Godhead, and the Trinity itself is sometimes thus described.[2] The Super-essential communicates Itself as a whole to those things which partake of It, and

[1] *On Divine Names*, IV, 10.
[2] *Ibid.*, II, 4.

if they share in It unequally, this is due to the imperfection of the participants and not to any imperfection in the Super-essential Godhead.[3]

We can speak of the endless procession from, indwelling of, and return to the Source as a divine yearning.[4] And it is worth noting here how Pseudo-Dionysius parallels the Neo-platonic flux and reflux of all from and back into the One. As with the Neoplatonists again, evil qua evil is nonexistent,[5] and can be characterized only as a lack of being and a lack of goodness.[6] That there should be such a thing as evil appears to be an inevitable consequence of hierarchy: nothing pro-ceeding from the One can be as perfect as its Source, and the more immediate processions are more perfect than the less immediate ones.

As all things proceed from the Super-essential, so do all things return thereunto, and the stages of return are the re-tracing of the procession from the Source. By means of self-knowledge, and by way of faith and the prayer of contempla-tion which is a yearning after union, the soul undergoes characteristic motions which elevate it toward its Source.

It was this work which exercised the chief influence on the first great attempt at a philosophical and religious synthesis which we encounter in the early medieval period: the system of John Scotus Eriugena. He was, of course, familiar with and influenced by both the Greek and the Latin Fathers. Augustine is quoted by him perhaps most often, but he also owed much to the Cappadocian Fathers,[7] especially St. Basil and St. Gregory of Nyssa.

John Scotus Eriugena was born in Ireland at the beginning of the ninth century (sometime around 810), and went to France between 840 and 847 at the request of King Charles

---

[3] *Ibid.*, II, 5.
[4] *Ibid.*, IV, 14.
[5] *Ibid.*, IV, 20.
[6] *Ibid.*, IV, 20.
[7] St. Basil (b. about 331–d. 379); St. Gregory of Nyssa (fl. 371–394).

the Bald. His knowledge of Greek enabled him to translate the works of Pseudo-Dionysius, as well as to read and appropriate other Greek Patristic writings. He also translated the *Commentary on Pseudo-Dionysius*, attributed to Maximus the Confessor, and the *On the Creation of Man* of Gregory of Nyssa. In 851, he wrote *On Predestination*, a refutation of the views of the monk Gottschalk, which was condemned a few years later by the Councils of Valence and Langres. After the death of his patron, Charles the Bald, in 877 nothing more is heard about him. His great work was *On the Division of Nature*, written after he had studied Pseudo-Dionysius, his commentator Maximus, and the Cappadocians (Gregory Nazianzen, Gregory of Nyssa, and Basil), but some of his characteristic views were already formulated in *On Predestination*. In addition to the influence of Greek Patristic writings, it is necessary to emphasize the great importance of Augustine for Eriugena. His main work was condemned by Pope Honorius III in 1225, probably because it had been circulating among, and influencing, members of heretical sects such as the Albigenses. It certainly influenced the heretical philosophy of Amalric of Bena and probably that of David of Dinant.[8]

The philosophy of Eriugena can best be conceived as a rationalization of Sacred Scripture. For it is the source of faith and faith precedes reason, although faith and reason come to the same end. This is justified by the passage in Isaiah (7:9) which Eriugena read as meaning "If you had not believed, you would not have understood." Moreover, Eriugena argued, when John and Peter ran to the tomb of Christ, although they both arrived there, Peter (who represents faith) entered before John (who represents reason). In the vision of God which St. Paul says is vouchsafed the Blessed, reason will replace faith. But true authority and true reason do not conflict, because they both flow from the same

[8] Amaury of Bène (d. 1206 or 1207); David of Dinant (lived some time before 1210).

fount of Divine Wisdom.[9] Philosophy, then, is a rational interpretation of Revelation so that true philosophy and true religion are the same.[10] In this sense we can say that reason is to be used before authority, since reason, radically considered, is the divine Logos from which all authority is derived.[11]

The justification of such an interpretation of the Sacred Text depends on the fact that it was figurative language and that it contains allegorical meanings. Thus although truth is contained in the Scriptures, the proper signs of words are not always used when the Scriptures insinuate the divine nature to man; rather there are similitudes and metaphors which condescend to our weakness.[12]

The Godhead is, in itself, utterly incomprehensible, and becomes comprehensible only by its manifestations in nature and by its symbolic language of Revelation. Thus when it is said that God wishes, loves, chooses, sees, hears, or does other things which are predicated of Him, we must suppose only that this ineffable Essence is being expressed by meanings which we can comprehend. Yet if we attempt, through charity, to ascend through the hierarchy of nature and the literal meaning of Scripture to the God of whom both are expressions, the Divine Wisdom descends through mercy to illumine us. This illumination is knowledge, and since the mind, in knowing, somehow becomes its object, the ultimate vision of God is a union with Him or a *deification* of man. As Maximus says, human nature, when it is joined to God, receives such a participation in divinity that, although it does not cease to be human nature, it seems to consist only of God. Wisdom, then, is the means by which union with God is achieved.

---

[9] On the *Division of Nature* (abbreviated hereafter *Div. Nat.*), I, 66, 555B; *Patrologia Latina*, Vol. 122.

[10] *On Predestination*, I, I. This comes from Augustine, *On True Religion*, v, 8.

[11] *Div. Nat.*, I, 69. Cf. Augustine, *De Ordine*, II, 9, 26.

[12] *Div. Nat.*, I, 64, 509 A.

The highest division of nature is into those things which are and those things which are not. Eriugena uses *not* and *nothing* in unusual ways. Those things are said *not to be* which surpass sense and understanding because they are superior to perception and cognition or because they fall so short of reality as to be beneath comprehension. *Nothing* is used to denote the Super-being of the Godhead and also the privation of being which characterizes everything which, in any way, falls short of this Super-being. In fact, everything among creatures can be said, in a wonderful manner of understanding, to be and not to be. If we affirm what is inferior, we negate what is superior in the hierarchy of things, whereas if we deny the inferior, we affirm the superior. The highest negation is God because no creature is equal or superior to God. Thus a thing is said *to be* insofar as it is known by itself or its superiors, and *not to be* insofar as it cannot be comprehended by beings inferior to itself. This dialectic of being and non-being operates throughout the division of nature although in different ways.

The first question to be asked, therefore, is whether these distinctions of being and non-being are distinctions of reason merely, or whether they are somehow aspects of reality. Eriugena evidently means both, for he speaks of affirmation and negation as applying to our comprehension, yet nature itself is said to consist of things which are and which are not. Even God is said to be ignorant of Himself because He cannot know *what* He is, since He is not a *what* (i.e., a determinate essence). Such a view implies that our negations are founded in the nature of things.

Eriugena also gives another division of nature which expresses more clearly the structure of the universe, and this division provides us with the order of matters discussed in his work. "The division of nature appears to me to receive four species by means of four differentiae: the first is that which creates but which is not created, the second that which is created and which also creates, the third that which is created but does not create, and finally, the fourth, that which neither creates nor is created."[13] The first is God as the original beginning of all things; the second, the Divine Word (Logos) in which are contained the primordial causes or exemplars of the created universe; the third, the created universe itself; and the fourth, God again, considered as the final goal or purpose of the universe and as its final place of repose.[14] The distinction between God as beginning and God as end of all things is due to our twofold way of considering that which is an indivisible unit, and so does not properly name God but only a relation of God to the things which are created. The second and third divisions, however, do not arise solely in our contemplation but are discovered also in the very nature of created things. In the creation, causes are separated from their effects, and some things are simply effects.

God as Super-essential cannot be understood as He is in Himself by any creature, not even by those in the Celestial Hierarchy. But He reveals Himself in, and by means of, *theophanies* or *divine appearances*. We can know that God is by knowing *what* these theophanies are.[15] In the large sense, a theophany means both the cognitive ascent of man to God and the descent of God to man.[16] Theophany as the expression of God is the procession or emanation of the created world.

Eriugena adopts the affirmative, negative, and symbolic or superlative theology of Pseudo-Dionysius. God as the most real and, indeed, the only absolutely real being transcends and reconciles all contrariety and distinction, so that affirmative and negative theology are reconciled in superlative theology. Since God is the essence of all things He may be called essence affirmatively, but since He transcends any limitation and

[13] *Div. Nat.*, I, 1, 441-442.
[14] *Div. Nat.*, I, 1, 442 and II, 2, 526-527.
[15] *Div. Nat.*, I, 45, 487.
[16] *Div. Nat.*, I, 9, 449.

definition we must also say that He is nothing.[17] We reconcile these by saying, in superlative theology, that God is Superessence.[18] The affirmation really contains negation, for God is called essence only as being the *origin* of essence. The negation really contains affirmation because God is not nothing as lacking being, but is only said to be nothing as lacking limitation. The superlative appellation of *Super-essence* is still a kind of negation, because God cannot be known or characterized. Thus Eriugena defends the *learned ignorance* of Pseudo-Dionysius: God is best known by our knowledge that He is forever unknown.[19]

Though God in Himself is forever unknown, He manifests Himself in the created universe. And since all that exists is in God, God can be said to be created in the things He creates. When it is said that God creates the universe from nothing this means that He did not use a preexisting matter which was distinct from, but coeternal with, Him. To say that He created the world from nothing must mean that God created the universe from His Super-essential being which is properly called "Nothing" since it is superior to every nature.

The manner of creation is simply God's vision of the whole universe, for to Him it is one and the same thing to see and to make. And since God can see only Himself, since nothing exists outside Him, and all that exists exists in Him, the universe is created by God's simple vision. The purpose of creation is more difficult to explain. On the one hand, God cannot be necessitated because there is will in Him, and where there is necessity, there is no will;[20] hence, God made whatever He made by His own will and not by necessity. On the other hand, the highest Good ought not to withhold from creating good things which are only good by means of and in the

17 I.e., "no thing."
18 *Div. Nat.*, I, 462.
19 *Div. Nat.*, III, 20, 684-685.
20 *On Predestination*, II, 1, 360 B.C.

highest Good.[21] Furthermore, if God had refrained from creating, He would have remained but a potential creator and would have been less than He is. This seems to say that the creation was a necessity of the Divine nature. It was not forced upon God from some source outside Him (for there is nothing outside of God), but it was, as Spinoza was later to say, a necessity of His nature.[22] It is true that Eriugena never stated this in so many words, but the passages certainly seem to imply it, and the Neoplatonic doctrine that the Source of Unity, Being, and Goodness overflows into finite existence by the sheer excess of Its Goodness without exhausting Itself is found in Pseudo-Dionysius, Proclus, and Plotinus. The conflict between the conception of Divine Freedom and the inevitability of procession was to cause difficulties for many of the philosophers throughout the medieval period.

The Logos (the second Person of the Trinity) is, according to Eriugena, the medium and instrument of creation.[23] Thus the Logos is the unity and residence of the "primordial causes" (that is, the Platonic Ideas) which constitute a sort of medium between God and the creatures.[24] They are coeternally created in the Logos, but are only in a limited sense coeternal with the Father, since He alone, as the cause of the Son and the Holy Spirit, has eternity in the strict sense. The Holy Spirit is the means by which the Father distributes the primordial causes in the manifested effects which are the results of creation. But Eriugena insists that the multiplicity of primordial causes is to be found only in their effects, so that this multiplicity and its order exist for our minds. The substances of created things thus proceed from the primordial causes into existence.

[21] *Div. Nat.*, v, 33, 952.
[22] The Procession of Creatures appears necessitated and Eriugena seems to hold also that the same is true of the return of all things into God.
[23] Here the author follows the Johannine Gospel I: 3.
[24] *Div. Nat.*, II, 20, 683. These *primordial causes* are also described as primordial exemplars, predestinations, definitions, divine wishes or intentions, ideas, species or forms, prototypes, etc., *Div. Nat.*, II, 3, 529.

The material world is constituted by a coming together of immaterial qualities which are sensibly perceptible only in their coagulation.[25] The spatiotemporal world of bodies, therefore, is constituted from incorporeal qualities. This doctrine is essential to Eriugena's view that the being of all created things consists in their being understood by God. God's knowledge, unlike ours, is causal, and, in knowing, God creates. Human knowledge on the other hand is entirely an effect of the things which are known.

Following a tradition which he found in the Greek Fathers (especially Gregory of Nyssa) and which goes back to Greek philosophy, Eriugena regards man as a microcosm, a lesser world, in which the whole creation is summed up. For the ideas of all inferior creatures exist in man, and, because the most essential being of things consists in their being understood, the whole creation may be said to exist in man. There is, in fact, a twofold existence of every creature inferior to man: first, as idea, and second, together with that composition of qualities which constitute body. In their higher existence, the creatures exist in man.

But man himself is a certain idea eternally formed or created in the Divine Mind. His knowledge of things and of the liberal disciplines (hidden as a result of the Fall) can be called forth if man is reformed by teaching and illuminated by Divine Grace. Man can know of himself *that* he exists, but not *what* he is. For what man is is concealed in the depths of Divine Wisdom which no man can comprehend. Man was created a rational animal because God wished to create every creature in him, that is, so that man would be a microcosm in which both the celestial and the terrestrial worlds are reflected. But we cannot explain why God wished every creature to be created in man. It seems that here one of the consequences of the principle of plenitude (that is to say, the principle that

[25] This idea is derived from the Cappadocian Fathers, Basil and Gregory of Nyssa.

every possible degree of being must be emanated from the Divine Goodness) is sidestepped in the interests of Christian theology. Although the doctrine of emanation in any form seriously compromises the freedom of the Christian deity, Eriugena is obliged to temper these consequences as much as possible.

As man is a microcosm so he is, as it were, in the midst of the created universe, and, as all things are created in man, so all things will return to their ultimate repose through man. The procession of creatures from God involves the return of all things into God at the end of time. Thus the material body will be resolved into the four elements, and body (as a concourse of immaterial qualities) will be resolved into spirit. The spirit, in turn, will be resolved into the primordial causes. The ultimate resolution of all things into God does not involve a loss of their individual natures. The restoration of all things in their causes is possible because the corporeal existence of things is but a trace or shadow of spiritual existence.

Eriugena represents human knowledge of things as both innate and sensibly acquired. Knowledge is, in its authentic form, innate in man, although the materials of knowledge come through sensation. But these sensations are unrelated until reason orders and unifies them.

We have seen that the attempt to combine a Neoplatonic system with Christianity is fraught with difficulties. Eriugena attempts to represent God as both transcendent of and yet immanent in the universe. God is free yet the procession from God and the return to God is necessitated. He carries this notion of the necessary return of all into God so far that he really abandons the usual doctrine of punishment of the damned. It is not surprising that his works were repeatedly condemned in the Middle Ages or that his works had a continued attraction. For there is a conflict, in the tendencies of Christian thought, between the plurality of free individuals and the necessary dependence of all beings on God. That

Eriugena was unsuccessful in reconciling these conflicts is wholly understandable. A radical pluralism of free individuals cannot be made consistent with the doctrine of dependence of all things on God, especially when this dependence is interpreted as Eriugena felt constrained to interpret it, for he could explain the dependence only by an identification of God with the created universe.

CHAPTER IV · ANSELM AND THE BEGINNINGS OF SCHOLASTICISM

LTHOUGH there was very little philosophy worthy of the name written in Europe from Eriugena to Anselm, there are some discussions that foreshadow the developments of the twelfth century. We may single out two problems of importance: the place of *dialectic* (or in more modern terms, logic) in theology, and the question about universals.

The problem of universals was introduced to the medieval Latin world in the following way: Porphyry, the disciple of Plotinus, wrote an *Introduction* [*Isagoge*] *to Aristotle's Categories* in which he proposed to discuss the nature of "genus, species, difference, property, and accident."[1] But Porphyry went on to say that "I shall refuse to say concerning genera and species whether they subsist, whether they are corporeal or incorporeal, and whether they are separated from sensible things or are placed in sensible things. For such questions are profound and require greater study." The translation and commentary of Boethius, and the problem of universals was commonly discussed in connection with Boethius' *Commentaries*.

One particular doctrine set forth in Porphyry's *Introduction* gave some of the earlier medieval students of that work a point of departure for the view known as extreme realism,

---

[1] In addition to the doctrine of *Categories*, i.e., the classification of different kinds of being or of "things said in an uncombined way"—namely, *substance, quantity, quality, relation, place, time, situation, condition, action,* and *passion*—Aristotle has a doctrine about the ways in which terms occur in the predicates of statements. Aristotle's own classification of these ways of predication was: *definition, genus, property,* and *accident.* This means that the predicate of a statement can stand to its subject as being either the definition of the subject (e.g., *a triangle is a plane figure bounded by three straight lines*), or its genus (e.g., a triangle is a *plane figure*), or a property of the subject (e.g., a triangle has *two right angles as sum of its interior angles*), or an accident of the subject (e.g., some triangle is *five inches on one side*).

58

that is to say, the view that universals are *things* which are in some way outside consciousness and prior to sensible individuals. For Porphyry had asserted that an individual is a unique collection of attributes. Thus the difference between two human beings, say Socrates and Plato, consists in the fact that Socrates is constituted by a collection of attributes which is different in at least one constituent from the collection of attributes which characterize Plato (or any other human individual). This was sometimes taken to mean that the individual can be constituted from the species by adding to it some unique set of attributes. On this view, the individual is literally derived from the species, so that the universal nature becomes individual simply by adding accidental characteristics to it.

Thus we find Remy of Auxerre (841-908) holding that "man is the substantial unity of many men," and Gerbert, echoing with evident agreement the words of Eriugena, maintained that the art which divides genera into species and resolves species into genera is not man-made but was used in the nature of things by the Author of all arts. Again, a certain Odo of Tournai (who wrote around 1092) maintained that the nature of man is one thing present in all human beings and that God produces a new human individual merely by creating a new attribute of the permanent substance which is man.

There is evidence from the writings attributed to Eric of Auxerre (841-876) and from some anonymous works[2] that the problem of universals was stated in such a way that the position known as nominalism could have easily arisen, but the first one known to have defended the position is Roscelinus (c. 1050–1120). He opposed the view that the universal is a real thing, and is said to have held that genera and species are

59

words or *vocal emissions* merely. Since nothing of his views remain in any writings, we are entirely dependent on the reports of his opponents—Anselm, Abelard, John of Salisbury —and on the accounts or notices of Otto of Freising and the author of *On Genera and Species*.[3] The outlines of an answer to the problem of universals had already been worked out in Boethius' *Commentaries on Porphyry* along lines which the nominalist Abelard was later to exploit.[4] I shall discuss this problem in detail when we come to Abelard.

The other question which disturbed the theological writers of the eleventh and twelfth centuries was the rôle of dialectic in theological and philosophical discussions. While some favored the application of logical rules of inference to the difficulties of religious dogma, there were strong voices against it. Chief among them was Peter Damian (1007-1072). In a tract *On Divine Omnipotence*, he argued that dialectic must be subservient to theology. He appeared to emphasize the divine omnipotence to such an extent that, not only the ordinary uniformities of nature, but also the principles of logic as applied to natural events are dependent on the absolutely omnipotent will of God. Thus St. Jerome had stated that, although God is omnipotent, he cannot undo what has already happened (e.g., God cannot restore virginity to a girl who has lost it). Damian replied that the laws of nature and of logic are founded by divine power, and that God is therefore not subject to the laws He has established. God can thus undo what is done, for He dwells in an eternal present, and to Him the past, present, and future in our transitory world are all equally present. Hence, while Damian rejects the proposition that what God has made, He will not have made, he still

[3] Sometimes identified as Joscelin of Soissons.

[4] Although Boethius explained that he was working out a solution along the lines of Aristotle "not in the least because we approved of it, but because this book has been written for the *Categories*, of which Aristotle is the author." (*The Second Edition of the Commentaries on the Isagoge of Porphyry*, translated in R. McKeon, *Selections from Medieval Philosophers*, New York 1929, I, 98.)

maintains that "God in His invariable and most constant eternity can so bring it about what will have been done in our transitory world may not be done; so that we can say: God can so act that Rome, which was founded in ancient times, will not have been founded."[5] The attribution of human logic to God is thus a strictly limited affair.

This discussion is but a part of Damian's general attack on dialectic and other disciplines. A religious man has little need of them, and in any case, philosophy must serve the Scriptures as a maid serves her mistress.

The place of dialectic and philosophy in the resolution of the problems of theologians in the eleventh and twelfth centuries is best illustrated by Anselm of Canterbury who represents a position between the extreme dialecticians and anti-dialecticians of his time, and is, in many ways, the beginner of the characteristic form which philosophy assumes in the twelfth and later centuries of the medieval period. As we shall see, his views on the use of reason and the status of logical principles in some ways resemble those of Damian and in other ways those of the great scholastics of the thirteenth and fourteenth centuries.

St. Anselm was born in 1033 in Piedmont. Joining the Benedictine order, he became Prior in 1063, Abbot of Bec in 1078, and Archbishop of Canterbury in 1093. He died in 1109. His main philosophical works are two treatises on the existence and nature of God (*Monologion* and *Proslogion*), a defense of his famous argument for the existence of God against his critic Gaunilon (*Liber Apologeticus*), and a dialogue (*De Veritate*). His theological tracts, however, often throw light on his philosophical views.[6]

[5] *On Divine Omnipotence*, ch. 15.
[6] The theological works are principally as follows: *De Fide Trinitatis* (On Faith in the Trinity), *De Incarnatione Verbi* (On the Incarnation of the Word), *Cur Deus Homo* (Why God Became Man), *De Libero Arbitrio* (On Free Will), and *De Concordia Praescientia Dei cum Libero Arbitrio* (On the Agreement between Divine Foreknowledge and Freedom of the Will).

Anselm adopted the view of Augustine that faith precedes understanding and provides the data of understanding. And, although we believe in order to understand rather than understand so that we may believe, we would be negligent if we do not try to understand that which we believe. It turns out, in fact, that we can give *necessary reasons* for some parts of our belief, which means that some of the constituents of faith can be demonstrated. Understanding is a stage of human consciousness midway between mere belief and the beatific vision of God promised by the Scriptures[7] to those who are saved. The desire to understand is a yearning to recover what was lost by Adam's Fall and this desire leads man from faith by way of understanding to the ultimate vision of God in Paradise. Beginning, then, with the data of faith which is an initial experience, we are to proceed by means of necessary reasons to understanding. While reason does not depend on faith, it must first be judged according to its agreement with faith. Thus, while Anselm speaks of proof by necessary reasons, he always qualifies this by his willingness to subject the results of his reasoning to ecclesiastical approbation.

We have first to ask what Anselm means by "necessary reasons." It is clear, I think, from the language he uses in stating his proofs and arguments, that, for Anselm, the *necessary reasons* are logically true propositions and logically valid inferences. Many of his arguments are in the form of reductions to absurdity, i.e., they show that the denial of a proposition or the rejection of a conclusion results in self-contradiction. It seems, therefore, that the necessity of a proposition or an inference depends on the self-contradictory character of its negation or rejection. It is clear that necessary propositions are true, but when we ask concerning the basis of these necessary truths, Anselm's views become somewhat incoherent.

Following Augustine, Anselm holds that our knowledge of

---

[7] St. Paul: "Now we see as in a mirror enigmatically, then we shall see face to face." *Corinthians* I: 13.

necessary truth comes from an illumination, from the Light which enlightens every man in this world. And he seems to believe that the very necessity of logical truth depends on the Divine Will: "And as, when God does a thing, since it has been done, it cannot be undone, but it is always true that it was done, still it is not rightly said that it is impossible for God that He make what is past not to be past. For in this case no necessity of not making or impossibility of making operates, but only the will of God which always wills that truth is ever immutable, as He is Truth."[8] We can suppose, of course, that Anselm did not intend this dependence of necessary truth on the Divine Will to apply as universally as the above quotation seems to imply. As the text stands, however, Anselm's view would appear to make necessary truth a consequence of the Divine Will. If so, this would weaken the force of his arguments for the existence of God, for all those arguments are based on necessary reasons which, as philosophical arguments, should be independent of assumptions about God if they are sufficient for proving that there is a God.

In order to have a full view of the assumptions which underlie Anselm's proofs for the existence of God, we must discuss his doctrine of truth. Anselm distinguishes several kind of truths. There is the truth of affirmative and negative judgments: A judgment or enunciation is true if it signifies correctly, i.e., when what is asserted is in fact the case. Then there is the truth of opinion or thought: A thought is likewise true when what is thought is the case, or when thought is as it should be. Anselm further finds a truth of will: A will is true when it is right, i.e., when one wills that which should be willed. There is also a truth in things: things are true when they are as they ought to be, i.e., when they are essences which conform to their archetypes in the supreme Truth which is God. All these truths have something in common, namely,

[8] *Cur Deus Homo*, II, 18.

a correctness or rectitude which is perceptible only to the mind. This correctness consists also in a conformity to a standard. We can therefore also say that God is *the Truth* because He is the ultimate cause of these several kinds of truth: things are effects of divine Truth and causes of the truth of thought and of judgments, while the truth of thought and judgment is merely the effect of the truth of things. The proof that there is, and must be, a supreme Truth is simply that if we say that there was a time before there was any truth and if we speak truly, then there was truth before there was truth which is inconsistent. Hence, an eternal Truth must exist, and, as all truth must have something by which it is true, there must be a Supreme Truth. The main interest which Anselm's views about truth has for us is their connection with his proof for the existence of God given in the *Proslogion*. Before I discuss this proof, known since Kant as the ontological proof, but often referred to by medieval philosophers as the Argument of Anselm (*Ratio Anselmi*), it will be well to examine the proofs given in his *Monologion*.

Whenever several things possess any attribute, whether in an equal or unequal degree, they possess it by virtue of something which is the same in all of them. That by virtue of which several things possess the same attribute (in equal or unequal degree) must be that attribute in its highest degree and it must be that attribute existing through itself (and not through some other thing). Now since we see several degrees of goodness in things, it follows that there must be something which is supremely good through itself. Again as we know that there are degrees of greatness, we can similarly infer that there is a maximum greatness, i.e., a being which is great through itself. Most important of all, we know that whatever exists exists either by virtue of something or by virtue of nothing. But it is out of the question that something can exist by virtue of nothing; therefore, whatever exists exists through (or by means of) something. Hence, either all things exist through many things which, in turn, exist through (or by means of) themselves, or there is exactly one thing existing through itself by means of which all other things exist. Now if there are several things each of which have the attribute of existing through itself, there must be something which *is* this very attribute of existing-through-itself, for we cannot suppose that a plurality of self-existing things give to each other this attribute of self-existence since this would mean that an independently existing thing derived its existence from another thing and so would be both independent and yet dependent. The only alternative remaining, then, is that there can be only one thing through which all other things exist. This Being is the maximum in the hierarchy of beings.

In all these arguments we notice the use of maxims of ancient philosophy, modified to suit the purposes of an essentially Augustinian metaphysics. The assumptions of Plato that a plurality of resembling things presupposes an attribute (or attributes) by means of which such resemblance is possible is combined with the causal assumption that whatever exists finitely must have a cause. This combination of the doctrine of Forms with the principle of causality is dictated by the Christian belief that the source of the attributes of things cannot be distinct from the source of their existence. Thus, in Anselm, the Platonic argument for Forms is combined with the causal argument for the existence of changing things. All this, of course, was implicitly or explicitly held by Augustine, but it achieves a deductive and systematic statement in Anselm's *Monologion*.

The proof for the existence of God in the *Proslogion* is the argument for which Anselm is famous in the history of philosophy, and he must be regarded as its inventor. Suggestions for the proof can be found in earlier philosophical literature, for both Augustine and Boethius had said that God is that than which no better can be thought.[9] There is a similar expression in Seneca.[10] It was, perhaps, such expressions which suggested the argument to Anselm. Anselm considered the arguments of the *Monologion* quite complicated, "The book was put together by connecting many arguments," and so he asked himself whether he could discover a single argument (*unum argumentum*), which required no other proofs for its support, by which the existence of God can be demonstrated. And he reported that, after a long struggle to put the matter out of mind, the proof suddenly occurred to him.

Faith provides us with the conception of "that than which nothing greater can be conceived." Yet the Psalmist asserts "The fool hath said in his heart, there is no God" (Psalms 14: 1). But the fool who hears of that than which no greater can be conceived understands what he hears. Now what we understand must, at least, exist in our understanding. But that than which nothing greater can be conceived cannot merely exist in the understanding, for if that than which no greater can be thought exists solely in the understanding it is not that than which no greater can be thought. For it is greater to exist in fact as well as in the mind than merely to exist in the mind; hence, that than which no greater can be conceived exists both in the understanding and in reality. This Being exists so truly that it cannot even be thought not to exist. Thus, if we can conceive of that than which no greater can be conceived, it must truly exist, for it is a contradiction to assert that that than which no greater can be conceived does not exist.

Anselm's argument seems to have the following form: if

[9] Augustine, *On Christian Doctrine*, I, 7, 7; *On Free Will*, II, 2, 5. Boethius, *De Consolatione Philosophiae*, Book III, Prosa 10: "Nam cum nihil deo melius excogitari queat, id quo melius nihil est bonum esse quis dubitet?"

[10] Seneca, *Natural Questions*, ii, Prologue 13. "Quid est Deus? Mens universi. Quid est Deus? Quod vides totum et quod non vides totum. Sic demum magnitudo sua redditur, qua nihil majus excogitari potest, si solus est omnia, opus suum, et extra et intra tenet."

that than which no greater can be conceived does not exist outside my understanding, then that than which no greater can be conceived is not that than which no greater can be conceived. Now since it is a contradiction to assert that a thing is not what it is, and since any statement which implies a self-contradiction must contain contradiction in itself, it follows that the nonexistence of that than which no greater can be conceived is impossible. Now since Anselm asserts, in effect, that it is because God exists so truly that He cannot even be conceived not to exist, I think we are entitled to suppose that we can be sure that God must exist from the fact that we cannot conceive that He does not exist. What is the cogency of this argument? Anselm appears to hold that God's existence is somehow manifested in our conception of Him as that than which no greater can be conceived, for he insists over and over again that that than which no greater can be conceived exists at least in our understanding. The contradiction which results from denying the existence of that than which no greater can be conceived must therefore be regarded as more than verbal. Because God exists in the maximal degree, because God is the Self-existent, it is impossible for anyone conceiving of God to conceive of Him as being merely a content of our thought. Thoughts, for Anselm, involve the presence of something in thought; hence, if that which is at least a content of thought cannot be conceived as merely a content of thought, what thus exists in thought must be more than a content of thought.

The force of the argument can be made out in yet another way. Necessary propositions, i.e., those propositions whose denials are self-contradictory, are true. Now true propositions must conform to their objects and must have objects with which to conform; hence, necessary propositions imply the existence of their objects. In this case, the necessary proposition is "That than which no greater can be thought cannot exist merely in thought." There must be an object which truly exists which this proposition correctly describes.

It is worth noticing that Anselm has two arguments here. The first professes to prove that God cannot fail to exist, and the second is intended to show that God cannot be thought not to exist. The second argument is subsidiary to the first, and should not be confused with it. The first argument can be stated more simply thus: Let T abbreviate "that than which no greater can be thought." Then the argument reads: If T does not exist, then T is not T. But since T is T, it follows that T exists.[11] The second argument reads: If T can be conceived not to exist then T is not T. But as T is T, it follows that T cannot be conceived not to exist. It is apparent that the second argument would not suffice to establish the first, for from the mere fact that I cannot conceive that God does not exist, it does not follow that there is a Being whose existence is such that its nonexistence cannot be conceived. Anselm must have regarded these proofs as distinct because he concluded them by saying "Thus, therefore, Something than which no greater can be thought exists so truly that it cannot be thought not to exist."

But this conclusion also suggests that it is the veritable existence of God which renders the thought of His nonexistence impossible. And this, as Anselm clearly allows in the proofs of the *Monologion*, can be interpreted to mean that God's nature and His existence are the same. This way of stating the case does not become prominent until the thirteenth-century Scholastics had exploited the distinction of es-

---

[11] The structure follows the logical schema: (*A* and *B* stand for any propositions) If A then B
But not B

Hence, not A.
Since the acceptance of the premisses is inconsistent with the denial of the conclusion, this is a valid schema. Hence if the premisses are true, the conclusion must be true. However, the mere validity of the argument in no way guarantees the truth of the premisses.

sence and existence derived from Avicenna.[12] Yet the essential
idea already occurs in Anselm and his critic Gaunilon. It is because God necessarily exists that He cannot be thought not to
exist. Whether Anselm was justified in using these arguments
has often been debated both in medieval and modern philosophy. He insists, for example, that God, being that than which
nothing greater can be thought, is *not* the greatest conceivable
being, but rather is a being who is greater than can be conceived. Indeed, this follows from the description "that than
which no greater can be thought." For if God were simply the
greatest being conceivable, we could suppose that a greater
than conceivable being exists, which is inconsistent with the
description "that than which no greater can be thought." But
if God is greater than can be conceived, in what sense can
Anselm hold that something is present in the understanding
which thinks of God? There is no reason to believe that Anselm's notion of divine illumination includes the actual presence of God in human thought. This being the case, it is hard
to escape the criticism of Gaunilon that to understand does
not necessarily mean to have *something* in the understanding.
Again the notion that *existence* is a kind of attribute which
God possesses (or *is*) in the highest degree has been doubted
or rejected by many philosophers.[13]

This *Argument of Anselm* was accepted by a number of
later philosophers in the Middle Ages (e.g., by Richard Fish-
acre [d. 1245], St. Bonaventure, and, with qualifications, Duns

[12] Avicenna (Ibn Sina, 980-1037), a Persian whose writings were very
influential in the Islamic and Christian worlds of the Middle Ages. No other
Islamic writer, save Averroes, is so often used by the Christian Scholastics.

[13] Notably Pierre Gassendi in his *Objections* to Descartes' *Meditations on
First Philosophy*, Kant in the *Critique of Pure Reason*, and Bertrand Russell.
According to Russell and others who follow him, *existence* is expressible only
by a logical quantifier, so that to say "the so-and-so exists" means simply
that "*there is* exactly one so-and-so," the "there is" phrase being the quantifier. "The Being than which no greater can be thought exists" thus means
"*There is* a being than which no greater can be thought," but to *exist* forms
no part of the content of the concept of such a being, because *to exist* is a
quantifying expression and not a qualifying predicate.

Scotus [d. 1308], to mention a few). But it was rejected by Thomas Aquinas, among others, on the ground that it assumes that we have some conception of God in Himself, a proposition Aquinas denies on the ground that all knowledge in the present life is derived by abstraction from sense-observation.

I must turn now to some questions concerning the relation of God to the world. The creatures have a sort of preexistence in the mind of God, their Creator, because creation is unthinkable unless there is in the mind of the creating agent an example or model or likeness or rule. These models comprise the inner-Speech of God and things are the copies thereof. The world was created from nothing and would perish without the constant conserving presence of God. This is, however, only one Speech or Word, and thus the question arises how can there be many copies of this one Word. The answer is that created things are more or less similar to the Divine Word. Thus, the plurality of degrees in which resemblance to God is possible explains the plurality of things in this world. There is thus no multiplicity of distinct ideas in the Word, but a plurality of distinct degrees in which God may be imitated. This is the so-called exemplarist doctrine of Augustine, and it is accepted in one form or another by practically all the Scholastics. Though it is phrased in different ways by Anselm's successors (depending on the requirements of their differing philosophical commitments), Abelard, St. Bonaventure, St. Thomas, Duns Scotus, and William Ockham all accept the exemplarist doctrine in some form. Exemplarism is required by the dogma of creation of the world by the free decree of God. The simplicity of the Divine nature prevents a plurality of distinct Ideas in God; hence, in some way or other, the plurality of Ideas must be explained by the different degrees of resemblance which creatures bear to their Creator. Anselm uses the language of *participation*[14] to express the relationship of creatures to God, but it is not clear how this is to be under-

14 *Monologion*, ch. 16.

stood. It is plain, however, that this is not intended in the Neoplatonic sense, for, although the characteristics and the existence of things must be explained in terms of their Creating Cause, Anselm's insistence on creation *ex nihilo* seems to exclude such an interpretation.

As all creatures are likenesses of their Creator so also is man. But as man is an image of God (and so more nearly like God than other terrestrial creatures), he can come to have some understanding of the Divine nature by coming to know himself. In fact, the soul's knowledge, remembrance, and love of itself is an image of the Trinity by which it was created. And in self-knowledge we have the closest approach we are capable of in the present life to knowing God. Since the soul exists for the purpose of loving God, and of loving Him eternally, it is clear that the good souls will exist eternally, and, because all souls are of the same nature, all will live eternally though not all will enjoy eternal blessedness.

CHAPTER V · ABELARD AND THE
PROBLEM OF UNIVERSALS

S WE have seen, the problem of universals was proposed to medieval thinkers by Porphyry. But as a matter of fact the problem arose in antiquity, and the main arguments for and against the doctrine that universals are objective things had been offered by Plato. Although Plato affirmed a doctrine of forms in order to explain, among other things, the meaning of general terms (*man, dog,* etc. in contradistinction to particular men, particular dogs, etc.), he had also set forth in one of his later dialogues (the *Parmenides*) most of the main arguments against the doctrine. One of the arguments which Plato brought against his own doctrine was as follows: Suppose that we apply the same general name (e.g., *man*), to a number of particular things on the ground that these several particulars are sufficiently alike to bear the same general name. This use of the same general term to apply to each of the particulars as well as the resemblance of these particulars is then explained by supposing that there is a single pattern or form in which the particulars participate, or, in other words, by the supposition that one and the same form is *in* these particulars. Now the individuals are distinct from one another yet one form is in them all. How can the form be single and undivided and still be *in* the several distinct individuals? Either the form will be divided and multiplied as many times as there are individuals, or the individuals will not be distinct. The one alternative destroys the form, while the other denies the data of the problem, namely the plurality of resembling individuals. This objection to the theory of forms, originated by Plato himself, was exploited by Aristotle,[1] and again by Boethius in his *Commentaries on Porphyry's*

[1] Aristotle, *Metaphysics*, Book Zeta, $1038^{b}1$–$1039^{b}20$.

Introduction. As we shall see, it was also used to great advantage by Abelard in his criticism of the Platonists of his own time.

Abelard was born in the year 1079 in the village of Palais, near Nantes. He studied with Roscelin, very probably also with Thierry of Chartres, and with William of Champeaux at Paris. Against William he successfully debated the problem of universals and forced his opponent to change his views. He then decided to study theology with Anselm of Laon. He soon became this Anselm's competitor, and returned to Paris and taught at the cathedral school. It was at this time that he fell in love with Heloise, the niece of the Canon of Notre Dame, to whom he arranged to be assigned as a tutor. The story of this affair is well known: the birth of their child, their marriage, Heloise's retirement to a convent, the mutilation of Abelard by her uncle's henchmen, and Abelard's retirement to the Abbey of St. Denys. After these events, Abelard began writing theological works, the first of which was *On the Unity and the Divine Trinity*. Abelard had always made enemies easily, and some of them contrived to have a council summoned at Soissons in 1121 at which Abelard's work was burned. He managed to establish an oratory at Quincey, to which students came in great numbers. About 1140-1141 he was again summoned to a council, this time at Sens, and St. Bernard appeared at the council and arranged Abelard's condemnation even before he had opportunity to defend himself. Abelard left the council and appealed to the Pope. On his way to Rome he stopped at Cluny, whose Abbot, Peter the Venerable, received him with kindness. Peter arranged a peace between Abelard and Bernard. Abelard, now old and in poor health, died at Châlons-sur-Saône, a religious house affiliated with Cluny, in 1142.

Abelard did not create the Scholastic method, as it has been called, but he greatly contributed to its later development. He composed a work[2] in which the conflicting opinions of the Fathers and authorities of the Church on various theological questions were set side by side. The purpose of the book was, as he wrote, to stimulate young readers to seek truth by exercising their minds and to improve their abilities by this exercise. There is no attempt to work out a systematic theology in the book and we have to accept Abelard's word that his purpose was simply didactic.[3] The remark made in the preface of his work that doubting leads to investigation which, in turn, leads to truth, occurs also in the *Glosses on the Categories*. This sort of remark was misunderstood in Abelard's own time, as it has been by modern interpreters. Abelard had certainly no intention of insinuating any doubts which would be destructive of existing orthodox Christianity. But it is generally true that he wished to employ logic and evidence to the extent which theological subjects admit. He was, then, championing reason, but not a reason directed against faith.

Abelard's well-known statement, "I do not wish to be a philosopher in order to contradict Paul, nor an Aristotle in order to be cut off from Christ,"[4] defines his attitude toward philosophy negatively. Positively, he wished to use philosophy to defend faith against heretics and unbelievers, and to elucidate the meaning of dogma as far as this is possible. In a letter to his son Astralabe, he asserted that faith comes, not by force, but by reason, but this again did not mean that a faith based only on the evidence of human reason has any merit. The merit of faith comes from the acceptance of divine authority. Yet, with Anselm, Abelard believed it a neglect if we do not attempt to understand that which is believed on the basis of such authority. Thus Abelard holds that we should attempt to understand the principles of faith. He distinguishes, however, between understanding (*intelligere*) and compre-

---

[2] The *Sic et Non*.
[3] See J. G. Sikes, *Peter Abailard*, Cambridge 1932, ch. 4.
[4] *Letter 17*.

hending (*comprehendere*). And he goes so far as to identify, for some purposes, understanding and faith, and contrasts this with *cognizing* or manifesting. "Faith," he writes, "is called an estimation of things not apparent, whereas cognition is an experience of those things by their very presence."[5] Thus faith involves some understanding and is an intermediate stage between ignorance and the beatific vision promised by St. Paul. It is, therefore, absurd for a teacher who wishes to inculcate faith in others to allow that he does not understand the things he wishes to communicate.

Faith, then, is to be reasoned about. Abelard uses several lines of persuasion to gain acceptance of this proposition. We must use reason because it is the quality by which man can be compared to God as being made in His image. Moreover, human reason is most suitable to investigate the Being in whose likeness it was made. Indeed, Christ as the *Logos* or *Sophia* of the Father is the source of logic (or dialectic) and reason.

The reason possessed by man is the recipient of Divine truth, even in the case of pre-Christian philosophers and inspired authors. Abelard frequently quotes them in order to show that they taught Christian truth even before the Incarnation. Thus, in his *Christian Theology* he held that Plato anticipated the doctrine of the Trinity, especially in the doctrine of the world soul, but he appears to have retracted this view later in his *Dialectic*.[6] He even supposed that these pagan philosophers had some anticipation of the Incarnation and Crucifixion. In fact, some of the philosophers led Christian lives, and many of them (Plato, Cicero, Anaxagoras) realized that the world owes its origin and direction to a providential Mind. The philosophers were for the heathen world what the prophets were for the Jews. All this illustrates a tendency which had its origin in the humanism of some of the apologetic Fathers.

[5] *Introduction to Theology*, II, 3.
[6] *Christian Theology*, I, 5; see edition of H. Ostlender in BGPM, Münster 1939, Band 35, Heft 2/3, and Petrus Abelardus, *Dialectica*, ed. L. M. de Rijk, Assen, Netherlands 1956, pp. 558, 559.

It is worth remarking that it is by no means restricted to medieval Christians, for we find similar praises of ancient philosophers in Islamic and Jewish philosophical writers in the Middle Ages.[7] It was, however, one of the grounds on which Abelard was attacked by Bernard of Clairvaux who maintained that Abelard's attempt to make Plato a Christian showed only that Abelard himself was a pagan. This was neither a just estimate of Abelard's intention nor, in general, of his convictions.

Abelard did not work out a systematic natural theology, but there are indications that he appealed to purely rational arguments to establish some of the principles of dogma. Thus, in his *Introduction to Theology*, he holds that the existence and unity of God can be established by reason. The things of the world, indeed the world itself, since they come into existence and are transitory, depend on some cause. This form of the principle of causality Abelard received from Chalcidius' translation of Plato's *Timaeus*. He adds that since rational beings could not have come from something irrational, the self-existing cause of all things must be a rational being.[8] From this and similar reasons, Abelard concludes that everything has a creator and director which men call God. All the features of this argument come from Abelard's antique sources.

The unity of God is argued along well-known lines. The greater the order, the fewer the rulers. The maximum order observed in the universe thus points to the unity of its ultimate cause. But it is difficult to ascertain the nature of God, because it is difficult to find in the world which is so far removed from the excellence of its Creator analogies appropriate to express God's nature.[9]

It is only when Abelard comes to the question of divine

[7] For example, in Averroes and Maimonides. See also *Hebrew Ethical Wills*, Schiff Classics, ed. I. Abrahams, Philadelphia 1920.

[8] *Introduction to Theology*, Book III.

[9] *Introduction to Theology*, Book II.

omnipotence that he introduces an original note. Here he sets forth a fundamental dilemma which has always disturbed theistic philosophers and which was a subject of controversy among the seventeenth-century philosophers, especially Leibniz and Spinoza. God who is the Good can produce only what is good. If He fails to produce some goods which He might have produced He must be called jealous or unjust. On the other hand, it seems that in His omnipotence He could have produced more or less than He actually has produced. Abelard attempts to resolve the dilemma in this way: God is determined to create individuals according to the particular goodness that they will contribute to the universe. This is intended to exclude a wholly arbitrary exercise of will. If this appears to necessitate God's action, it is a necessity arising from the divine nature itself, not some constraint coming upon God from something outside Himself. In other words, God's freedom is restricted only by the requirements of His own nature; hence, as determined by the choice of what is best, God could not have made another world containing fewer or more or better things.[10]

The *Epitome of Christian Theology*, written by one of Abelard's students, and perhaps partially representative of his views, includes a theodicy which recalls the attempts of the ancient Stoics. The main doctrine that God could create only what He has in fact created was attacked by St. Bernard, and rejected by the major Scholastics of the thirteenth and fourteenth centuries.

In a number of passages of his logical and theological writings, Abelard plainly accepts some form of exemplarism. Depending on Augustine, Boethius, Macrobius, and Priscian as sources and quoting them for support, he expounds the idea that Ideas preexist the creation as patterns which determine divine Providence in creating the best possible world. This exemplarism is not, so far as Abelard was concerned, inconsist-

---

[10] *Introduction to Theology*, Book III.

ent with his denial that there are any universal essences in the nature of things, for he denied that such exemplars were things, and regarded them as concepts in the divine understanding.[11] In fact his optimism implies some form of exemplarism, just as his nominalism in logic obliges him to deny that exemplary forms are things. Whether these views are consistent with one another cannot be discussed until Abelard's logical doctrines are set forth.

Although dialectic was, for Abelard, mainly a means of elucidating dogma, defending faith against detractors, and supporting authority by reason, it was in his logical writings that he made his greatest contribution to philosophy. Even though he did not create the Scholastic method or originate many of the logical doctrines developed in his works, he is highly original in the statement of the nominalist position, and it is to this aspect of his work that we now turn.

The task of logic is the discovery and the judging of arguments (i.e., the discovery of the kinds of inference) and the testing of inferences for validity. In some arguments, the validity depends on the subject matter of the argument, while in others only the pure form of the argument is involved. Now in order to understand an argument, it is necessary to understand the propositions of which it is composed. But, as the propositions consist of terms, these must be studied first. The order of logical inquiry consists in the study of terms, propositions, and finally arguments. Logical study concerns the use of language and is thus distinguished from physics which concerns the nature of things.[12]

It is in his *Glosses on Porphyry*,[13] that Abelard attempts to

[11] *Logica Ingredientibus*, ed. B. Geyer, BGPM, Band 21, pp. 22, 314. The important parts are translated by R. McKeon, *Selection from Medieval Philosophers*, New York 1929, Vol. I.

[12] These points are made in diverse places, e.g., in the *Logica Ingredientibus*, pp. 1-3, in the *Logica Nostrorum Petitione*, p. 508, and in the *Dialectica*, ed. de Rijk, p. 286.

[13] These glosses exist in three forms: the short paraphrases without comment (recently published by Mario dal Pra); the *Logica Ingredientibus* of

solve the problem of universals to which allusion has already been made. Abelard asks the three questions put by Porphyry: (1) whether genera and species subsist or are placed only in the understanding; (2) if they subsist, whether they are corporeal or incorporeal; (3) whether they are separated from sensibles or are placed in sensibles. To these he adds a fourth question, whether genera and species must refer to something or whether, if their normal referents are destroyed, these universals could consist of the mere meaning of the concept. We shall see that this last question takes on considerable importance for Abelard. His nominalistic solution of the problem of universals requires him to deny that universals are things and to affirm that they are significant words or concepts merely, and he finds a problem in the existence of a significant term which has no normal extradiscursive referent. The answer to his fourth question is designed to solve this problem.

We are fortunate in having from John of Salisbury, a younger contemporary and one-time pupil of Abelard, a fairly complete account of the major views on the problem of universals which were held by Abelard and his contemporary opponents.[14] This account enables us to identify those whose views Abelard opposes, when he does not do so himself. Salisbury can be corroborated by Abelard's autobiography, by Otto of Freising, and by the anonymous author (probably Joscelin of Soissons) of *"De Generibus et Speciebus."*

The first view considered was that held by William of Champeaux before Abelard compelled him to abandon it. According to this doctrine, there is one substance or "material essence" in the several different individuals of a kind. These individuals differ from one another by a diversity of accidents

---

which the first part is a commentary on Porphyry's *Isagoge*, and a second edition of this commentary, the *Logica Nostrorum Petitione*, both published by Geyer. See B. Geyer, *Peter Abaelards Philosophische Schriften*, BGPM, Münster 1919-1933, Band 21.

[14] John of Salisbury, *Metalogicon*, II, 17, trans. D. D. McGarry, Berkeley 1955, pp. 111-116.

(also called, at this time, *forms or properties*). Thus Socrates and Plato are substantially one, because in them there is one and the same substance, viz., man. But they differ because in Socrates there is a quality peculiar to Socrates, and by the same token in Plato a quality peculiar to Plato. This doctrine was first stated by Porphyry in the *Isagoge*, and, as I indicated in a previous chapter, had been defended by Odo of Tournai. Abelard had little difficulty in refuting this view. Supplied with arguments from Boethius' *Commentaries*,[15] he shows that one and the same substance would, on such a view, have mutually inconsistent qualities. For since *animal* is present in Socrates and also in an ass, the substance animal will be simultaneously rational and irrational. Again, since the common universal is at the same time in many individuals, it will be at once one and many. These and like contradictions require us to reject this view.

William of Champeaux retreated to another position in which he held that individuals of a kind are discrete from one another, not only in the fact that their accidents are different but also in that their natures or essences are not the same. Yet two men can be called the same *indifferently*. Because they are both men they are indifferently men or do not differ insofar as they are men. It is hard to see how this formula is to be interpreted.[16] As Abelard regards this view as closer

[15] Boethius, *The Second Edition of the Commentaries on the Isagoge of Porphyry*, translated in R. McKeon, *Selections from Medieval Philosophers*, I, 70-99. The arguments of Boethius are traceable to Aristotle's *Metaphysics*, Book Zeta, and ultimately to Plato's *Parmenides*. Perhaps some Stoic sources are also involved. It is worth noting that the nominalist view of universals was adopted by some Stoics and goes back to the Cynic Antisthenes of the fifth and fourth centuries B.C.

[16] "You see that I take these two words, *one* and the *same*, in two senses, according to indifference and according to the identity of exactly the same essence; according to indifference, as we say that Peter and Paul are the same in this, that they are men; for as far as it pertains to humanity, as this and that is mortal and as this and that is rational. But if we wish to confess the truth, the humanity of each is not the same but similar, since they are two men. . . . Wherever persons are many, substances are also many. . . . But this mode of *one* must not be referred to the nature of

to the truth, we may regard it as the beginning both of moderate realism and nominalism. We can so use the terms *one and the same* that two different individuals who are exactly similar to one another are one and the same as far as this similarity is concerned. But the use of identity to describe both the unity of an individual and the similarity of different individuals of a kind leads to trouble.

It seems likely that the *indifferentist* doctrine was developed in several ways by others. Joscelin of Soissons, according to John of Salisbury, maintained the doctrine that the universal is a *collection*. We have several statements of this doctrine. One is defended by the anonymous author of *De Generibus et Speciebus*: "Just as *Socrateity* which formally constitutes Socrates is nowhere outside Socrates, so also the essence of man which sustains *Socrateity* in Socrates is nowhere except in Socrates. Hence, I say that the species is not that essence of man alone which is in Socrates, or which is in any other of the

---

divinity."—*Sentences*, William of Champeaux (Lef'evre, pp. 14, 25).

"There are some who assign universality to things, and who assert that the same thing is both universal and particular. These people assert that the same thing is in many *indifferenter*, but that it is not in its inferiors *essentialiter*. For example, when they say that the same thing is in Socrates and Plato, they understand 'same' to mean indifferent or consimilar. And when they say that the same is predicated of many or that it exists in certain things, such is as if it were said: certain things agree in some nature, that is to say that these are similar things, in so far as they are bodies, for example, of animals."—*Lunel Logic*, Abelard (f 13v, 9-27).

"But Socrates may be regarded *simpliciter*, not as Socrates, that is to say, in every property of Socrates, but rather in a certain property, namely, in the fact that he is a rational, mortal animal, and according to this status he is different and indifferent: different from any other existing thing in this way, that Socrates himself is neither, essentially speaking, any of the others according to the status of man, nor is he essentially any of the others according to anything else; however, he is indifferent, that is consimilar, with certain others, namely with Plato and with other human individuals in the fact that in any of these things is rational, mortal animal, and observe Socrates and any other individual man, in so far as any of them in a rational mortal animal, are *unum et idem*."—Bibliotheque Nationale, Anonymous, ed. Haureau (Latin Section, v, 313, Paris 1892). It will be observed that all statements of the indifferentist view use the formula "eadem rem in diversis indifferenter," or something similar.

individuals, but I say that the species is the whole *collection* from other singular things conjoined with the nature of Socrates. This whole collection although it is many *essentially*,[17] is nevertheless called by the authorities one species, one universal, or one nature; just as *people*, although it is collected from many persons, is said to be one."[18] Abelard expounds this view very simply: "Some people maintain that the universal thing only exists in the *collection* of many. They do not call Socrates and Plato species by themselves, but they say that all men taken together are the species which is man, and likewise all animals taken together are the genus which is animal, and thus in the case of others."[19]

Abelard has little difficulty in showing that this theory will not stand. The universal is that which is naturally apt to be predicated of many. But a collection, as a collection, cannot be predicated of any of its members because it lacks the sort of commonness required for this. Moreover, any individual can be considered as a collection since it consists of parts, so that, for example, Socrates would be a universal. Again, if a universal is nothing but a collection, any arbitrarily designated collection will be a universal. Again, a collection is not logically prior to its parts so that its members cannot be characterized until the collection is formed.

Still another view was expressed by Walter of Mortagne and by Adelard of Bath. According to John of Salisbury, the adherents of Walter's view "distinguish [various] states [of existence], and say that Plato is an individual in so far as he is Plato; a species in so far as he is a man; a genus of a subaltern [subordinate] kind in so far as he is an animal; and a most general genus in so far as he is a substance."[20] According to

[17] I.e., with reference to essence.
[18] *De Generibus et Speciebus*, in V. Cousin, *Ouvrages Inedites. Abelard*, Paris 1836, pp. 524-525.
[19] *Logica Ingredientibus*, p. 14 of Geyer's edition.
[20] *Metalogicon*, trans. McGarry, II, 17, 113. In the *Polycraticus* (VII, 12) John of Salisbury explains the doctrine as follows: "several singular sensible

Adelard of Bath, "The names of genus, of species, and of individual are imposed on the same essence but each of these is imposed in a diverse *respect*. . . . Since, therefore, the very same thing which you see is at once genus, species, and individual, Aristotle correctly said that genus and species only exist in sensible things. And they are in fact the sensible thing itself, although they are considered more acutely."[21] Abelard explains these theories of *state* and *respect* in much the same way, and he finds them unacceptable. The division of an individual into several respects or states requires that the same thing is both peculiar and common: as peculiar, a thing is predicable of itself; as common, it is predicable of many. But this would mean that one and the same individual is both predicable and not predicable of itself as individual, and, again, both predicable and not predicable of another as universal. While the motivation of this theory is clearly the attempt to locate universality in individual things, it fails in the attempt to predicate a thing of a thing.

Now as all attempts to predicate things of things have failed, Abelard concludes that universality can be ascribed only to words or (as in the revised edition of this commentary, i.e., the *Nostrorum Sociorum Petitioni*) to *significant words* or *sermons*. One significant word or concept can be applied to or predicated of many things because of their common likeness. But does not the mention of a common likeness involve ascribing universality to things? Abelard does not think so. Individual men, for example, are distinct from one another both in their individual essences and in the diversity of their accidental differences. Yet they agree (or are alike) *in that they are men*. "I do not say that they agree *in man*, since no

---

things having been apprehended, since these alone are truly said to exist, a given singular brings in diverse *states* by means of which it constitutes *for reason* the most special and the most general in the singular things themselves."

[21] Adelard of Bath, *De Eodem et Diverso*, in BGPM, Münster 1903, Band 4, Heft 1, pp. 11-12.

thing is man save a discrete thing [i.e., the individual], but in *being man.*"[22] Now *to be man* is not a thing. As Abelard points out, likeness or agreement is often asserted in the case of negative predicates, as when we say that all substances are alike in *not inhering in some subject,* and we would not call *not inhering in a subject* a thing. Thus when we say that two men are alike *in being man* we are not invoking an essence. The common reason for imposing the same universal term on several different individuals is that they *themselves* are like each other (*ipsi ad invicem conveniunt*). The status of man is *to be man* but this feature of the nature of each individual man is not a common essence. Thus Abelard's explanation of resemblance is in terms of the individuals themselves and does not involve any thing distinct from the individuals in virtue of which they resemble one another. The individuals by their very own selves are in mutual agreement or mutual likeness.[23] Likeness, therefore, can be explained without appeal to a common nature or a shared essence. Abelard's negative critique of realism owed something to Boethius, but his refutation of the twelfth-century views and his positive account of resemblance is his own contribution.

In order to understand Abelard's doctrine of abstraction we must look for a moment at some of his psychological theories. Although he had no firsthand knowledge of Aristotle's psychological writings, he shows remarkable acquaintance with some of the main points of Aristotle's views. The senses, he tells us, perceive bodies or what is in bodies by means of corporeal organs. The intellect (or understanding) needs no body or corporeal organ. It is concerned only with the likeness of things, of which likeness it constructs for itself

[22] "Non dico 'in homine' cum res nulla est homo nisi discreta, sed in esse hominem," *Logica Ingredientibus,* p. 19, lines 24-25.

[23] P. Vignaux, in the article *Nominalisme* in *Dictionnaire de théologie Catholique,* Tome 11, and in his *La Pensée au moyen âge,* Paris 1948, pp. 46-47 states that Abelard's position is very like that of William Ockham in the fourteenth century. Indeed, some of their formulations are verbally almost the same.

a duplicate which remains in the mind. Thus the form to which the understanding directs itself is an imaginary and *fictive* thing which the mind constructs for itself whenever it so desires. Some of these fictive constructions are universal, others particular. In any case, the form or fictive construction is different both from the understanding itself and from the external physical things. This third thing, the form, is what a noun signifies. The point of Abelard's insistence that the form (or fictive construct) is distinct is simply that universal nouns must have some significance in certain cases in which they cannot have a normal referent. Thus "roses" in the sentence "There are no roses" must have significance but it cannot derive this significance from denoting roses if the sentence is true, i.e., if in fact there are no roses.[24]

Because man learns things through the senses, he rarely if ever has a simple understanding of things because "the exterior sensuality of accidents prevents man from conceiving the natures of things purely." God, on the other hand, may be accredited with a pure knowledge of things. Man, indeed, can know the artifacts resulting from his own ingenuity, but he has not a complete knowledge of natural objects. Nevertheless, the constructs which the mind makes can be described as *opinions* of the intrinsic forms of things which are not accessible to the senses, such as *rationality, paternity, sitting*, etc.

The commonness of universal words thus depends on two factors, (1) the resemblance of those individuals on which the universal word is imposed, and (2) the existence in consciousness of a common conception. But because universals are said to be formed by abstraction we must ask how abstrac-

---

[24] I.e., in winter (at least where Abelard lived) there are no roses. But a further explanation is necessary here. The medieval logicians, following Aristotle, have thought of some propositions as being sometimes true and at other times false. This is in sharp contrast to the practice of contemporary logicians. See J. R. Weinberg, Review of P. Boehner's edition of Ockham's *Tractatus de Praedestinatione et de Praescientia Dei, etc., Philosophical Review* (July 1947) pp. 446-448, and William and Martha Kneale, *The Development of Logic*, London 1962, p. 238 and *passim*.

tion occurs. Matter and form are always mixed together in physical things. The mind can consider one without attending to the other. Thus, if I remove or circumscribe all accidental features of a man, I can consider his essence, and thus I have a concept obtained by this abstraction. But it is said that such abstraction falsifies the thing because it considers the thing as different from what it actually is. A man is both matter and form (i.e., both essence and accidents together),[25] and the consideration of one without the other falsifies the thing. Abelard replies, "When I say that I consider only this one among thé qualities the nature has, the *only* refers to the attention alone, not to the mode of subsisting, otherwise the understanding would be empty. For the thing does not have only it, but is considered only as having it."[26] Thus, although the manner of existing is other than the manner of being understood, there is no falsification, for by abstraction the understanding considers one aspect of a thing separately but does not consider that aspect as separated from the thing in reality.

Now universal conceptions are obtained by such abstractions. A conception of the nature of a lion which is adequate to represent any other lion will have in it only that which is common. All particularizing features will be omitted. If we wish to form a concept peculiar to a given lion, such particularizing features will be included. In the case of a common conception, hearing the noun which calls up this conception does not recall any of the particular features of one individual rather than another. The word "man," for example, depends on a form common to all men. The very commonness of this form produces a confusion in order that we understand that it applies

<hr />

[25] Note that this use of matter and form is quite different from Aristotle's use, a point which will perhaps be clearer later when we discuss some of the philosophers who use Aristotle's own distinction.

[26] *Logica Ingredientibus*, p. 25, lines 25-28, translation in McKeon, *Selections from Medieval Philosophers*, I, 246.

to all men, and not to any one in particular. Thus common nouns call up common concepts, whereas proper nouns call up proper concepts. The word "confusion" should not mislead us, for although some interpreters of the ancient and medieval doctrines of abstraction have suggested that the common concept results from a running together of several particular images, this does not seem to be involved in Abelard's account. The confusion is only in the manner of understanding the simple nature or quality abstracted. Thus a confused image is a concept of confused signification, that is, a concept which does not produce the understanding of one single, discrete individual as over against another. Common concepts do, however, nominate (stand for) particular things.

There are obvious resemblances between Abelard's account of abstraction and that of later Scholastics, especially St. Thomas Aquinas, where the similarity of the language used is striking. But, as Vignaux has pointed out, there are important and decisive differences. Abelard's account is a psychological theory which does not presuppose the Aristotelian doctrine of matter and form nor the Avicennian doctrine of a common nature. Abelard's doctrine that concentrated attention or simple consideration enables us to apprehend one feature of a composite individual to the neglect of another has its difficulties. The consideration of the nature of an individual apart from its accidental features can be justified only by a metaphysics which permits a nature and its accidents to exist separately in fact (if only by an especial exercise of divine power). Abelard barely goes into these metaphysical problems, but his nominalist successor of the fourteenth century, William Ockham, argues this point in detail. The account of abstraction which Abelard gives is obviously incomplete without some such argument.

Abelard answers Porphyry's questions in terms of the foregoing doctrine. Universals *signify* things which really exist by denoting (Abelard says "nominating") singulars among which there is resemblance. Universal terms are corporeal with respect to things denoted, but incorporeal in respect to their manner of signifying, since they are words associated with concepts which signify indeterminately. Again, universals denote something existing in sensible individuals, but are understood outside the sensible things because the thing denoted in the individual can exist apart from its accidents.

Finally, because the universal word signifies not only the sensible individuals subject to it (i.e., those it denotes) but also the common conception, Abelard can answer his fourth question. If there are no longer any individuals of a sort normally denoted by the common universal word, there is still the common conception which continues to provide the universal word with significance. By this means, we can significantly and truly say "There are no roses," when in fact there are no longer roses.

The nominalistic doctrine thus requires that the normal referent of a universal term be one or more existing individuals. But since sometimes there are true negative propositions of the form "There are no so-and-so's" (e.g., "There are no roses here and now"), the universal term must derive its significance from something. Abelard found this permanent source of significance in the common conception formed by the mind. The full answer to Abelard's fourth question probably is connected with another doctrine which he devised to deal with the meanings of sentences.

In order to account for the logical necessity which we find in logically true propositions Abelard feels obliged to assume the existence of something distinct from thoughts on the one hand and from physical things on the other. Thus suppose we say: "If there is a rose, there is a flower." This proposition is both true and necessary. But we cannot locate this necessity either in thoughts or in things, for both thoughts and things are transitory.[27] In fact, such conditional propositions or "consequences" as "If there is a rose there is a flower," "If there is a man there is an animal," are true and necessary and eternal. Even before man existed, it was eternally true that "if there is a man, there is an animal." And although for *proving* that *man is animal* it is necessary that man exist, the existence of man is not the cause of the truth of the proposition "If there is a man there is an animal." For this proposition is true whether or not a man exists, and, in general, the necessity of implication does not require the presence or absence of any thing.

It is not open to us to say that the necessary truth of implications depends on thoughts and their connections. For not only is the transitory character of thought incompatible with the eternal necessity of implication, but it is not even true to say that the thought of the antecedent cannot occur unless the thought of the consequent also occurs. (A person can understand a proposition without understanding what follows logically from it.) We *can*, however, say the following:

It cannot happen that what the antecedent thought asserts is the case and what the consequent thought asserts is not the case if the implication is true and necessary; hence, that which is asserted by propositions is other than thoughts and other than things. We can call "that which is asserted by a proposition" a "quasi-thing of the proposition."[28] But these "quasi-things" of propositions are absolutely not essences. Thus it is true that what is asserted by a proposition is not any *thing*. If it is asked how can that which is not a thing or essence be the cause of the truth of a proposition, one can reply, as Abelard has already argued in his *Glosses on Porphyry* in explaining

[27] See Abelard, *Glosses on Aristotle's De Interpretatione* in B. Geyer's *Abaelards Philosophische Schriften*, BGPM, Band 21, Heft 2, p. 366, lines 1-10, and, for the whole discussion, pp. 365, lines 30-370, and line 33. See also Petrus Abaelardus, *Dialectica*, ed. L. M. de Rijk, pp. 160, 264ff., and 282, lines 25-29.

[28] *Logica Ingredientibus*, ed. B. Geyer, BGPM, Band 21, p. 366. The *dicta propositionum* are called "*quasi res propositionum*."

the resemblance between two men. Socrates and Plato are alike *in being man* or *in being substance*, yet no *thing* can be designated in virtue of which they are alike.

Abelard insists that nothing can be stated affirmatively of the "that which is asserted by a proposition"; that is, of the sense of a proposition. Instead of saying affirmatively that the sense of a proposition is nothing, therefore, it would be better to say that it is not something. For I cannot say that nothing happens when I say "it happens that Socrates runs."

Abelard is evidently attempting to provide us with some referent for propositions (which term, in medieval philosophy always means either a written or spoken sentence or a thought) in order to account for the facts that (1) some propositions are true and necessary and therefore eternal whereas both thoughts and things are transitory, and (2) some true propositions are purely negative as, e.g., "A chimaera does not exist" and so have no *things* as referents. The referent of a proposition may be called a quasi-thing but, as he tirelessly insists, not an essence (i.e., not an existing substance). His nominalism prohibits him from appealing to any things other than the natural or artificial objects which comprise the world, and his clear realization that the referent of a necessary or a true negative assertion cannot be thoughts require the assumption of "that which the proposition asserts" (*dictum propositionis*) as a referent.

We may conjecture that Aristotle's distinction[29] between affirmation and negation, on the one hand, and what is affirmed and denied, on the other, was one of the sources of Abelard's doctrine on the dictum of a proposition. It is also possible that Augustine's doctrine that the eternal laws of numbers are in the divine mind contributed to Abelard's reflections. But whatever its historical source, the theory is an original conception

[29] See *Categories*, ch. 10, 12^{b}6-15; *Metaphysics* 1051^{b}33-35; and Abelard, in BGPM, Band 21, Heft 2, p. 275, lines 4-6.

of the theory of meaning which is required to complete Abelard's doctrine about universals.

The contributions of Abelard to logic and theory of knowledge are the more remarkable when we consider that he had so little of Aristotle's writings to draw upon. His discussion of universals and abstraction and his use of the method of contrasting authorities in theology in his *Sic et Non* make him one of the founders of the Scholastic method of the later centuries of medieval thought.

CHAPTER VI · PHILOSOPHY IN THE
ISLAMIC MIDDLE AGES

HOUGH the position of philosophy in the Judaeo-Islamic world of medieval times was superficially analogous to the situation in Christendom, there were several important and profound differences, the most important of which were the place of a formal creed and the character of religious authority. While creeds were formulated by the several different sects in Islam and by the medieval Jews, these creeds never enjoyed universal acceptance by the faithful. And, again, while religious authority was often powerful in a given locality or country, there was never any central authority comparable in power and scope with that of Rome in the Christian West.[1]

On the other hand, it cannot be too strongly emphasized that the position of the philosopher in the Islamic world of the Middle Ages was precarious. After Al-Ghazali's refutation of philosophy, it ceased to develop in the East, and it did not fare well in Muslim Spain after Averroes and Maimonides. Although there were periods favorable to the development of philosophical inquiry (especially when politico-religious authority was limited to a local potentate), there were periods when fanatics engaged in inquisition, imprisonment, execution, confiscation of libraries, destruction of books, and other excesses.[2] In fact, the existence of books by philosophers on the

[1] Another difference, emphasized by Professor Strauss, was the fact that the Roman Catholic Church explicitly used philosophy as *ancilla theologiae* and thus assumed control of it, whereas this was never done in Islam, so that Islamic philosophers enjoyed an autonomy which was not enjoyed by their Christian counterparts. See Leo Strauss, *Persecution and the Art of Writing*, Glencoe, Ill. 1952.

[2] Cf. Leon Gauthier, *Ibn Rochd*, Paris 1948, pp. 17-19; E. I. J. Rosenthal, *Political Thought in Medieval Islam*, Cambridge 1958, p. 177 and *passim*. Even Ibn Rushd (Averroes) said that heretics must be killed. See his *Tahafut al-tahafut* (*The Incoherence of the Incoherent*), trans. S. Van den Bergh, 2 vols., London 1955. My references will be to this work.

"agreement of philosophy and religion" attests, not simply to the twofold interests of their authors, but especially to the necessity of justifying philosophical inquiry in an environment which, at the very best, merely suffered it to exist. In some ways, therefore, although some of the Islamic philosophers went further in the development of doctrines that were in fact inconsistent with any reasonable reading of revealed religion, philosophy in the long run fared better in the Christian world where ecclesiastical limitations on philosophical activity were far more effective and organized.

Among the Muslims, the main sources of authority were generally considered to be the Koran, tradition, the universal agreement of the faithful, and the principle of analogy (legal reasoning by which a general principle could be applied to parallel cases).[3] Universal agreement, however, meant consensus among the religious authorities, and even this principle some Muslim leaders in the Middle Ages rejected in favor of the authority of specially designated Imams. Insofar as it is possible to extract any set of common beliefs, we can designate the following as practically universal: The Koran was the work of God and, by the end of the reign of the Omayades, it was a general dogma that the Koran was eternal.[4] The Eternal Koran was more or less consciously regarded as the Islamic counterpart of the Divine Word of Christendom. This Koran was dictated to the last and most important of the prophets, Mohammed. Although Islam is uncompromisingly monotheistic, the Koran and the Throne of God are co-eternal with the Deity Himself. There are, in addition, mediate beings such as angels as well as the principal evil spirit, Iblis (perhaps from *diabolos*) or Shaitan (cf. Satan), and subsidiary demons, the jinns. Although there are miraculous stories concerning Mohammed (and some of the holy men) which are a part of the "tradition," the great miracle of Islam is the Koran

[3] Cf. Alfred Guillaume, *Islam*, New York 1954, p. 101.
[4] Cf. Carra de Vaux, *Les Penseurs de l'Islam*, Paris 1923, Tome 4, p. 145.

itself; how could a book of such great beauty be the work of the semiliterate Prophet?[5] The Koran had to be the revelation of Allah.

The religious doctrines of the Koran being largely adaptations of Judaic and Christian religious dogmas, a minimal creed involving belief in Resurrection, Judgment, Paradise, and Hell was accordingly general in Islam. In addition to these theoretical principles, the practical obligations of the devout Muslim are essentially prayers, pilgrimage, almsgiving, and fasting. For present purposes, the theoretical principles are most important. The one God created the world by fiat and with a foreknowledge which was also predestinating. This predestinating foreknowledge is contained in the "Preserved Tablet" or eternal Koran. Despite this predestination, man's will is somehow free. These conflicting dogmas produced both philosophical and theological controversies. The Koran speaks as if God has a plurality of attributes, viz., Life, Knowledge, Hearing, Sight, Will, and Speech. The attempt to reconcile this plurality with the absolute unity of God also occasioned intellectual difficulties.

The contact of Islam with Judaic, Greek, and Christian doctrines, both theological and philosophical, made these controversies inevitable. It will be well to sketch the character of these influences and the consequent effects on the development of philosophy. The Christian school of Edessa in Mesopotamia, founded in 363 by St. Ephraim of Nisibis (who taught part of Aristotle's logic), was closed in 489. Its professors continued their work in Persia under the Sassanide King Chosroës. In Syria in the sixth century at Risaina and Kinnesrin, Aristotle and Greek science were cultivated. Thus Greek thought was established in the Near East before the

---

[5] Cf. Majid Fakhry, *Islamic Occasionalism*, London 1958, p. 133. "It is baffling that this claim for stylistic perfection (sc. of the Koran) should have been accepted with such docility by the greatest of Arabian authors . . . when its legitimacy is all too unwarranted, even from a purely formal point of view."

rise of Islam. The Abbassides of the eighth century patronized
the Syrian scholars, and, under this patronage, Euclid, Galen,
Aristotle, Theophrastus, and Alexander of Aphrodisias were
translated. In the reign of Al-Mamun (813-833), the son of
Haroun Al-Raschid, Aristotle was translated from Greek with
the help of Syriac into Arabic. The Syrian Honein Ibn Ishaq
(d. 876) directed the translations, epitomes, and the writing
of Aristotle and the Greek commentators at Bagdad. It is
worth remarking that his methods of translation were exact
and scholarly. Many Greek manuscripts of a given work were
collated in the process of translation.[6] In the ninth and tenth
centuries new translations of Aristotle, Theophrastus, Alexander, Themistius, Syrianus, and Anmonius were produced
by the Nestorian Syrians. There was a fairly continuous contact between Islamic theologians and Christian theology, and
there is little doubt that ideas of Greek and Syrian Christians
were responsible for some of the important theological speculations in Islam (this is true of the "liberal" theologians, the
Mutazilites, and particularly true of the more "orthodox"
Mutakallimun). It should be mentioned here also that the
influence of Aristotle was tinged deeply by Neoplatonism.
This was due, in part at least, to the fact that some of the
Greek commentators had already interpreted some of Aristotle's views Neoplatonically and to the further fact that an
epitome of Plotinus' *Enneads* (IV-VI) had been given the
mistaken title of *Theology of Aristotle*.[7] Another Neoplatonic
work, the so-called *Book of Causes*, actually an epitome of
Proclus' *Elements of Theology*, was also ascribed to Aristotle.[8]
The antique intellectual heritage of the Judaeo-Islamic world

[6] Cf. *Isis*, VIII (1926), 690.
[7] The source of this confusion is not wholly understood but the mistake
already appears in the title of the Arabic version.
[8] Many other pseudonymous works of this sort were in wide circulation in
the Judaeo-Islamic world (e.g., pseudo-Empedocles, *On the Five Substances*,
a work from which Ibn Gabirol, the Spanish Jewish Philosopher of the
eleventh century, drew much of his philosophical inspiration).

thus contained much of the best philosophy, theology, and science but sometimes in a confused form.

The earliest form of philosophical speculation in Islam was probably brought about by the attempt to make the religious doctrines of the Koran internally consistent and intellectually respectable. Doubtless the attitude of the learned Jews and Christians (e.g., John Damascene) spurred on some of the faithful to debate religious issues in the attempt to extend the faith of Islam, or at least to defend it against detractors from outside. One group of theologians, the Mutazilites, attempted to formulate the main principles of Islam somewhat as follows:

1) God is an absolute Unity—a fact which entails His incorporeality. This principle was probably directed against polytheism, but also to some extent against the Trinitarian Doctrine of Christianity.

2) Man's will is free. (God does not like evil, He does not create the actions of men, but God gives man the power to obey the divine precepts.)

3) There are promises of reward and threats of punishment in the Divine revelation.

4) The sinner is in a state intermediate between the infidel and the true believer.

5) Man is under obligation to do good and prevent evil, so that the obligation to engage in the Holy War is, in principle, no different from the obligation to combat the sinner.[9]

The most important of the orthodox groups of the theologians was established by Al-Ashari (d. 935).[10] As the views of Al Ashari and his followers are of some importance in later development of thought both in Islam and in Latin Christendom, I want to discuss them in more detail. First of all Al-

---

[9] Cf. Carra de Vaux, *Les Penseurs de l'Islam*, Tome 4, p. 135.

[10] Al-Ashari was at first a pupil of one of the important Mutazilite teachers in Bagdad, but he made a public rejection of this rationalistic movement when he was forty years old and defended orthodoxy by the dialectical methods of his Mutazilite antecedents.

Ashari insisted on the literal interpretation of the Koran with all its anthropomorphic language applied to Allah, yet, with equal insistence, held that God is totally unlike anything else. The literal interpretation of the Throne of God, the Pool of the Prophet where the believers drink, the beatific vision—all these are to be accepted. He also adopted the view (derived ultimately from Neoplatonic or Stoic sources) that the eternal Word of God is an idea in His mind. What is good or evil is wholly determined by God's decree. In fact man's will is the creation of God and (inconsistent with this) only man's appropriation (*kasb*) by which he accepts the choice divinely created for him is within his power. It therefore appears that the central tenet of Al-Ashari and his school is the absolute omnipotence of God and the complete dependence of all creatures and their activities on God.[11]

There are two principal contentions which distinguished the Asharite school of Mutakallimun (literally, "Speakers"),[12] the absolute omnipotence of God which means for them that God is the *only* cause, and an unusual version of the atomic theory.[13] The atomic theory amounts to something like the following (although it should be noticed that there was disagreement about the more minute details of doctrine): The universe consists of extensionless particles[14] which are exactly like one another, and the gross bodies are conglomerates of these ultimate particles. Unlike the atoms of Democritus, however, these atoms are not eternal. The doctrine that God is the sole cause of existence and change required the continuous recreation of the atoms and of their accidents (qualities).

[11] See the creed of Al-Ashari in *Al-Ibānah 'an 'Usal al-Dujānah*, Hayderabad, 1321 A.H.

[12] The Latin philosophers of medieval Christendom (e.g., St. Albert and St. Thomas) refer to them as *loquentes in lege Maurorum.*

[13] For speculation as to the origin of *this* atomism, see S. Pines, *Beiträge zur islamischen Atomenlehre*, Berlin 1936, pp. 95-123.

[14] See H. A. Wolfson, *An Unknown Pseudo-Democritean Fragment and the Muslim Unextended Atoms*, Festgabe für Eric Voegelin, Munich 1962, pp. 593-606.

The word for accident was applied in the broadest sense to refer to everything truly assertible of atoms so that some Asharites held that annihilation of a body is produced when God created the accident of extinction in it. Even time and space were atomized. Motion consists, according to these theologians, of the displacement of an atom of body from one point of space to another in an atom of time. This would seem to mean that an atom was successively recreated in successive positions in successive moments of time. Difference of velocity then consists in the fact that some atoms are recreated more often in a given fixed position than others. The accidents of a gross body are accidents of the atoms composing it. Again there is a difference between this atomism and that of Democritus or that of Epicurus. The former denied that atoms had any qualitative accidents, whereas the latter supposed that qualitative accidents belong only to composites of atoms.

From the accounts of the Asharite doctrines preserved by Sharastani, Maimonides, Averroes, *et al.*, it is clear that both the doctrine about causality and the atomic theory were defended on logical and epistemological grounds. The main point here was the so-called "Maxim of Admissibility"[15] according to which "everything conceived by the imagination is admitted by the intellect as possible." This means that whatever is free from contradiction must be admitted as possible for God to accomplish; hence, the ordinary routines in the natural world, the order of the various parts of the universe, and the like are only the result of God's customary way of acting. Without any absurdity resulting therefrom, God could change His custom or habit and the universe would be different. We shall observe later how Al-Ghazali used this view in an attack on the "Philosophers" in Islam (particularly directed against Avicenna).

The views of the Asharites exerted considerable influence

---

[15] See Moses Maimonides, *Guide to the Perplexed*, Pt. I, ch. 73, proposition 10.

not only in medieval Islam but among the Jews living in countries dominated by Islamic culture. Maimonides devoted many pages of his *Guide to the Perplexed* to a refutation of their doctrines, and his Islamic contemporary, Averroes (Ibn Rushd), attacked them in his *Incoherence of the Incoherence*.[16] Aquinas attempted to refute the causal theory of the Asharites in his *Summa Theologiae* and especially in his *Summa Contra Gentiles*, and there is some evidence of influence even among the philosophers of the seventeenth century.[17]

The philosophical ideas of the Mutakallimun have most often been described as naive. This has been due, in part, to the fact that our knowledge of their speculations has come largely from hostile critics. Yet I venture to suggest that when we have a better understanding of their views and arguments they will appear to us as subtle critics of the philosophical notions of *their* opponents.[18]

The kind of philosophy which most influenced the intellectual currents of the thirteenth century in the Christian West is represented by a series of Islamic writers who have been miscalled Aristotelians. It is true that their language and many of their interests are determined by the works of Aristotle. But it is more correct to call them Neoplatonists (Averroes is, to a great extent at least, an exception). The first important writer of this group was Al-Kindi (d. 873). A series of his works survive in Latin form: *On Intellect and What is Understood*,

[16] *Tahafut al-tahafut*, trans. S. Van den Bergh.

[17] Cf. Leibniz, *Discourse on Metaphysics*, §7.

[18] I understand that H. A. Wolfson will soon publish a volume devoted to the Mutakallimum. Meanwhile, I shall give but one example of this subtlety: Aristotle (*Physics*, VIII, 1, 251^{a}15–251^{b}28 and Simplicius in *Physics*, 466, 13f. See Sir Thomas L. Heath, *Mathematics in Aristotle*, Oxford 1949, p. 103) had argued that it is logically impossible for time and motion to begin. The careful wording of a passage from Shahrastani [*Summa Philosophiae*, ed. Alfred Guillaume, p. 4.], viz., "Something that temporal things do not precede is itself temporal," suggests to me a clear understanding that there is no contradiction involved in the temporal beginning of the universe. This seems confirmed by Al-Ghazali, *Tahafut*, *al-Falasifah*, Lahore 1958, pp. 40-41; S. Van den Bergh, *Averroes' Tahafut al-tahafut*, 1, 41-48.

On Sleep and Vision, On the Five Essences, Introduction to the Art of Logical Demonstration, as well as a *Treatise on the Magical Arts.*[19] According to the title of the work known as the *Theology of Aristotle,* Al-Kindi corrected the first Arabic translation (the book is actually not, as the title states, a commentary, but an epitome of Plotinus *Enneads* IV to VI). Although the full title makes it plain that the work is not by Aristotle, it seems to have been attributed to him in Islam, if not when it first appeared, then sometime later.[20] This is of great importance for understanding Al-Kindi and his "peripatetic" successors in Islam. He attributes to Aristotle, or at least finds no incongruity in accepting as compatible with Aristotelian thought, notions which are plainly Neoplatonic.

His treatise *On the Intellect* is one of a long series of works by that title, or with the same subject matter, which came from Islamic philosophers, such as those of Al-Farabi, Avicenna, and Averroes. The theme common to these treatises is the explanation of Aristotle's doctrine of the active reason (νους ποιητικός). Following the lead of Neoplatonic doctrines of emanation, these philosophers explain the active reason as a separate spiritual being, the last of the Intelligences emanated from God. This doctrine in Averroes is associated with the notion that there is but one active reason for all human beings. The logical consequence of this view is the doctrine that there is no personal survival. Whether Averroes actually denied the idea of personal survival is another question.

In the case of Al-Kindi, there is certainly a plurality of individual souls which, as he says,[21] survive the death of the

[19] There are extensive quotations from the last-mentioned work in Giles of Rome, *Errores Philosophorum,* ed. J. Koch and trans. J. O. Riedl, Milwaukee 1944, pp. 47-55. The other works are in BGPM, Münster 1897, Band II, Heft 5.

[20] See Alfred Guillaume, *Legacy of Islam,* London 1931, p. 252. See also F. Dieterici, *Die Sogenannte Theologie des Aristotles,* Leipzig 1883.

[21] *Liber Introductorium in Artem Logicae Demonstrationis,* BGPM, Band II, Heft 5, p. 62, "Et post mortem fit anima Angeli caelestis spiritualis, sempiterni esse, delectabilis guadere semper."

body. Nonetheless there is an Intelligence always actual from which man acquires his intellect.[22] Al-Kindi also divides intellect into four species: the intellect which is always in act, the intellect which is in potency in the soul, the intellect which passes from potency to act, and finally the demonstrative intellect. This doctrine is explicitly attributed to Plato and Aristotle, but it hardly need be said that it is not to be found there. Aristotle only distinguishes the active from the passive intellect. Al-Kindi's more elaborate classification, however, seems to be the prototype of similar distinctions made by Al-Farabi and Avicenna.

The influence of Neoplatonic ideas on Al-Kindi is nowhere better illustrated than by the *Treatise on the Magical Arts*. In this treatise he holds that if it were given to anyone to comprehend the whole condition of the celestial harmony, he would know the world of the elements with all its contents in every place and every time, as that which is caused is known by the cause. If indeed he knew anything of this world in its entire condition, the condition of the celestial harmony would not be hidden from him, since he would comprehend the cause by means of its effect—for all things acting in the world of elements, however small, are effects of the heavenly harmony. And things, whatever they are and whatever they are to be, are denoted in that harmony. Wherefore one who would have complete knowledge of the heavenly harmony would know the past and the future completely. This doctrine is elucidated in terms of the theory that everything which exists in the physical world sends out rays in every direction so that everything contains rays derived from everything else. Thus the complete knowledge of any single thing in the world represents, as a mirror, the total condition of the heavenly harmony.[23] Thus

[22] *Ibid.*, pp. 5-7.
[23] The "mirror" figure of speech (which occurs later, e.g., in Cusanus and Leibniz) as well as the whole doctrine, is derived from the Neoplatonists. Cf. especially Proclus, *Elements of Theology*, ed. Dodds, p. 254 and Plotinus, *Enneads*, v, 8, 4, and is ultimately traceable to the Stoics.

everything is necessitated. He also held that the heavenly harmony is the true cause of everything although people popularly suppose that one thing acts on another by its own rays. This doctrine is connected with a belief in the efficacy of natural magic.

The tendency to reconcile Plato and Aristotle is characteristic of the early philosophers in Islam. Al-Kindi wrote a short tract "reconciling" the Aristotelian and Platonic definitions of the soul,[24] and Al-Farabi wrote a more extensive *Harmony between Plato and Aristotle*.[25] Works of this sort seem to be attempts to reconcile Aristotle and Neoplatonism.

But Al-Kindi is a Muslim and therefore has several problems which are characteristic of religious philosophy in the Middle Ages. Creation is dealt with in part in a short treatise on *The Agent in the Proper Sense and in the Metaphorical Sense*, in which creation from nothing is distinguished from other kinds of natural causation.[26] The language suggests a modification of the Neoplatonic system of emanation and some of the statements in this little tract also suggest that, properly speaking, God alone is cause in the sense that reminds us of the doctrines of the Mutakallimun. There is also the problem of the nature and value of philosophy. Al-Kindi gives several definitions of philosophy derived from "the ancients," viz., the love of wisdom, attainment of moral perfection, contemplation of death, science of sciences, man's knowing himself (a Socratic maxim which Al-Kindi turns into the study of one's self as the study of the microcosm), and, finally, philosophy as knowledge of the eternal universal things.

[24] This tract is translated in full in *Isaac Israeli* by A. Altmann and S. M. Stern, London 1958, p. 43.

[25] There is some division of opinion as whether Arabic translations of any of the Platonic dialogues existed. There were paraphrases and epitomes (e.g., Galen's), but F. Rosenthal (*Islamic Culture*, XIV [1940] 387-422) has produced convincing evidence that the Islamic philosophers were mainly, and perhaps exclusively, dependent on indirect sources for their knowledge of Plato's dialogues.

[26] See Altmann and Stern, *Isaac Israeli*, pp. 68-69 where this treatise is translated in full.

These conceptions are closely connected in Al-Kindi's mind: self-knowledge involves a knowledge of the contents of the active Intelligence which, for Al-Kindi, is the totality of the forms of things.[27]

Religious philosophy must explain the phenomena of prophetic revelation (this is especially true of Islam, a religion in which prophecy is the greatest miracle). Accordingly Al-Kindi explains that the knowledge of the prophets is obtained directly and requires neither research nor acquired logical skill. It is, in fact, dependent upon the will of God and the purification of the prophets.

Al-Kindi employs several methods for proving the existence of God. Since man is a microcosm, i.e., a small-scale replica of the universe, he sees in himself indications of the nature of things as a whole, and the analogy between the individual human being and the universe leads Al-Kindi to employ the argument from design, that is, from the evidences of order and arrangement in the sensible world, to establish the existence of a Divine Arranger. For every organization there is an organizer.

He goes on to argue that the universe could not have existed from eternity. Otherwise an infinite sequence of events would have been realized, a conclusion Al-Kindi regarded as absurd. Since time (as well as body and motion) is limited, the universe has limited duration; hence, it must have been created, and since a created thing entails a creator, there must have been a creator.

While he adheres to the general Neoplatonic scheme which we find in the pseudo-Aristotelian writings (*Theology of Aristotle*, etc.), he modifies it "in a small but not unimportant detail."[28] "The highest sphere of the heavens . . . , having been created from nothing by God, will last as long as God so wills,"[29] so that the universe will perish when God wishes.

[27] Altmann and Stern, *ibid.*, pp. 37, 159.
[28] R. Walzer, *Oriens*, 1950, pp. 7ff.   [29] R. Walzer, *ibid.*, p. 8.

Although he makes no attempt to prove the limited temporality of the universe, just as he does not attempt a philosophical justification of the resurrection of the flesh, he evidently, as a Muslim and a Mutazilite, felt obliged to accept these dogmas.

It is clear from his views about the extraphilosophical nature and origin of prophecy that Al-Kindi believed that there is a source of knowledge superior to philosophy which requires no philosophical preparation. This not only makes philosophy ancillary to theology but also connects Al-Kindi, historically, with the Athenian Neoplatonists rather than with the Alexandrines for whom philosophy was not essentially distinct from religion.[30]

Al-Farabi (d. 950) appears to have presented a more systematic form of philosophy. His works cover the systematic treatises of Aristotle and some works on Plato, whom Al-Farabi appears to have known only through epitomes. He also wrote some works on the *Ideal State* and on *The Ideas of the People of the Virtuous City*. For a long time, the *Gems of Wisdom* and the *Sources of Questions* were attributed to him, but the attribution of the second is very doubtful, and of the first almost certainly wrong.[31] It is, therefore, very difficult to say what ideas may safely be attributed to him. The famous distinction between essence and existence which has an important place in the Christian philosophy of the thirteenth century was attributed to him but, as this comes from doubtful or wrongly ascribed works, it is no longer safe to say much about this in connection with Al-Farabi.

It seems reasonably clear that Al-Farabi placed philosophy in the highest position of human aspiration. Not only does

[30] R. Walzer, *op.cit.*

[31] See S. Pines in *Revue des Études Islamiques* (1951), pp. 120ff. and F. Rahman, *Prophecy in Islam*, London 1958, pp. 21-22. My use of the "Sources of Questions" has been sparing, and I would have avoided it altogether had some other of Al-Farabi's genuine writings been available to me.

he deny the resurrection of the flesh, but he explicitly accords to metaphysics the highest rank. Theology (i.e., Kalam) is secondary because it employs dialectical methods whereas metaphysics uses demonstration. This distinction foreshadows that of Ibn Rushd (Averroes). The idea lying behind it is the distinction between philosophers and ordinary people. The latter cannot be expected to comprehend philosophical truth and so must be instructed in concrete and picturesque language.[32] Thus the "lurid escatology"[33] was treated by many enlightened Muslims as figurative language suited to the uncultivated nomads to whom Mohammed brought the Revelation. Ibn Al-ʿArabi of Murcia (1164-1240), Ibn Tofail (1100-1184), Ibn Rushd (1126-1198), all take this view which, as Walzer has observed, is an inheritance from the Alexandrine Neoplatonists. Perhaps this is the closest that medieval philosophers came to any independence of philosophy from revealed religion. This does not mean that genuine philosophical independence was achieved. For, although their thought may have been relatively free from limitations imposed by religion and its authorities, most of these Islamic philosophers were limited by their dependence on their Greek sources. I do not mean that they were all consciously intellectual subjects of the Greek philosophers. (This might apply, however, to Averroes.) Nevertheless, their problems and solutions move within the boundaries of Aristotelian and Neoplatonic conceptions.

Being is the most universal concept (although some other concepts, such as Unity, Truth, Goodness, are coextensive and therefore convertible with *Being*). It is also the simplest concept and cannot, strictly speaking, be defined. Some things can be regarded as *possible* beings since their essence does not imply the necessity that they exist. Another thing is such that,

---

[32] *The History of Hayy ibn Yaqzan*, trans. S. Ockley, revised and introduced by A. S. Fulton, London 1929, p. 30.

[33] The distinction between "the learned and the vulgar" is, of course, very old and can be traced back to Greek Antiquity. The distinction among rhetorical, dialectical, and demonstrative arguments is derived from Aristotle.

when its essence is considered, its existence is seen to be necessary. Now if something exists which is merely possible it must exist through (or by means of) another thing. In other words, the existence of possible beings implies the existence of a being whose nonexistence involves contradiction.[34] For there can neither be an infinite regression of things (whose existence is only possible) standing in cause and effect relations to one another nor can these beings be mutually interdependent in a circular way (i.e., such that A is caused by B, B by C, C by D, ... and Z by A). The self-subsisting necessary Being which stands at the beginning of the causal chain must be the most perfect of things and thus unaffected by any of the four kinds of cause (material, formal, efficient, or final).[35] The existence of all things comes from this perfect Being, but not by way of a purpose similar to human purposes; hence, things emanate from this Being solely because He knows His own essence. His knowledge is therefore the cause of the existence of the things which He knows. But this is not a temporal knowledge, and hence the reception of existence by finite things is an eternal process. That God is anterior to the world is the statement of a logical dependence, not of a temporal relation. Al-Farabi has a number of proofs that God is one and absolutely simple.[36] The only way in which the plurality of contingent beings can be derived from such an absolutely simple unity is as follows:[37] The First Being is good, wise, etc. Insofar as It thinks, there emerges from It a second wholly incorporeal

[34] Al-Farabi, *'Uyun al Masä'il-Fontes Questionum*, ed. Miguel Cruz Hernandez, AHDL XII (1951), 303ff., and F. Dieterici, *Alfarabis Philosophische Abhandlungen*, Leiden 1892, p. 94. Cf. Al-Kindi (quoted by Altmann and Stern, *op.cit.*, p. 60) and Ibn Sina, *Kitab al-Najāt*, p. 366 (quoted by A. M. Goichon, *La Distinction de l'essence et de l'existence*, Paris 1937, pp. 159ff.).

[35] See Goichon, *La Distinction*, pp. 152ff. It was generally argued that the necessary being would be perfect in the sense of lacking any defect.

[36] See Al-Farabi, trans. F. Dieterici, *Der Musterstaat*, Leiden 1900, pp. 8-14.

[37] That this is the *only* way was argued because it was held that an absolutely simple being could have only one *immediate* effect.

Being (the first of a series of Intelligences or pure forms) in which there is a plurality. For it thinks both of itself and its Source. Insofar as it thinks of its source it emanates a second Intelligence, and insofar as it thinks of itself it emanates the outermost sphere of the heavens. The second Intelligence, in a similar manner, radiates a third Intelligence and the sphere of the fixed stars. This process continues until we reach the sphere of the moon. In the *Sources of Question* (*Uyūn al-masā'il*) the number of Intelligences and spheres is left undecided. But in the *Model City* (*Arā ahl Madīna al-fadila*), the number of spheres is fixed at nine and the number of Intelligences at ten: the outermost sphere, the sphere of the fixed stars, the spheres of Saturn, Jupiter, Mars, Sun, Venus, Mercury, Moon, and the process is terminated in the Agent Intelligence. This last Intelligence is the cause of the existence of terrestrial souls on the one hand and of the four elements on the other.[38] From the elements result various mixtures, and these mixtures are, according to the proportions of the constituent elements, prepared to receive various kinds of souls, viz., vegetable, animal, and human.

Our knowledge of the First Being (God) is radically and incurably deficient and it is high wisdom to know that the human understanding cannot fully understand God (the learned ignorance of Neoplatonic origin which we have already encountered in Pseudo-Dionysius and Eriugena and which is a persisting theme of medieval thought in the Judaeo-Islamic as well as the Christian world of the Middle Ages). God can in a sense be known negatively (the *via negativa or via remotionis* of the Christian Scholastics) and also by preeminence (cf. the Superlative Theology of Pseudo-Dionysius

[38] This account is based on the *Model City* and *The Sources of Questions*. See Goichon, *La Distinction*, pp. 152-155, and pp. 227-228nn., for translation of the pertinent sections of the latter, and F. Dieterici, *Der Musterstaat*, pp. 23-31, or *Ara ahl Madīna al-fadila* (Publication of the Institut français d'Archeologie Orientale du Caire, 1949) for translation of the former work.

and Eriugena and also certain views of the thirteenth-century Christian theologians, e.g., Thomas Aquinas).[39] Yet Al-Farabi does not hesitate to say of God that He is Infinite, Immutable, Simple, One, Intelligent, the Truth, Life, etc.[40]

The main aim of man is to become like God. This Al-Farabi elaborates in terms of self-improvement and then the improvement of the community (i.e., the family or the political community). There is no doubt that he, like the several other philosophers (*falāsifah*) of Islam,[41] held that happiness can be found only in the political community and that the intellectual life can be perfected only within the community. But there is also no doubt that intellectual perfection is the ultimate aim.[42] How this intellectual perfection is to be achieved and the condition of consciousness which characterizes it can be understood only in terms of Al-Farabi's theory of the intellect.

The Islamic philosophers in general, and Al-Farabi is no exception, assume that whatever exists free from matter is an intellectual being.[43] In the *Model City* Al-Farabi gives an argument for this to the effect that God, because He has nothing of the material in His nature, is an intellect. The argument is: That which prevents forms from being intellects and from engaging in actual thinking is matter. Now if a thing does not require matter in its being, then it is already an actual intellect.[44] Moreover matter is the cause of the fact

---

[39] See SCG, I, 14 and 34.

[40] *Der Musterstaat, op.cit.*, pp. 13-23.

[41] Excepting Ibn Bajja (Avempace) who is a special case. See E. I. J. Rosenthal, *Political Thought in Medieval Islam*, ch. 8.

[42] See Rosenthal, *op.cit.* ch 6, and p. 274 n.30. This view has its ultimate origins in Plato, Aristotle, and Plotinus.

[43] In the Latin translations the single Arabic word for intellect ('aql) is sometimes rendered by "Intelligentia" (intelligence) and sometimes by "intellectus" (intellect) depending on the context. Very frequently, *Intelligentia* is used to denote the celestial emanations and *intellectus* to denote the human mind.

[44] This goes back ultimately to Aristotle, *Metaphysics*, Book Delta, 9, 1075^a3-5: "Since thought and the object of thought do not differ in things containing no material, they will be identical and the act of thinking will be identical with theorized thought."

that a thing is not immediately and entirely intelligible. But since God is free from matter, He is also essentially intelligible; hence, since God is also absolutely simple, His intellect, Its intelligible object, and the act of understanding are identical.[45]

Now in the case of man who is material as well as spiritual in nature, thinking is not originally identical with the object of thought. Indeed, Al-Farabi holds, as did Al-Kindi, that there are several intellects (or, better, several stages in the development of intellect) in man. Man has, at first, a merely potential intellect which is gradually perfected until a contact is made with the Agent Intelligence, which is the last of the purely spiritual beings in the hierarchy of intelligences emanated from God. These several stages of the intellect are: the potential intellect, the *intellectus in effectu* (i.e., in act), and the acquired intellect. Some forms are abstracted from matter, while others do not exist in matter and hence need not be abstracted therefrom. When these separate forms become forms for the human intellect, it becomes the acquired intellect. The Agent Intellect abstracts forms from sensible material things for us and, when it becomes an object of thought for us, our intellect reaches the stage of acquired intellect. It seems, then, that this contact with the Agent Intelligence is the highest achievement for man and human beatitude consists in this conjunction or union with the Agent Intelligence.

What this means for human immortality is not easy to see. Ibn Tofail[46] complained that Al-Farabi in a work on morality asserted that the souls of evil men would be subject to eternal torments whereas in other writings he held that such souls cease to exist and that perfect souls alone are immortal.

[45] *Die Musterstaat*, p. 13. This doctrine is related, as is obvious, to Aristotle's description of God's activity as being a "thinking about (his own) thinking." Cf. Aristotle, *Metaphysics*, XII, 9, 1074^{b}35.

[46] Spanish philosopher of the twelfth century, an older contemporary and friend of Averroes (Ibn Rushd).

Ibn Rushd (Averroes) had similar complaints, and even held that Al-Farabi denied personal immortality altogether.[47] In the *Model City* Al-Farabi states that when good men die their souls join similar souls and, in this blessed state, the arrival of new souls increases the happiness of those already in Paradise. This is in direct conflict with a statement of Ibn Rushd to the effect that the survival of the individual as a separate form is an old wives' tale. It is possible, as R. Walzer has suggested, that Al-Farabi was capable of giving out an orthodox view for popular consumption, and concealed his actual beliefs from the masses.[48] In any case, ambiguity on this question of personal immortality, deliberate or inadvertent, is to be encountered in many of the Islamic philosophers. One of Al-Farabi's accusers, Ibn Tofail himself, is very vague on this point.[49] There is something about Al-Farabi's statement in the *Model City* which suggests absorption of the individual into the Agent Intelligence.

Another interpretation of Al-Farabi's psychological theory given recently by F. Rahman makes the theory more consistent and removes some of the grounds for the criticism which later Islamic philosophers directed against it. According to Rahman, the intelligible forms which the human intellect becomes are abstracted from sensibles. The Agent Intelligence only illuminates the sensibles and the intellect of man, but does not actually radiate forms into the human mind. This clearly differentiates Al-Farabi's doctrine from that of Avicenna (according to whom the forms themselves are radiated into the human mind by and from the Agent Intelligence).

Again, according to Rahman, Al-Farabi "consistently and boldly declares that those human beings in whom this potential intellect does not become actual perish with the death of

[47] See S. Munk, *Melánges de philosophie juive et arabe* (reprint, 1927), pp. 347-349.
[48] R. Walzer, *Islamic Culture*, XIV (1940), 387ff.
[49] See his *History of Hayy ibn Yaqzan, op.cit.*, pp. 88-93.

the body,"[50] and Rahman supports this with a text of Al-Farabi which seems conclusive. Thus Al-Farabi seems to hold that (1) only the souls of intellectually cultivated individuals survive bodily death,[51] and (2) this survival is individual, i.e., there is no absorption of the individuals into the Agent Intelligence. This interpretation of the doctrine, while not wholly consonant with orthodoxy, comes closer to it than the other interpretation.

Perhaps the most important philosopher in Islam, Avicenna (Ibn Sina, 980-1037) owes much to Al-Farabi. On his own admission[52] it was Al-Farabi's work *On the Objects of the Metaphysics* which made clear to Avicenna the meaning of Aristotle. And many details, especially of metaphysics and psychology, are common to the two men. Yet there are important differences, and Avicenna's influence both in the Islamic and the Christian world of the Middle Ages was far more extensive (indeed it can hardly be overestimated). Avicenna's philosophy is taken as representative of the philosophers whom Al-Ghazali attempts to refute in his *Incoherence of Philosophers*. Shahrastani devotes to Avicenna an extensive section of his *Religious and Philosophical Sects in Islam*. In the Christian West, he is, as Gilson has demonstrated, the chief influence on the development of early thirteenth-century Scholasticism. He was as famous as a scientist and physician as well as a philosopher, and his medical writings were widely used down to modern times.

According to Avicenna, it is in the science of Being (metaphysics) that the existence of God must be demonstrated. Therefore, he prefers the proof for the existence of God from the possible character of things in the world rather than from

[50] F. Rahman, *Prophecy in Islam*, p. 25.
[51] The degree of beatitude is thus a function of the degree of cultivation. This becomes quite clear in later writers, e.g., Levi ben Gerson.
[52] See his autobiography, trans. A. J. Arberry, in *Avicenna on Theology*, London 1951. Another translation into French is in Avicenna, *Le Livre de Science*, Paris 1955, Vol. I.

arguments taken from natural science (e.g., the argument from physical motion to a First Mover). Accordingly, he begins his reflections by a careful and detailed analysis of the notion of *Being*.[53] This part of Avicenna's philosophy is both the most important and the most difficult to grasp. For it is clear from all his writings on the subject of metaphysics that Being, as well as the principal terms associated with it (*necessary*, *possible*, etc.), does not admit of either definition or description. *Being* cannot be defined because there is no concept more general than *Being* in terms of which it could be defined; again it cannot be described because nothing is better known than *Being* (and *descriptions*, according to Avicenna, state properties of a thing in order that we may have some knowledge of it when we do not know its essence. Since there is nothing cognitively more primitive than *Being*, a description leading to a knowledge of *Being* cannot be found).[54]

That *Being* is the primary notion is argued by Avicenna in a number of ways. One of these, while not entirely original, is elaborated by Avicenna in his own way and is of importance for his psychology as well as his metaphysics. This is the argument of the "flying man." Suppose that a man were to exist anew with full powers of understanding but suspended in space in such a way that he could not perceive any part of his body nor be stimulated by any of his senses, he would still know that he *existed*.[55] This shows, not only that man's

[53] Avicenna gives several statements of his metaphysical views: The main and longest account is in *The Book of Healing* (sc. of the Soul) (*Kitab al-Šifā*), an encyclopaedia which contains a metaphysics, physics, psychology, etc. The short compendium of this work is the *Book of Salvation* (*Kitab al-Najāt*). In addition, there are two other outlines of his entire philosophy: *The Books of Directives and Remarks* (*Kitab al-Išarat wa-l-Tanbihat*) and a work in Persian *The Book of Science* (*Danesh-nâmè*). The metaphysical, physical, psychological parts of the "Book of Healing" were translated into Latin in the twelfth century, parts of the "Salvation" into Latin and French in recent times. There are also French translations of the other aforementioned works.

[54] *Le Livre de Science* (*Danesh nâmè*), I, 94.

[55] Ibn Sina, *Le Livre des directives et remarques*, trans. A. M. Goichon, Paris 1951, pp. 303-309; cf. the same argument used in Avicenna's great

self-knowledge does not depend on a prior knowledge of his actions or sense-experiences, but also that the primary concept is that of *Being*. Now as primary and nongeneric, *Being* can and must be known without definition. We can, of course, say something about *Being* and the concepts of *Unity*, *Possibility*, *Necessity*, and *Essence* which are associated with *Being*. But we cannot give either a definition or descriptions.[56]

Being is used, in its most general sense, to include any object of discourse and is applied in an analogical sense to each member of the hierarchy of *Being* starting from God, and going on through created substances without matter, substances conjoined to matter, forms of corporal things, and matter. *Being* is applied also to objects of consciousness even though they have no counterpart in the world outside of consciousness (e.g., fictions of imagination).

Now *Being* belongs to a thing *per se* in which case it is a substance, or accidentally, in which case it is an accident. These represent degrees of being. The most important division of *Being*, however, is between essence and existence. Avicenna deals with this distinction at length in all his philosophical works. A few characterizations of this distinction must suffice here.

In order to grasp the distinction[57] we must consider that some characteristics belong to the nature of a thing as explicitly

Metaphysics, which is translated by Goichon (*La Distinction*, p. 14) and E. Gilson (*Les Sources greco-arabes de l'augustinisme avicennisant*, Archives d'histoire litteraire et doctrinale du moyen âge, 1929-1930, pp. 40-41 for the Latin text). It also occurs in the psychological part of the Najāt (See F. Rahman, *Avicenna's Psychology*, London 1952, pp. 10-11.) The source of this argument is Plotinus (*Enneads*, IV, 8, 1) and, ultimately, perhaps Plato (cf. *Theaetetus*, 185-186).

[56] The difference between *definition* and *description* was introduced by the Stoics, and was well-known in Islam through Galen and Alexandrian commentators. See *'Išārāt*, trans. Goichon, pp. 106-107; *Danesh nâmè*, *Le Livre de Science*, vol. 1, p. 94.

[57] Goichon, *La Distinction*. For a criticism of this point of view, see F. Rahman, *Essence and Existence in Avicenna*, Medieval and Renaissance Studies, Warburg Institute, London 1958, IV, 1-16. The distinction appears to have been derived from Aristotle, *Posterior Analytics*, II, $92^{b}9$-20; I, 2,

constituting its nature, others belong to it as properties which are logically connected with this nature. But from the definition of such a nature it cannot be discovered whether or not such a nature exists, i.e., whether it is concretely realized or instantiated. A nature or essence is simply what it is and we cannot know, merely by knowing this "what," whether or not it is instantiated or realized. Hence, because *that something of a given kind exists* is different from *what its nature is*, Avicenna argues that existence is extrinsic to essence. For Avicenna this in turn implies that everything whose essence and existence are thus distinct requires a cause which gives such an essence existence, i.e., brings it into concrete being.

Now to say that existence is external to essence seems to treat existence as an accident and, therefore, as some sort of attribute. But it is not wholly clear that this is Avicenna's intention.[58] What is meant by existence, then, remains somewhat obscure. It is nonetheless true that Avicenna repeatedly asserts in his various philosophical works that existence is an accidental attribute of essence.

Another distinction of *being* related to the one just mentioned is the difference between possible and necessary being. The necessary being (literally "the necessary of existence")[59] is that being, the supposition of whose nonexistence implies a contradiction, whereas in the case of a possible being, no contradiction results whether we suppose it to exist or not to exist.[60] Every being whose essence is not its existence is thus a possible being, whereas a being in which essence and existence are the same is an absolutely necessary being. Yet Avicenna also holds that beings, possible when considered in themselves, are necessary when they are caused to exist by a being which

---

72ª23-24; Goichon also calls attention to Plotinus, *Enneads*, VI, II, 6. See her translation of *'Išārāt, Le Livre des directives et remarques*, p. 356, n. 1.

[58] See F. Rahman, *op.cit.*, pp. 8-9.

[59] *Wājib al-Wujūd* or *al-Wājib al-Wujūd*.

[60] *Kitab al-Najāt*, 366 (*Metaphysices Compendium*, Lib. I, 2 Pars, 1 Tract. Cap. 1, Carame 66-68); see Goichon, *La Distinction*, pp. 159ff.

is absolutely necessary. From this it seems to follow that whatever exists and is caused is possible in itself and necessary in virtue of its cause. And so, it would seem, there is no real contingency in Avicenna's universe.

There are two ways by which the existence of the necessary being is established. Usually Avicenna argues from the existence of possible beings to that of a necessary being.[61] We are certain that in this world below (i.e., in the sublunar part of the universe) something exists. Either this thing which exists is possible or absolutely necessary. If it is absolutely necessary then we have proved that there is an absolutely necessary being. Suppose that it is possible. We can show that the existence of anything that, in itself, is possible, ultimately derives from the existence of an absolutely necessary being. For there cannot be an infinite series of merely possible beings each responsible for the existence of another. Since every possible being requires a cause, we must ultimately assume a necessary being which causes all beings which in themselves are merely possible and which yet exist.

Avicenna also suggests another way[62] in one of his works. Although this work was not translated into Latin and so had no influence on the Christian philosophers, it is of interest because it finds a parallel in Duns Scotus[63] whose principal inspiration in metaphysics was certainly those works of Avicenna which were translated into Latin. To prove the existence of

[61] This argument, *ex possibilitate*, is used by Moses Maimonides, *Guide to the Perplexed*, Pt. 2, ch. 10, pp. 152-153 of M. Friedländer's translation, London 1928. It is the third of the "Five Ways" of Thomas Aquinas; see his *S.th.*, I, q. 2, a. 3. It occurs in Avicenna in the *Metaphysics of the Sifā'*, II, 521; see the translation of M. Horten. In the metaphysics of the *Najāt* (Carame, 91-93), the *Išārāt* (Goichon's translation, pp. 357-360) Goichon also translates the argument from the *Najāt* (*La Distinction*, ch. 35, pp. 166-167, n. 4).

[62] *Išārāt* (Goichon's translation, *Le Livre des directives et remarques*, pp. 371-372).

[63] See Duns Scotus, *De Primo Principio, Text and Translation*, Evan Roche, Franciscan Institute, St. Bonaventure, N.Y., 1949. E. Gilson, *Avicenne et le point de Départ de Duns Scotus*, AHDL, II (1927), 89-149.

the Necessary Being we need only analyze the idea of Being; we do not have to reflect on anything other than Being itself. Here we understand that Necessary Being contains its own existence, and we see Necessary Being as such. When we contemplate the nature of Being, it attests its own existence. Now since we can obtain the idea of being by knowing our own existence without the aid of our senses, we have a direct intuition of the Necessary Being. Avicenna seems to have supposed that this method is available only to the most just individuals,[64] while others less good must employ the argument from possibility.

The Necessary Being is absolutely *one* and absolutely simple. This Being, identified with God, Allah, is without any essence, properly speaking, and, properly speaking, is not a Substance. Only one such Being is possible. The question arises how the multiplicity of the world can be derived from this unique and absolutely simple Source.

Avicenna's system of the emanation of the universe is clearly derived from Al-Farabi with, of course, some further elaborations. Following the principle that a single simple cause can have but one effect, Avicenna holds that but one being can proceed from the First Being. Plurality is, then, the result of a differentiation existing in the first emanated being. Since it is entirely free from corporeality, it will be an Intellect (or *Intelligence*). God also is an Intelligence, on this consideration, but in God, the knower, the known, and knowing are all one. In the first emanated Intelligence, however, there is an intrinsic multiplicity. For insofar as this Intelligence thinks of its Source, it emanates a second Intelligence. Thinking of itself as necessary (in virtue of the fact that it is necessarily emanated from the absolutely Necessary Being) it emanates the form of the outermost celestial sphere, and thinking of itself as possible (since all but God is, in itself, only possible) it emanates the body of the outermost celestial

---

[64] Siddīqīn (similar to *zaddukim* in Hebrew).

sphere.[65] This process goes on: the second Intelligence generates a Third Intelligence as well as the matter and form (= soul) of the next outermost sphere (the sphere of the fixed stars), and so on as the Intelligences, souls, and spheres of the five planets, the Sun, and the moon are produced. From the Intelligence which has generated the sphere of the moon comes a final Intelligence which is too far removed from the Source of existence to generate another Intelligence. Each stage in this hierarchy is, so to speak, causally feebler than its predecessor so that the last Intelligence lacks the power to produce another Intelligence. Nevertheless, the last Intelligence is a very important part of Avicenna's cosmology, for from it comes the world of terrestrial matter with its forms.[66] In fact, this last Intelligence, the so-called Agent Intelligence, plays a crucial role in Avicenna's psychology and epistemology.

It must be understood that the emanation of the world from the First Cause is an *eternal* and a *necessitated* process. Hence the dependence of the world upon God is causal, not temporal. This, though formally incompatible with the literal meaning of the Koran, is very clear in Avicenna's discussion. God, by knowing his own essence, knows the effects which necessarily follow from Him. He knows the singular things insofar as they are universal, that is to say, by knowing the universal causes and their mutual concurrences.[67]

[65] The account of this process can be found in the *Metaphysics of the Sifā'* (*Metaphysica*, IX, 6); see M. Horten's translation *Die Metaphysik Avicennas*, pp. 602-603; in the *Nājāt* (see trans. of Carame, *Metaphysices Compendium*, pp. 194ff). The best discussions I have found are in E. Gilson, AHDL, I (1926), especially pp. 37ff.; and Goichon, *La Distinction*, pp. 238-244. As Mlle Goichon remarks, this is perhaps the best-known part of Avicenna. It is expounded by Al-Ghazali (in his *Tendencies of Philosophers* and in his *Incoherences of Philosophers*; see *Averroes' Tahafut al-tahafut*, trans. S. Van den Bergh, p. 109), and discussed and rejected by Averroes (*Tahafut, op.cit.* p. 111), and expounded and rejected by Thomas Aquinas (SCG, II, q. 42).

[66] See *Isārāt*, p. 175 (Goichon, *Livre des directives et remarques*, p. 431).

[67] The text of the *Sifā'* and *Nājāt* on this subject is translated by Goichon, *La Distinction*, pp. 266-272; cf. Carame, pp. 118-125. M. Horten, *Die*

But this view of things is impossible for an orthodox Muslim to accept, and the eternity and necessity of the world as well as the doctrine that God knows particulars only by knowing their universal causes will be attacked by Al-Ghazali.[68] Certainly Avicenna emphatically affirms that God knows *all* particular things and events. At the same time, it is difficult to see how his system can prove this or even make a place for it. Some of the Christian Scholastics (e.g., Thomas Aquinas), will object that knowledge of particulars through their universal causes is unsatisfactory.[69] The main difference between Aquinas and Avicenna is that, for the former, God acts freely and man's-actions are not all necessitated, whereas Avicenna holds to the absolute necessitation of all events.

The sublunar world of matter is a world in which there is constant change, the coming-into-being and perishing of individual material things. How does this come about? Avicenna must explain (1) how there is a plurality of individuals of the same form, and (2) how a given form comes to characterize a given part of matter.

Avicenna accounts for the plurality of individuals of the same nature by matter existing under determined dimensions. Thus when matter is determinate in quantity, position, etc., it suffices to differentiate one individual from another in the same species. In a word, determinate matter is the principle of individuation. The forms of all material things are radiated from the agent Intelligence, the Giver of Forms (*Donator Formarum*). That a given bit of matter will receive one such form is determined by its "preparation," i.e., when there is a particular mixture (of determinate proportions) of the four elements, this material mixture is prepared to receive one of

---

Metaphysik Avicennas, Halle 1907, p. 522, lines 16-22, and generally pp. 522-528.

[68] See his "Deliverance from Error," translated by W. Montgomery Watt in *The Faith and Practice of Al-Ghāzali*, London 1953, pp. 37-38.

[69] See SCG, I, 63; *S.th.*, I, q. 14, a. 11.

the forms constantly radiated from the Agent Intelligence.[70]

Avicenna's doctrine of the human soul and of human knowledge must now concern us. I have already alluded to the argument that man can know that he exists without recourse to his bodily senses. For Avicenna this not only supplies man with a direct knowledge of existence but also assures him that his soul is a substance capable of existing apart from the body. His argumentation reminds the reader of Descartes's radical distinction of body and mind and of Descartes's proof of his own existence. Avicenna devotes some time, in fact, to proving the substantiality of the soul from the unity of consciousness. From this substantial character of the soul, Avicenna deduces its immortality.[71]

There are vegetative souls (of plants), animal souls (with motive and perceptive powers), and rational souls (of human beings). Now the rational human soul has, so to speak, two faces. The one face, the practical faculty, looks down to the body and the external physical world. Its function is to govern and direct the body. The other face, the theoretical faculty, has the function of looking upward to the celestial world whence come knowledge and, ultimately, blessedness.

The human intellect begins as a material intellect and, under the action of sense experience and the illumination of the Agent Intelligence, becomes necessarily the intellect in effect, the intellect in habit, and the acquired intellect. In this final stage, human potentiality effects some kind of contact with "the first principles of all existence."[72] This will be clearer when an account of the relation of perception and knowledge is set forth.

[70] For some further details of this complex theory see E. Gilson, *Pourquoi St. Thomas a critiqué St. Augustin*, AHDL, I (1926), p. 38.

[71] He denies the Platonic doctrines of preexistence of the soul and transmigration. See, for all this, F. Rahman's *Avicenna's Psychology*, London 1952, chs. 10-15. (This is a translation of the psychological part of the *Najāt*.)

[72] Rahman, *op.cit.*, ch. 5.

The external senses are affected by the action of physical objects, and leave impressions in the imagination. Man has a further capacity (the estimative faculty, which is shared with other animals) of discerning "nonmaterial intentions," that is, that certain external objects are beneficial and that others are to be avoided. While imagination can represent objects even in their absence, the images of things in consciousness are presented with all their sensible details. In other words, these faculties cannot separate the forms in abstraction from their material and accidental accompaniments. Now while perception and induction are certainly aids to human reason in acquiring knowledge, the forms of things must be abstracted to perfect this knowledge. Avicenna speaks of the human reason abstracting these forms, but this, as Rahman has pointed out,[73] is only a figure of speech. For the images in consciousness only "prepare" the soul for the reception of these forms which are radiated into human consciousness by the Agent Intelligence. Thus the Agent Intelligence not only gives forms to things in the material world, but is also the source of forms as we cognize them in our consciousness. When, therefore, we cease to be actually thinking of a given form (e.g., the form of horse), the human intellect ceases to have that form in itself. In order to think of such a form again, consciousness must be again prepared by the images of things in order to receive the appropriate radiation from the Agent Intelligence.

The form which is thus received is considered in itself as an essence. From the standpoint of the concept in the mind this essence is *one*; as duplicated in the physical world (as many times as there are individuals possessing such a form), it is many. But considered as an essence, it is neither one nor many but simply the essence or common nature. Avicenna's famous formula: *Equinitas est equinitas tantum* (Horseness is simply horseness) means that an essence, considered in itself

[73] F. Rahman, *Prophecy in Islam*, London 1958, p. 15.

(i.e., in its content), is neither one nor many but simply what its logical content reveals.[74]

This doctrine that a common nature considered in itself is neither one nor many is part of the solution of the problem of universals which was to be adopted by many scholastics in Christendom in the thirteenth century. Both Aquinas and Scotus use it in different ways to deal with the question. On the other side, both Al-Ghazali and William Ockham reject it in their nominalistic resolutions of the problem.

The Islamic philosophers of the Eastern part of the Islamic world were constantly opposed by the orthodox. Perhaps the effective culmination of this opposition is to be seen in the attack on philosophy by Abu Hamid Muhammad al-Ghazali (b. 1058 in Persia–d. 1111). The nature and purpose of this attack was explained by Al-Ghazali in an autobiographical account of his intellectual career, the "Deliverance from Error."[75] In the interests of orthodox Muslim doctrine, Al-Ghazali set out to master the doctrines of the philosophers and the several philosophical sciences (logic, physics, and metaphysics). The three points of the philosophers which he singled out for criticism and refutation are: the denial of bodily resurrection; the denial that God knows particulars (i.e., that God's knowledge comprises only universals); and the affirmation that the world is eternal.[76] Al-Ghazali also engaged in criticizing certain religious sects in Islam but this is of little interest to philosophy.

[74] F. Rahman, *Avicenna's Psychology*, ch. 7, p. 38; see Goichon, *La Distinction*, pp. 71 ff. for translations of the passages in the *Šifā'* pertinent to this question.

[75] Translated in Watt's *The Faith and Practice of Al-Ghāzalī*, pp. 19-86.

[76] See *The Faith and Practice of Al-Ghāzalī*, pp. 37-38, and also Averroes' *Traité Décisif (Fasl al-maqâl)*, ed. and trans. Léon Gauthier, 3rd edition, Alger 1948, p. 11. "Abu-Hāmid [Al-Ghazali] has formally accused [Al-Farabi and Ibn Sina] of infidelity in his *Incoherence of Philosophers* on three points, namely, the affirmation of the eternity of the world, that God does not know particulars, and about the interpretation of passages of the Revelation with regard to the resurrection of the body and with regard to several matters of the future life."

As he explained in the *Deliverance from Error*, it is necessary first to expound the doctrines accurately and then to criticize them. Accordingly he wrote an extensive work *The Tendencies of the Philosophers* which is mainly an exposition of Avicenna's views. This was followed by *The Incoherence of the Philosophers* (*Tahafut al-falasifah*).[77]

This attack on philosophy is a very remarkable work. Its earliest modern students recognized the similarity of Al-Ghazali's critique of causality with that of the French Occasionalists and Hume.[78] But it is replete with acute criticisms of many other philosophical doctrines, such as the doctrine of potentiality and actuality, the doctrine of real universals, and so on. I shall restrict myself to an account of the attack on causality which best illustrates the acuteness of Al-Ghazali as a critic.

Following the line already taken by the Asharite Mutakallimun, Al-Ghazali holds that God is the only real cause, and that the apparent and alleged causal connections among things other than God are really due to God's direct action.

On the other hand, one of the essential doctrines of the philosophers is that necessary causal connections are to be encountered throughout the universe. We must not forget that Avicenna regarded causal connection as necessary. Al-Ghazali attempts to show that the arguments of the philosophers to this end come short. The philosophers, especially

[77] The *Tendencies* was translated into Latin by Dominic Gundisalvi in the twelfth century and so was known to the thirteenth-century Scholastics. The *Incoherence*, however, was not translated into Latin until 1328. As the preface of the former work was omitted from Gundisalvi's translation (a preface which explained the purely preliminary and expository character of the work), the thirteenth-century scholastics read Al-Ghazali as one of the "Philosophers" and did not realize that he was actually an enemy of philosophy. The *Tahafut* has recently been translated by A. Kamali: *Al-Ghazali, Tahafut al-Falasifah*, Pakistan Philosophical Congress (Mohammed Ashraf Darr, 8 Meleo Road, Lahore, India), 1958. The important sections are reproduced by Averroes. See *Averroes' Tahafut al-tahafut*, trans. S. Van den Bergh.

[78] E. G. Renan's famous statement about the critique of causality: "Hume n'a dit plus." Cf. Sir William Hamilton, *Lectures on Metaphysics*, Boston 1859, pp. 541-542.

Al-Farabi and Avicenna, held that the connection between causes and effects is one of logical necessity, in other words, that the existence of a cause without its appropriate effect (or *vice versa*) is impossible. In the interests of the religion of Islam this argument must be contested. For unless it is false, miracles are impossible, since a miracle consists of the divine interruption of the common course of nature.

There are a number of arguments which serve our purpose. First of all there is the logical argument. Impossibility consists in the simultaneous affirmation and negation of the same thing, and all impossibilities ultimately amount solely to the assertion of a self-contradictory statement.[79] It is also the case that all necessity reduces to logical necessity[80] since the necessary is that the denial of which is impossible. If we apply this to the causal nexus we get the following result: "According to us the connection between what is usually believed to be a cause and what is believed to be an effect is not a necessary connection; each of the two things has its own individuality and is not the other, and neither the affirmation nor the negation, neither the existence nor non-existence of the one is implied in the affirmation, negation, existence and non-existence of the other. . . ."[81] Attempts to meet this argument are countered by pointing out that the necessity of causal connection (i.e., the impossibility that a certain event is not causally connected with another event), depends on what is conceptually included in the descriptions of the events in question. Events can be so described that the existence of one involves that of the other.[82] But this depends on the description, not on the events themselves.[83]

There is also an empirical argument against the alleged

---

[79] Van den Bergh, *op.cit.*, pp. 52-53, 328-329.

[80] Van den Bergh, *op.cit.*, p. 60.

[81] Van den Bergh, *op.cit.*, p. 316.

[82] Van den Bergh, *op.cit.*, p. 329.

[83] Thus, if we describe a man as a father, this description logically connects that man with a child.

empirical evidence for causal connection. The philosophers appeal to observation to show, for example, that it is the contact of a flame with a piece of cotton that brings about combustion of the cotton. But "observation proves only a simultaneity, not a causation, and in reality there is no other cause but God."[84] Some passages of the *Incoherence* seem to suggest that causal belief is associated with habit, but it is not wholly clear that Al-Ghazali has anticipated Hume to this extent.[85]

This illustrates the sort of destructive criticism which Al-Ghazali brings against all of the contentions of philosophers. The use of philosophical methods to discredit philosophy was not invented by Al-Ghazali. Not only was he indebted to the Mutakallimun, but they, in turn, to the Christians and ultimately to the Greeks. The phenomenon of a philosophical attack on philosophy is itself not unique. The ancient Sceptics used it, Judah Halevi later imitated Al-Ghazali in this endeavor, and we find several instances in the fourteenth century (especially, Nicolas of Autrecourt). Scepticism in the interests of religion occur again in the sixteenth and seventeenth centuries in Italy, France, and England.

Al-Ghazali's critique was certainly one of the causes of the decline of philosophical speculation in the Islamic East. He achieved great fame for his *Revival of the Religious Sciences* and encouraged orthodoxy and mysticism at the expense of philosophy. The next important philosophers in Islam flourished in Muslim Spain in the twelfth century.

The earliest philosophers in Spain were, like those of the Islamic East deeply influenced by Neoplatonic works. But, in

[84] Van den Bergh, *op.cit.*, p. 317; see also the Latin translation of Averroes' *Tahafut*: *Destructio Destructionis* in *Aristotelis Opera*, Venice 1574 (Junta) Vol. IX, "Et ipsi (sc. philosophi) non habent rationem visi testimonium adventus combustionis cum tactu ignis. Sed testimonium indicat, quod advenit cum eo, et non indicat, quod advenit ex eo, et quod non sit causa alia praeter eum."

[85] See Van den Bergh, *op.cit.*, p. 324, and M. C. Hernandez, *Historia de la filosofia español*, Madrid 1957, I, 164.

the case of the Spanish philosophers, a work ascribed to Empedocles (actually a Neoplatonic compilation) was very influential. The main difference between the emanation theories which were adopted in the East and those which came out of Pseudo-Empedocles was the theory that the first emanation from God was prime matter. This doctrine is defended by Ibn Masarra of Cordova (883-931). It was also adopted by the Jewish philosopher, Ibn Gabirol, of whom I shall say something later.

The first important Islamic philosopher in Spain was Ibn Bajja (Avempace) who lived from about 1070 until 1138. Many of his writings are lost, but there remain two works of importance: *The Regime of the Solitary* and *Treatise on the Union of the Intellect with Man.*[86] He was one of the links between Al-Farabi and Ibn Rushd (Averroes), and his views on physical questions are discussed by the latter. The main concern of Ibn Bajja is how man can achieve his ultimate aim, blessedness, which is to know and love God. While the other philosophers in Islam all maintained that human happiness can be achieved only in existing political states and had made it clear that the philosopher shares political responsibilities with other members of the community in which he finds himself, Ibn Bajja is almost or entirely alone in holding that the quest for happiness must be the result of the philosopher's own efforts. The imperfection of existing states forces the philosopher to pursue his ultimate happiness by himself or with a few like himself who share his aims.

Only human actions can determine purposes or ends. Now the solitary philosopher should set for himself the goal of perceiving spiritual things. The further a substance is removed

[86] The first part of Ibn Bajja's treatise on the "Regime of the Solitary" has been translated by Dunlop, in the *Journal of the Royal Asiatic Society* (1945), pp. 61-81; E. I. J. Rosenthal "The Place of Politics in the Philosophy of Ibn Bajja," *Islamic Culture*, xxv (1951), 187ff., has discussed the doctrine in general terms. S. Munk, *Mélanges de philosophie juive et arabe*, pp. 383ff. gives an extensive analysis.

from anything corporeal, the more it merits the term spiritual; and the things which most merit such a designation are the Agent Intelligence (also called "Active Intellect") and the substances which move the heavenly spheres. Altogether there are four kinds of spiritual forms: the Intelligences which move the spheres; the active and emanated intellect; the forms of material things, which are abstracted from physical objects; and finally the ideas of the common sense (*sensus communis*), of imagination, and of memory.

By means of sensation, memory, etc., we are led to the higher forms. Now, whereas forms abstracted from matter exist in the human mind in a condition different from their existence combined with matter, it is altogether different in the case of forms which never existed in matter. If we know such completely separate forms, their existence in our consciousness is the same as their existence in themselves. Hence, when man's potential intellect is actualized and becomes acquired intellect, man knows himself as an intellectual substance. But the acquired intellect now is, as it were, the substratum for the higher spiritual forms, especially for the Agent Intelligence.

The Agent Intelligence is an indivisible purely spiritual form and all the specific forms of material things are in it as one undivided form. When, therefore, we finally arrive at a conception of this unity of all specific forms, namely, the conception of the Agent Intelligence, we know it as it is in itself, we are united with it, and thus have achieved the final end, and human blessedness. So by essentially intellectual means and without any antiphilosophical mysticism,[87] Ibn Bajja holds man can achieve union with the Agent Intelligence and so beatitude. The two characteristics which appear to differentiate the views of Ibn Bajja from most of the other

[87] It is true, of course, that prophetic inspiration achieves this union without the usual intellectual stages of the process. Cf. Munk's translations of ch. 6 of the "Regime" in *Mélanges de philosophie juive et arabe*, p. 399. Munk's account of Ibn Bajja is the best I am acquainted with.

philosophers (*falasifah*) of Islam are that (1) philosophical knowledge *can* be achieved outside existing society, and (2) it can be achieved rationally and without special benefit of Islam.

The Spanish philosopher Ibn Tofail (1100-1184), known to the Latin world as Abubacer, provides a version of the solitary metaphysician, doubtless influenced by Ibn Bajja, but presenting some interesting features of its own. In the form of a philosophical novel, Ibn Tofail presents his philosophy in the biography of *Hayy ibn Yaqzan* (The Living One, Son of the Vigilant).[88]

Again and again, Ibn Tofail emphasizes that multiplicity reduces to unity so that the multiplicity of individuals reduces to the unity of their species, and, by the extension of this notion, the whole world, vital as well as inanimate, has a unity.[89] This world requires a cause because all its contents are produced anew. It makes no difference whether the world as a whole is eternal or not, for in either case there must be an Agent (which is neither a body nor something joined to a body) to which all things owe their existence. Hence, the world is logically, if not temporally, dependent on God. Moreover, the design we discover in the world attests to the intelligence of its cause. God is pure existence, a Being existing necessarily by its essence. Since man can comprehend this completely incorporeal Being, his own essence must be incorporeal, and because the incorporeal is incorruptible, man's essence cannot be dissolved. Knowing that God exists, man desires to behold God continuously. The method of coming

[88] For an English translation, see *The History of Hayy ibn Yaqzan*, trans. S. Ockley, revised by A. S. Fulton, London 1929. This has the defect that it lacks Ibn Tofail's important introduction. The best and most reliable translation is that of Léon Gauthier, *Hayy ibn Yaqdhân, roman philosophique d'Ibn Thofaïl*, Beirut 1936. The Latin translation of Pococke of 1671 and 1700 is thought by some to have influenced Defoe in his *Robinson Crusoe*.

[89] "That all multiplicity reduces to unity" is the Neoplatonic doctrine that the reality of the multiple depends on some unity. See, e.g., Proclus, *Elements of Theology*, I, 1.

to know God consists in abstracting from one's own and all other limited essences so as to see only the one permanent Being.

The problem of the complete identification of the individual human self with God now confronts Ibn Tofail. On the one hand, it can be argued that one who has knowledge of the Divine Essence, has that essence, and since this Essence can be nowhere save with Itself, and as the presence of the Essence is the Essence, it would appear that the individual is identical with the divine Essence. On the other hand, "We cannot say of these separate essences which know the essence of this True One, that they are *many* or *one*, because they are immaterial. There is *multiplicity* because of the separation of one essence from another, and there can be no unity but by *conjunction*, and none of these can be understood without compound notions which are mixed with matter. But the explication of things in this place is very straight and difficult; because if you go about to express, by way of multitude, or in the plural, according to our present way of speaking, this insinuates a notion of *multiplicity*, whereas they are far from being many; and if you speak of them by separation, or in the singular, this insinuates a notion of *unity*, whereas they are far from being one."[90] So Ibn Tofail concludes that there is, in some sense, a union with the Divine Essence, and in some sense a multiplicity of human essences each, in someway, united with the Divine Essence.

Ibn Rushd (Averroes) is, after Avicenna, the Muslim philosopher whose works had the greatest influence in medieval Christendom. A younger contemporary of Ibn Tofail, with whom he was associated, Ibn Rushd (born in Cordova in 1126), was a judge and a physician as well as a philosopher, and the greatest commentator on Aristotle since the close of

[90] Ockley-Fulton translation, p. 144; cf. Plotinus, *Enneads*, V, 7, 1. See *Plotinus*, by A. H. Armstrong, London 1953, p. 82, "We ought not to be afraid of the infinity which this introduces into the intelligible world; for it is all in an indivisible unity. . . ."

the schools in Athens in the sixth century. Although the jurists and the theologians of his time made Muslim Spain an uncongenial place for philosophy, Ibn Rushd was protected by his royal patrons. His temporary disgrace and exile must be explained as a political gesture of his patrons to protect him from the zealots. He died in 1198.

His commentaries on Aristotle won him the title of "The Commentator" (Dante, who imaginatively encountered him along with Euclid, Galen, Aristotle, Avicenna, Plato, *et al.* in Limbo, calls him the one "who wrote the great comment.")[91] His attitude toward Aristotle was evidently one of unbounded admiration. Scattered throughout his commentaries are extravagant praises of the Philosopher. The passages most often referred to in this connection are in the prologue to his commentary on Aristotle's *Physics*. There are other instances of it in his commentary on Aristotle's *On the Parts of Animals* and *On the Generation of Animals*.[92] Ibn Rushd expresses himself on the matter as follows: Aristotle discovered physics, logic, and metaphysics because nothing written on these subjects before him could be considered a satisfactory foundation of these sciences. Moreover, Aristotle has completed these sciences, for, when his works appeared, men turned away from earlier investigations and no one in fifteen hundred years has been able to add anything to them that is worthy of notice. To find all this in one man is so remarkable that one must consider him almost divine. We incessantly thank God who has given

[91] Dante, *Inferno*, Canto IV, line 144. Ibn Rushd wrote three kinds of commentary on each of Aristotle's main works; The *Lesser Commentary* (or Epitome), the *Middle Commentary* which paraphrases the text, and the *Great Commentary* which is a detailed discussion of every paragraph. The style of the *Lesser Commentary* was adopted by earlier thirteenth-century Christian writers (e.g., Albertus Magnus), while Thomas Aquinas adopted the style and method of the *Greater Commentary* in his *Commentaries on Aristotle*. The Jewish philosophical authors of the thirteenth and later centuries also adopted the style of Averroes' commentaries.

[92] See S. Munk, *Mélanges de philosophie juive et arabe*, pp. 316, 411. See also, E. Gilson, *History of Christian Philosophy in the Middle Ages*, New York 1954, p. 220 and p. 642 n. 17.

us such a man, from whose works we can learn all that can be known. As Aristotle reached the pinnacle of human intellectual perfection, so is his doctrine the supreme truth. The reason for this is simple: Aristotle discovered both the art of demonstration and the basic premisses of the sciences, that is, he found propositions that are necessary, essential, and primary from which, by absolutely certain deductions, the irrefutable conclusions follow. No perception of the senses, therefore, can conflict with these demonstrations.

The question immediately posed by such approbation from an avowed Muslim is whether there can be a conflict between scientifically demonstrated propositions and the tenets of Islam. This question has been answered in many ways.[93] The important point to make here is the difference between the Ibn Rushd of legend and the Ibn Rushd of fact. In the Christian world of the thirteenth century he was made responsible for the doctrine that the world was eternal, that God does not know singulars (individual things) and does not exercise particular providence, that there is only one intellect for all men, that personal survival after death is impossible, and that there are truths of philosophy which are theologically false (and *vice versa*).[94] We shall indicate how the Ibn Rushd of fact stands in the face of these indictments. It is necessary to say that the interpretation offered here is only one of many possible interpretations, and that there is a profound division of opinion among the closest students of the subject.[95]

The first point to be made is that Ibn Rushd explicitly

---

[93] For a summary of the several *recent* interpretations, see Hernandez, *Historia de la filosofia española*, II, 81-103.

[94] See, e.g., Thomas Aquinas, SCG, III, 76 and I, 63; *S.th.*, I, 76, 2; I, 117, 1; and I, 46, 1.

[95] See E. I. J. Rosenthal, *Political Thought in Medieval Islam*, p. 177. "(Ibn Rushd) was a Moslem first and a disciple of Plato, Aristotle and their commentators second, but I do not deny that Ibn Rushd is not always constant and unambiguous." See also Léon Gauthier, *Ibn Rochd*, pp. 32-33 and S. Van den Bergh, *op.cit.*, II, 203-204 and *passim*.

denied the so-called doctrine of double truth, i.e., that there are truths of philosophy which are formally inconsistent with truths of theology. "If these religious precepts are of good quality and if they invite us to the speculation which leads to the knowledge of true Being, then we Muslims know decisively that speculation based on demonstration cannot lead to contradiction of the teachings of the Divine Law. For truth cannot contradict truth; rather truth agrees with truth and truth testifies in favor of truth."[96] If there is an apparent conflict between the Divine Law (Koran) and proved philosophical truth, the Law admits of an interpretation according to the canons of interpreting the Arabic tongue. Such an interpretation sometimes involves passing from the literal to the metaphorical or figurative use of an expression. But there is no possibility of a genuine conflict. We may well wonder how Ibn Rushd was thought to have held to the double-truth doctrine. Max Horten has shown how some of the later translations of Ibn Rushd may have led to such a misinterpretation. Averroes was an avowed enemy of the Mutakallimun, the followers of Kalam or orthodox theology. When the Arabic text states that some philosophically untenable doctrine is valid according to theology, i.e., Kalam, the Latin text reads *"Hoc est verum secundum theologiam,"* and it was perhaps such misleading renderings that were partially responsible for the misapprehension. But this is not the whole story. Some of the philosophers in thirteenth-century medieval universities were said to have professed that certain propositions of Aristotle, though demonstrable according to natural reason, were plainly contradictory to the Christian faith. There is little doubt that this doctrine was actually maintained, although it is difficult to identify those who maintained it. There is, likewise, little doubt that the commentaries of Ibn Rushd in their Latin version were partially responsible for this view.

This possibility of holding that Aristotle's philosophy is

[96] Averroes' *Traité Décisif*, ed. and trans. Gauthier, p. 8.

true and yet does not conflict with Islamic beliefs has been explained lucidly by Leon Gauthier, and it will make Ibn Rushd's position clearer if Gauthier's theory is set forth. The only way recognized in Islam to resolve conflicts about belief was to appeal to *ijma* (the universal consensus of Islam, which for practical expediency was interpreted to mean the consensus of the learned and competent men of a given epoch). In cases of dogmatic conflict over theoretical principles, in contrast to matters of religious practice, the consensus had to be *proved*. But this law again was practically impossible to administer because it was impossible to set precise limits to the epoch, to determine who was competent: because of the plurality of sects and political authorities in the Islamic world (which at Ibn Rushd's time extended from Muslim Spain to China) there was no *de facto* religious authority qualified and empowered to interpret ambiguous texts, define dogmas, and make adjustments between religion and philosophy. Furthermore, there is, according to Gauthier (although here some authorities are in disagreement) nothing in Islam to correspond to the Mysteries of the Christian faith; hence, Gauthier concludes, the Muslim philosopher was free to interpret the Koran in the light of reason. Now it is true that the zealots among the jurists and theologians as well as a fanatical caliph or emir were free to denounce or persecute the philosopher. But the situation in medieval Islam was sufficiently different from that of medieval Christendom to account for the possibility of an Al-Farabi, an Ibn Sina, or, above all, an Ibn Rushd.

In his treatise on the agreement between religion and philosophy, Ibn Rushd devised an unusual theory about the nature of revelation (Koran). In the effort to end theological debates which had produced a multiplicity of warring sects, as well as to defend philosophy against charges of heresy, Ibn Rushd held the following views: The Koran exhorts us to study philosophy. It makes no difference whether our predecessors were Muslims or not if they discovered truth which can aid a Muslim in his philosophical pursuits. The ancient philosophers had made a thorough investigation of the sciences, and we must examine what they said, accept what is true, and reject the false.

There are three different kinds of men, i.e., three different human temperaments: those who form judgments by philosophically demonstrative reasoning, those who are convinced by dialectical arguments, and finally those who are brought to assent by exhortation.[97] The Koran was intended for all men and so invites all to study it, according to their capacities and temperaments. Here we must remember that, as a Muslim, Ibn Rushd held to the equality of all members of Islam and as a student of Plato and Aristotle, to the importance of the community for all human life. As he also maintained that religion, in addition to being true, was indispensable to the welfare of the state, he was obliged to adopt some view that would make a place for the philosopher without jeopardizing civil peace and without weakening the effect of religion on the masses. It is just as well then, he maintains, to restrict philosophy to those who are capable of it, and to appeal to men of other capacities by dialectic or exhortation. The Mutakallimun are objectionable precisely because they attempted to bring philosophical issues to the masses who were incapable of understanding them.[98] The deepest truths of religion are understood in their purest form only by the philosophers. But as few can attain to this, the Koran was deliberately revealed so that the humblest intellects could benefit by it.

This doctrine does not mean that there are no limits to the philosopher's interpretation of revelation. Ibn Rushd explicitly states that anyone who holds that the doctrine of future

[97] The origin of this classification is probably due to Aristotle, *Metaphysics*, Book Alpha, 3, 995^{a}6, and to the Stoics. See S. Van den Bergh, *op.cit.*, II, p. 98.

[98] Of course, Ibn Rushd also objects to the Mutakallimun because they used arguments that were, in his opinion, at best dialectical and at worst sophistic.

rewards and punishments was taught merely in order to safeguard the stability of society is an infidel and deserves to be
executed. He defends the philosophers against the charges
of Al-Ghazali, and holds firmly that God both knows and
provides for particular things in the world, and that there is
an afterlife.[99]

In his philosophy, Ibn Rushd follows Aristotle as closely as
possible. He rejects Al-Ghazali's denial of causal connection
on the grounds that (1) "one who denies the effect of the
causes or the results of them, also denies philosophy and all
the sciences. For science is the knowledge of things by their
causes, and philosophy is the knowledge of hidden causes.
To deny the causes altogether is a thing altogether unintelligible to human reason. It is to deny the creator, not seen by
us. For the unseen in this matter must always be understood
by a reference to the seen,"[100] i.e., a knowledge that there is
a God can be obtained only by an inference from observed
causal connection to the First Cause; (2) the occurrence of necessary causal connection is self-evident, i.e., the existence of
causes and effects is a primitive principle whose denial leads to
absurdities.[101] Thus Ibn Rushd does not attempt to prove the

[99] The sources of this account are principally:
1) Ibn Rochd, *Traité Décisif*, ed. and trans. Léon Gauthier, *op.cit.*
2) Averroes' *Tahafut al-tahafut*, trans. S. Van den Bergh, *op.cit.*
3) *The Philosophy and Theology of Averroes*, trans. Mohammed Jamil-
Ur-Rehman, Baroda 1921. (This is a translation of the *Decisive Treatise,
The Appendix*, and *An Exposition of the Methods of Arguments Concerning the Belief of the Truth*, etc. There is also a more reliable Spanish
translation by M. Alfonso (*Teologia de Averroes*, Madrid 1947). Only
one of these tracts, the *Exposition of Methods of Arguments* was available to
the Christians in the Middle Ages in Raymond Martin's *Pugio fidei*.
[100] *Exposition of the Methods of Arguments*, (Rehman, *op.cit.*) pp.
276-277.
[101] See Van den Bergh, *op.cit.*, pp. 318-319, 273: "If life could proceed
from the lifeless, then the existent might proceed from anything whatever,
and there would be no congruity between causes and effects. . . ." This
argument has its origin in the Aristotelian principle that the effect must be
like its cause, as Van den Bergh (II, 150, n. 4) observes. In statement,
however, it is much closer to Epicurus, in *Diogenes Laertius*, X, 39 (cf.
Lucretius, *De rerum natura*, I, 125).

principle of causality, but rather defends it dialectically, since he holds (following Aristotle here) that absolutely first principles cannot be proved. He simply takes it as self-evident.[102]

With the principle of causality, Ibn Rushd proceeds to establish the existence of God. Against Avicenna he argues that the existence of God should be proved in physics, not in meta physics, for he rejects the distinction of essence and existence on which the metaphysical proofs of Avicenna depend.[103] Against some of his predecessors, he holds that the arguments from the order and mutual adjustment of things, while instructive and persuasive, are not absolutely conclusive; it does not absolutely prove the existence of God but rather enables us better to understand the divine wisdom.[104] The only absolutely demonstrative argument for the existence of God is Aristotle's proof in the eighth book of his *Physics* to the effect that the eternity of matter, motion, and time require a first unmoved mover, a pure form.[105]

God is an Intelligence because (as with other Islamic philosophers) every Pure Form (i.e., form unmixed with matter) is an Intelligence.[106] He is active in some way for otherwise He would be superfluous and the highest imitation of Him could not be a form of activity.[107]

As the First Mover, God is the cause of all celestial movements. Ibn Rushd opposes the emanation doctrines of Al-Farabi and Avicenna, and holds instead that a multiplicity of

---

[102] Cf. M. Horten, *Die Hauptehren Averroes nach seiner Widerlegung Gazalis*, Bonn 1913, p. 296: "Eine Ableitungsmöglichkeit des Kausalgesetzes leugnet Averroes also; denn der hier genannte Syllogismus würde den Grund für das Kausalgesetz enthalten, dieses also erwiesen. Für Averroes ist das Kausalgesetz also etwas innerlich Evidentes, Unerweisbares."

[103] Van den Bergh, *op.cit.*, p. 236.

[104] *Exposition of the Methods of Arguments*, (Rehman, *op.cit.*) pp. 207-220; Gauthier, *Ibn Rochd*, p. 145. See also Averroes, *Die Epitome der Metaphysik*, trans. S. Van den Bergh, Leiden 1924; E. Gilson, *History of Christian Philosophy in the Middle Ages*, p. 644.

[105] Van den Bergh, *Tahafut*, p. 261.

[106] Gauthier, *Ibn Rochd*, pp. 145ff.

[107] Van den Bergh, *Tahafut*, p. 300; also Ibn Rushd, in *Metaphysicorum XII*, comment 44.

Intelligences can come directly from the First Being.[108] With respect to the existence of these Intelligences nothing more can be understood save the idea of their connection and dependence.

We can say, speaking analogically, that God has a *nature*[109] and that He can be described,[110] we can attribute Intellect to God and say that, in knowing Himself he knows other things including particular things and events.[111] His eternity requires the eternity of the world but this does not mean that the world is eternal by itself.

God's absolute unity and uniqueness are proved by showing that any multiplicity in God or of gods would be logically incompatible with the Simplicity of the Divine Nature.[112] Hence the multiplicity of divine attributes must be "constituted through relation," i.e., many different things may be attributed to God in terms of the relations of the world to God.[113]

The problem of the relation of the Agent Intelligence to human minds is one of the most difficult points in Ibn Rushd's philosophy.[114] The solution he gave to it, as understood in thirteenth-century Christendom, earned for him the reputation of having denied individual immortality. Ibn Rushd attempts to explain one of the most obscure passages in Aristotle's *De Anima* (III, 4, 5) which asserts that the part of the soul which thinks cannot be mixed with the body. Now throughout nature we find the distinction between the agent and the patient. A similar distinction must exist in the soul ($\dot{\epsilon}\nu$ $\tau\hat{\eta}$ $\psi\nu\chi\hat{\eta}$).[115] Intellect ($\nu o\nu\varsigma$) must therefore be regarded as one thing insofar

[108] See H. A. Wolfson, *Crescas' Critique of Aristotle*, Cambridge, Mass. 1929, p. 667.

[109] Van den Bergh, *Tahafut*, p. 272; Gauthier, *Ibn Rochd*, p. 147.

[110] Here Ibn Rushd seems to differ from Avicenna and others among the "philosophers." See Van den Bergh, p. 222.

[111] Van den Bergh, *Tahafut*, pp. 206-207, 261-265, 280.

[112] *Ibid.*, p. 173.

[113] *Ibid.*, II, p. 115.

[114] See Ibn Rushd's *Commentary on de Anima*, III, comment 5, where he insists on the great difficulty of the subject.

[115] Aristotle, *De Anima*, III, V, 430ª10-14.

as it becomes everything (i.e., becomes the *forms* of the objects it contemplates) and it must be regarded as another thing insofar as it makes all things (ὁ δὲ τῷ πάντα ποιεῖν), i.e., insofar as it actualizes the forms of things perceived. Now intellect in the sense of agent is separable from the body, unmixed with the body, and is not the recipient of any action of the body (ἀπαθής). Now only intellect in the active sense is immortal but, because it cannot be acted upon, we do not remember (our present life). This seems to mean that survival of the individual personality with its memories, etc., is out of the question. Aristotle goes on to say that the mind as passive is destructible and cannot think without the active intellect. It is possible also to read the last line of Aristotle's chapter (430ª24-25)[116] as meaning that nothing can know without the intellect considered as passive. The Greek commentators, especially Alexander of Aphrodisias and Themistius, strongly disagreed on the matter. Alexander held that the passive intellect is a mere potentiality which does not survive the body, whereas Themistius maintained that the passive intellect "is a real spiritual entity, or substance independent of the lower parts of the soul, though associated with them during life, and hence is not subject to generation and corruption, but is eternal."[117] Alexander identified the Active Intellect with God.

Ibn Rushd expounds the views of these commentators and then attempts a synthesis of the parts of each which he regards as correct.[118] The Active Intellect comes from the Sphere of the Moon and is, therefore, not God. Its function is to actual-

[116] As W. D. Ross (*Aristotle*, 5th ed., London 1949, p. 152) observes, the last words of the chapter may be interpreted in at least four different ways.

[117] I. Husik, *History of Medieval Jewish Philosophy*, New York 1916, pp. 332-333.

[118] The clearest easily accessible accounts of this matter are: Munk, *Mélanges de philosophie juive et arabe*, pp. 445-455 (only the last sentence on p. 454 seems to me erroneous); Husik, *op.cit.*; Léon Gauthier, *Ibn Rochd*, pp. 238-245; *The Summary of Cajetan of Thiene*, translated in Gilson, *History of Christian Philosophy in the Middle Ages*, pp. 645-646.

ize forms in human consciousness and to actualize forms in material things. The passive Intellect is only the Active Intellect when the latter is conjoined to the human soul. When the imaginative power of man is supplied with images from the operation of the senses, it furnishes these images to the passive intellect. The forms, existing potentially in such images are actualized by the Active Intellect. The result of this is that human consciousness is supplied with concepts, judgments, inferences and so has become the *acquired intellect*.

Now this means that the only beings which are *purely spiritual* in nature and which enjoys a *purely spiritual immortality* are the Intelligences. The denial of Themistius' view that the passive intellect is a purely spiritual substance, one for each human being, would, therefore, seem to involve Ibn Rushd in a denial of human survival after death. Yet, as we shall see, this is not the case.

Ibn Rushd holds that, because matter is the principle of individuation, it is impossible that many forms specifically identical and free from matter should exist. From this it follows that a plurality of human souls could not survive without any bodies while retaining their individuality.[119] On the other hand, Ibn Rushd holds that those who deny individual immortality should be put to death as being wrong, irreligious, and a threat to the community. Consequently, those who hold to "the survival and numerical plurality of souls" must maintain that they survive "in a subtle matter, namely the animal warmth which emanates from the heavenly bodies."[120] Now these parts of subtle matter (which are associated with individual souls) preserve their numerical distinction and must be images of the earthly bodies of men because "that which has perished does not return individually."[121]

Ibn Rushd insists that the individual survival guaranteed

[119] Van den Bergh, *Tahafut*, p. 14.   [120] *Ibid.*, p. 357.
[121] *Ibid.*, p. 362.

by Revelation is a fact. On the other hand, he holds with Aristotle that the soul, qua perfection of the organic body, cannot exist without a body. The doctrine of the Resurrection of the body came to his rescue here. For if bodily resurrection (or, more correctly, the celestial body taking the place of the corrupted physical body) occurs, the continuity of individual personality is possible on terms which are consistent both with Aristotle and with Revelation. Thus although the Averroes of medieval Christendom denied personal immortality, the Ibn Rushd of fact affirmed it. It must be said by way of explaining this discrepancy that the work in which Ibn Rushd makes his position clear was not available in Latin until the fourteenth century.

Ibn Rushd was the last of the great philosophers in Islam, or at least, the last of those who had any influence on Western Christendom. His interpretations of Aristotle in their Latin form influenced philosophers in the Christian West from the thirteenth to the seventeenth century, and, as we shall see, played a decisive rôle in the crucial change of thought which took place after 1277 when the Bishop of Paris, Étienne Tempier, condemned the propositions which were associated with the name of Averroes.

CHAPTER VII · THE PHILOSOPHY
OF THE JEWS IN THE MIDDLE AGES

HE Jewish writers of the Biblical period were moralists, poets, historians, and legislators rather than philosophers. Still, many of their views about God, man, and the influence of God in history suggested philosophical questions which were asked and answered when Judaism came under the influence of Greek thought. Moreover, before the advent of anything among the Jews that can properly be called philosophy, such doctrines as the eternity of the Law (Torah) and the quasi-personification of Wisdom (Hochma) in the so-called Wisdom Literature (Proverbs, Wisdom of Solomon, Sayings of Jesus Son of Sirach) were points of departure for philosophical discussions. In the period of the formation of the Talmud, the questions concerning the indispensable theoretical elements of belief, as well as practical questions, occupied the attention of the Talmudic scholars. We find, for example, some of the authors of the Gemara maintaining that the belief in certain dogmas is one of the conditions for a "Portion of the Future World."[1] At the same time it was early maintained that "the righteous of all peoples have a portion of the World to come,"[2] the *righteous* defined as those who observe the ethical commandments of the Decalogue.[3] The search for the basic dogmas

[1] Gemara, ch. Helek, tract. Synhedrin; see David Neumark, *The Principles of Judaism*, Cincinnati 1919, pp. 38-39.

[2] See the Soncino edition of Genesis, *Genesis*, p. 33.

[3] This doctrine of general salvation of the righteous of all nations is connected with the doctrine of the Noachite laws. The covenant with Noah (considered as representative of mankind) guaranteed God's favor with the righteous men of all peoples: hence the notion of the Noachite laws, i.e., the fundamental religious and moral precepts for mankind. See also *Tosefta Sanhedrin*, xiii, 2, and *Mishnat Rabbi Eliezar* (ed. H. G. Enelow, New York 1934, p. 121). The "righteous," however, are those who accept the Laws of the Sons of Noah as divinely revealed. See also Steven Schwarzschild, "Do Noachites Have to Believe in Revelation?", *Jewish*

of Judaism has, therefore, a somewhat different significance than that of the attempts to formulate a creed in the Christian or Islamic world. Moreover, though the notion of a heretic occurs, it applies in practice to the members of the Jewish community. There are several somewhat conflicting definitions of "heresy." For instance, the "Shulkan Aruch" defines heretic (*Apikoros*, from *Epicurus*) as one who does not believe in the divine origin of the Law (Torah) or Prophecy;[4] Maimonides includes among heretics those who hold that there is no God and that the world is without a governor; the Mishnah (Sanh. x. 1, Gem. 90ᵃ) states "He who says that there is no resurrection, he who says that the Law has not been given by God, and an Apikoros will not have a share in the future world." Yet it is clear (from *Sifra, Behukkotai*, iii, 2) that rejection of the "laws and ordinances" was the decisive criterion for atheism. Although a creed or body of dogma was not a completely settled affair, and was not as important for medieval Judaism as it was for Christianity, the contact of Jews with other civilizations made the eventual development of a religious philosophy a necessity.[5]

As already mentioned, Philo of Alexandria was the first important Jewish philosopher. His use of the allegorical method to make Scripture concordant with reason and experience and his view that philosophy is the servant of theology have already been discussed. Philo's philosophical theology is a blend of Platonism and Judaism: God is the most general .

Quarterly Review, Vol. LII, no. 4, pp. 298ff., Vol. LIII, no. 1, pp. 30ff., and Jacob Katz, *Exclusiveness and Tolerance*, London 1961, especially pp. 115ff. and ch. 14.

[4] Josephus, *Antiquities*, 158, 2, refers to Epicureans as those who deny Providence. See *Jewish Encyclopedia*, New York 1901-1906, Vol. I, Article *Apikoros*.

[5] Yet it should be added that some of the medieval Jewish philosophers approved the view that heretics should be put to death. See Maimonides' *Epistle to Yemen*, trans. Boas Cohen, Academy for Jewish Research, New York, 1952, and reproduced, in part, in *Introduction to Contemporary Civilization*, 3rd ed., New York 1960, Vol. I, especially pp. 40-41.

and the highest existence; He is above knowledge, virtue or goodness. We do not reach God by reasoning (i.e., demonstration) but by an immediate subjective certainty. Still, the principle of causality leads us to some knowledge of God. As Philo sometimes argues, no work of skill makes itself; hence, we must necessarily assume a divine Artificer. God is simple, one, free and omnipotent. He is the place of the world because He encompasses all things.[6] The highest of the divine forces is the Logos (*Sophia, Hochma*). This is the divine Reason encompassing all Forms. This modification of Plato was required by the monotheistic commitments of Philo and is one of the prototypes of those Neoplatonic schemes in which the Realm of Forms is united with the Divine Mind. The Forms are also described in Stoic terms as Powers ($\delta v v \acute{a} \mu \epsilon \iota \varsigma$, $\lambda \acute{o} \gamma o \iota$) and Philo said that they were produced before the creation.[7] The aggregate and unity of these forms are called the Logos and Intelligible Cosmos ($\kappa \acute{o} \sigma \mu o \varsigma$ $v o \eta \tau \acute{o} \varsigma$) and also the divine Reason. Unfortunately and inconsistently, it is described also as a being distinct from God. On the one hand, the absolute transcendence of God makes any description of Him impossible, but on the other hand, the doctrine of Providence requires that there be Ideas in God. Again, as the Forms (Ideas) are instrumentalities of God they must somehow be in God, yet, as God must be distinct from the world, Forms must function as intermediaries and intervene between God and the world. The difficulty recurs throughout philosophy and we find medieval Jewish philosophers (e.g., Gabirol and Maimonides) troubled by it.

In *On the Creation of the World* (*De Opificio Mundi*) God is described as having created the world from a preexisting matter,[8] yet a little later in the same tract Philo writes as if

[6] Cf. Philo, *De Somniis*, I, II. Cf. H. A. Wolfson, *The Philosophy of Spinoza*, Cambridge, Mass. 1924, I, 297-298.

[7] Cf. Philo, *De Opificio Mundi*, Book IV, where the forms are called "the elder Creation."

[8] *Ibid.*, Book V.

matter itself had been created.[9] In any case Philo holds that time either originated with the world or after it was created.[10] Only *one* world was created.[11] The human soul is treated as distinct from the body and as an emanation of God.

The question of Philo's *direct* influence on the subsequent development of philosophy is still *sub judico*,[12] but there is little question of some kind of indirect influence. Most of the main themes of religious philosophy in the Middle Ages are foreshadowed or adumbrated in Philo's writings, as H. A. Wolfson has copiously demonstrated.

Medieval philosophy among the Jews begins properly with Isaac Israeli (about 855 to 955, born and lived in Egypt). His works are largely compilations from other authors[13] yet he has some importance in the history of medieval Christian philosophy because his writings were translated into Latin and frequently quoted by the Christian Scholastics of the thirteenth century. He is mainly influenced by Neoplatonism and shows especial dependence on Al-Kindi. Another and far more important philosopher was the Egyptian-born Jew, Saadia ben Joseph Al-Fayyumi (892-942) who became head of the religious academy at Sura. It will be worth while to indicate some of his thoughts on religious philosophy. Saadia is interesting as a religious philosopher for a number of reasons. While the larger part of his work is devoted to questions that are particularly or exclusively concerned with Judaism, his point of departure is that of the religious philosophers generally. Moreover, he is influenced to a large extent by the Mutakallimun but little, if at all, by Neoplatonism.

---

[9] *Ibid.*, Book VII. Nevertheless, most authorities seem to think that Philo accepts a world-formation out of a matter originally without qualitative determination.

[10] *Ibid.*   [11] *Ibid.*, Book LXI.

[12] See H. A. Wolfson, *Philo*, Cambridge, Mass. 1947, II, 158 and E. R. Dodds, *The Parmenides of Plato and the Origin of the Neoplatonic "One,"* *Classical Quarterly*, XXII (1928), 140.

[13] See A. Altmann and S. Stern, *Isaac Israeli*, London 1959, for translations of and commentaries on his work.

Saadia begins his philosophy by an investigation of the sources of knowledge,[14] by what has been called his "quest for certainty."[15] The main "roots" of knowledge are sense-perception, reason, inference, and reliable Tradition (this last includes both the Written Law (Scriptures) and the Oral Law (Talmud). In order to refute Scepticism, Saadia employs a number of familiar arguments, one similar to the *cogito* argument already encountered in Augustine, Plotinus, and Avicenna.[16] His defense of inference is especially illuminating. In addition to the truth vouchsafed by perception and the self-evident deliverances of Reason, knowledge can be obtained about things not immediately accessible by means of logically necessary inference.[17] If anything discovered by sense-perception is such that its existence logically necessitates the existence of other things, we must acknowledge the other things. Thus by logically necessary inference we infer the existence of the unknown causes of the events we perceive. Saadia adds that we must be sure that only one cause can explain the observed event, that our inference does not contradict known facts, that further it is self-consistent, and finally that in accepting the theoretically inferred things we have not adopted a theory worse than those we have rejected.

After these preliminary investigations which are intended to provide a firm foundation for knowledge, Saadia raises the question: why should we speculate about religious and moral questions? Since we have been given a revelation, why should we investigate further? Because we can then discover by our reason what has already been vouchsafed by revelation and

[14] The principal literature accessible to the reader will be: (1) The complete translation of Saadia's main philosophical work: *The Book of Beliefs and Opinions*, trans. S. Rosenblatt, New Haven 1948; (2) an abridged translation of the same: *The Book of Doctrines and Beliefs*; (3) M. Ventura, *La Philosophie de Saadia Gaon*, Paris 1934.

[15] See the excellent monograph by A. Heschel "The Quest for Certainty in Saadia's Philosophy," *Jewish Quarterly Review*, N.S., Vol. XXXIII, and the literature cited there, especially the essays of H. A. Wolfson.

[16] See A. Heschel, *op.cit.*, p. 273, n. 43.   [17] Rosenblatt, *op.cit.*, p. 21.

we can thus defend Revealed Doctrine against its detractors. Yet if reason can do this, why was there a Revelation at all? Here Saadia anticipates an answer, given in several variants by later medieval philosophers, e.g., Maimonides and Thomas Aquinas. Revelation was given in advance of rational argument because rational argument (which comprises the sciences) takes a long time to be discovered and elaborated and "we should have existed without religion for some time until the work of speculation was completed"; many people are unwilling or unable, or lack sufficient time, or are assailed by intellectually crippling doubts.[18] Thus revelation must precede reason, while reason can complete and perfect our knowledge of what has already been revealed.

Saadia's arguments for the existence of God owe much to the Kalam. He begins by discussing whether or not the world was created. Saadia, using the last of four theories on this subject (eternity of the world in its present form, Manichean dualism, eternity of matter, and creation from nothing), attempts to prove that the world was created from nothing. His arguments depend *inter alia* on the denial of the possibility that an infinite series of events precedes the present state of things, and on a kind of argument to design.[19] Since things cannot create themselves, there must be a Creator who created them from nothing.[20] The fact that Saadia examines and rejects the theory of emanation is indication that he does not mean by "creation from nothing" a creation out of the divine substance.

Having proved the existence of a Creator, Saadia turns to the question of the attributes of God. He attempts to prove that God has such attributes as *Unity, Life, Power, Wisdom, Incomparability* (a list that is fairly typical: we find similar

[18] Cf. Altmann and Stern, *op.cit.*, pp. 44-47; Rosenblatt, *op.cit.*, pp. 27-33.

[19] For the details, see H. A. Wolfson, *Kalam Arguments for Creation in Saadia, Averroes, Maimonides, and St. Thomas*, Saadya Anniversary Volume, New York 1943, pp. 197ff.

[20] Altmann, *op.cit.*, pp. 58-62. And M. Ventura, *op.cit.*, pp. 113-171.

lists in both Islamic and Christian authors). How can such a plurality of attributes be consistent with the divine unity and simplicity? According to Saadia, these attributes elucidate the meaning of *Creator* and then denote the ways the creature is related to God. In other words, Saadia's theory of attributes foreshadows Maimonides' doctrine that they are "attributes of action" and not a plurality of characteristics in the divine Nature.[21]

Saadia also deals with the anthropomorphisms in the Scriptures by holding that some of them can be interpreted allegorically. Some must, however, be taken literally, especially the visions of Daniel and Ezekiel. These mystical visions do not mean that any of the prophets actually saw God, but only that they beheld an appearance of light created by God.

As to the soul, Saadia seems to take a dualistic view, and his language suggests that the soul consists of a subtle matter.[22] From the introspective evidence that we choose without felt compulsion he argues that the human will is free.[23] There is a discussion of human freedom in connection with divine foreknowledge. The bulk of Saadia's work concerns religious and moral questions, some of which are restricted in their interest to Judaism. Saadia is primarily of interest because he was far more original than any of his predecessors and exhibits a freedom from Neoplatonism that is rare among philosophers in the early Middle Ages.

Of far greater interest and influence is Solomon Ibn Gabirol (born about 1021 and died about 1058). He was one of the first philosophers in Andalusian Spain, preceded only by Ibn Masarra of Cordova (883-931), and flourished at a time when Jewish intellectual culture had moved from Babylonia to Spain. His fame among the Jews as a poet outlived his reputation as a philosopher although his greatest poem, "The Royal

[21] But, as Altmann (*op.cit.*, p. 84, n. 1) observes, Saadia is not very consistent on this subject.
[22] Altmann and Stern, *op.cit.*, p. 152; Rosenblatt, *op.cit.*, p. 256.
[23] Altmann and Stern, *op.cit.*, pp. 118-125; Rosenblatt, *op.cit.*, 188ff.

Crown," contains important features of his philosophy. His philosophical work is contained in *The Fountain of Life*, originally written in Arabic, translated into Latin in the twelfth century under the title *Fons Vitae* and attributed to Avicebron, Avencebrol, etc. (all corruptions of Ibn Gabirol). This work is so free of any specifically or uniquely Jewish elements that some of the medieval Christian theologians who read it were inclined to think it was written by a Christian.[24] The only important Jewish philosopher who mentions Gabirol's *Fountain of Life* criticizes it severely as being non-Jewish.

Gabirol is a Neoplatonist, but the variety of Neoplatonism he expounds differs in certain ways from the systems most common in the Judaeo-Islamic world of the Middle Ages. One of the chief influences on him, and also on Ibn Masarra, was the pseudo-Empedoclean *Book of the Five Substances*.[25] According to this Neoplatonic work, matter and form are to be found throughout all the created world so that even incorporeal substances have in them matter and form. The matter of the subhuman (i.e., terrestrial) world is distinguished by the form of corporeity. As Altmann remarks, there is no place in the pseudo-Empedoclean system for the division of the universal soul into a series of hypostases (i.e., distinct substantial emanations).[26]

The main features of the universe, according to Ibn Gabirol are: God, the divine Will (or Creative Word), universal mat-

[24] E.g., William of Auvergne, *De Universo* I, p. I, cap. 25, quoted by J. Guttmann, *Die Scholastik des dreizehnten jahrhunderts, etc.*, Breslau 1902, p. 26. It was not until 1845 that S. Munk discovered the true authorship of the "*Fons Vitae*."

[25] The best secondary accounts of Gabirol are: S. Munk, *Mélanges de philosophie juive et arabe*, reprint, Paris 1927, pp. 151-306; J. Guttmann, *Die Philosophie des Judenthums*, Munich 1933, pp. 102-119; I. Husik, *History of Medieval Jewish Philosophy*, New York 1916, pp. 59-80. The Hebrew abbreviation of the *Fountain of Life* is translated in Munk, *op.cit.*, pp. 3-148, and the entire third book is translated by F. Brunner, *La Source de Vie, Livre III*, Paris 1950.

[26] Altmann and Stern, *op.cit.*, p. 168.

ter and universal form, universal intellect, universal soul, universal nature, and finally the substance of the categories. Excepting God, matter and form, as noted before, are encountered throughout the series of emanations. Now this doctrine that matter is to be found throughout the universe (God excepted, of course) has its origin in Plotinus.[27] It is the doctrine of hylomorphism which many of the Christian Scholastics, especially the Franciscans, were to adopt. Another closely related doctrine which the Scholastics later debated is the plurality of substantial forms, and this, too, is to be traced to Ibn Gabirol. According to this doctrine, there are several different forms determining a single substance, e.g., the corporeal, vital, and rational form in man. Universal hylomorphism and the plurality of substantial forms are thus usually found together in the doctrinal syntheses of the thirteenth and fourteenth centuries.

Matter is, then, the underlying substratum for all beings excepting God. It emanates from the creative Will and forms the basis for all subsequent emanations.[28] The spiritual substances of the celestial (= intelligible) world have matter underlying their forms.[29] For matter is intelligible or spiritual, with the exception of the matter having the form of body (or corporeity). Thus there are gradations of matter of which only the lowest is corporeal.[30]

Man is a microcosm or little world and all the features of the great world or macrocosm are found in man.[31] The Will is the force which holds matter and form together throughout the universe. This force suffers diminution as we proceed down through the hierarchy of beings and when we reach the lowest part, body, we find it inert and incapable of exercising any action.

[27] *Enneads*, II, 4.
[28] *Fons Vitae*, V, 333-335; Munk's translation of the Hebrew abbreviated version, V, 67-69.
[29] *Fons Vitae*, IV, 8ff.; Munk, *op.cit.*, IV, 1. [30] *Fons Vitae*, IV, 243.
[31] *Fons Vitae*, III, 200; Munk, *op.cit.*, III, 27ff.

Since man is a microcosm, it is possible for man to know the universe. If man succeeds in knowing himself he will understand the universe. This is because man's nature encompasses all things and somehow penetrates all things. Man's ultimate end is to know the Universal Will. Man cannot hope to know God because the finite cannot encompass the Infinite. God can, therefore, be known only through His effects especially as they are exhibited on the working of the Will. The soul of man may know the Universal Reason (because it is somehow similar to it). It can even, by a suprarational intuition, attain to Universal Matter. The somewhat mystical and poetic description of the stage of human consciousness when it reaches this highest stage claims that man will see himself as contained in the spiritual substance of the higher world. In knowing universal matter we know the most immediate expression of God.

The point of originality in Gabirol's philosophy is the doctrine of Will. But it is also the most ambiguous feature. On the one hand, it seems to be identical with God when we forget about its activities. Considered as the active cause of all things and the force holding the world together, it is represented as distinct from God. Thus Ibn Gabirol appears to vacillate between a view of the divine Will which would be pantheism and a view which does not explain the relationship between Will and God. Perhaps the notion of Will as the instrument of creation was intended to emphasize Ibn Gabirol's desire to avoid the necessitarian character of Neoplatonism.[32] Indeed, he states that the world has just the existence which God freely wishes to confer upon it. But it is difficult to introduce this free volition of God into a framework originally designed by Plotinus for whom the emanation of the world was necessitated by the divine nature.

[32] Cf. H. A. Wolfson, *The Problem of the Origin of Matter in Medieval Jewish Philosophy*, Proceedings of the Sixth International Congress of Philosophy, New York 1927, pp. 604-605.

It is necessary to pass over very able philosophers such as Joseph Ibn Zaddik, Abraham Ibn Daud, and Judah Halevi (this last the Jewish counterpart of Al-Ghazali by whom he was much influenced) to discuss the most significant figure in medieval Jewish thought: Moses Maimonides.

Maimonides (b. Cordova 1135–d. Egypt 1204) wrote his main philosophical work, the *Guide to the Perplexed*, for the purpose of removing the doubts and perplexities of learned Jews who were troubled by the apparent conflict between philosophical and scientific doctrines and the doctrines of the Bible and the Rabbinic treatises. Thus his work is primarily theological, its purpose is "apologetic and concordistic,"[33] and involves philosophy only when this suits the occasion. Yet it does contain a philosophical doctrine which was to be influential, not only among his coreligionists, but also, in its Latin version, in the Christian world of the thirteenth century and after. His influence among the Jews was permanent and decisive, and the saying, "From Moses (the Law giver) to Moses (Maimonides) there was none like unto Moses (Maimonides)," expresses this well.

Like his great contemporary in Muslim Spain, Ibn Rushd, he does not recommend the study of metaphysics for the mass of mankind. The subject itself, he tells us, is very difficult, human intelligence at the outset is inadequate, and the preparatory studies require a long time to complete. Moreover, the moral virtues or moral perfection must precede the study of philosophy (a point derived from Aristotle and frequently emphasized by many of the Islamic philosophers). Finally, the cares of life as well as the distraction of luxuries prevent most people from the successful pursuit of the subject. If one is to pursue the truth in philosophy he must be free from passion and, disregarding custom, follow reason and evidence. The preliminary conditions for philosophical study, therefore, are: the ability to reason logically, the grasp of the natural

[33] I. Husik, *History of Medieval Jewish Philosophy*, p. 239.

sciences, and moral perfection (since one cannot judge soundly if he is the victim of unruly passions).[34]

One of the sources of difficulty in reconciling the Scriptures with the theories of the philosophers is the failure to understand that many words of the Bible applied to God are really homonyms, i.e., equivocal words, which is to say, words which have several meanings which have nothing in common with one another. We must not, therefore, expect a literal agreement between revelation and science. On the other hand, correct exegesis must identify and explain these homonyms. When this is done we shall see whether revelation and science are in conflict.

Among the Jews, Maimonides states, there have been two main philosophical affiliations: some have followed the Kalam; others, Aristotle's views. In order to discover which of these philosophical systems is to be preferred we must ask first of all how successful they are in establishing what they propose to show. Accordingly, Maimonides gives a systematic account of the Kalam and of the Aristotelian system as he understood it.

The system of the Mutakallimun when examined is found to be defective on two principal counts: Its theory is internally defective and its attempt to prove the existence of God is built on shaky foundations. If the temporal finitude of the world could be conclusively proved, the existence of a Creator would be assured. But the arguments the Mutakallimun employ do not really prove the newness of the world.

On the other side, the Aristotelians claim that the world is eternal and insist that this very fact requires an eternal unmoved mover whom they identify with the God of Scripture. Yet when the Aristotelian system is confronted with the facts of celestial motion, it is unable to provide a completely satisfactory theory. More important than this is the fact that the

[34] *Guide to the Perplexed*, II, 23, M. Friedländer's translation, London, 1928, p. 195.

Aristotelians do not provide a conclusive proof of the eternity of the world.

In the face of this deficiency on both sides, what are we to do? The Scripture teaches the creation of the world in time, but Maimonides thinks that perhaps exegetical devices might bring about a reconciliation if such were demanded by philosophical demonstrations of the eternity of the world. It is not clear, however, that we must resort to such stratagems because the eternity has not been definitely shown. We may, however, take the doctrine of the eternity of the world as a *provisional* aid in the proof of God's existence. If we can prove the existence of God on this provisional hypothesis, we know that it can be proved in any case, because it is admitted that a Creator is required if the world has endured for only a finite time in the past. It will then be appropriate to inquire what can be said in favor of the creation-hypothesis.

Maimonides then expounds several proofs which he derived from his Greek and Islamic predecessors. The first is the proof from motion given by Aristotle in the eighth book of the *Physics* based on the eternity of time and motion. This proof is elaborately prefaced by twenty-five propositions which are established by Aristotle (in the *Physics* and *Metaphysics*) and by his commentators. The eternity of movement and these twenty-five propositions together imply that a first unmoved mover must be assumed. It follows, by some additional elucidation, that the unmoved mover is *one* and *incorporeal*.

The second proof is derived from Al-Farabi and Avicenna, namely, the argument for the existence of a necessary Being. There is a third proof based on the notion of potentiality and actuality, and a fourth which depends again on the notions of "moving" and "being moved." These proofs also establish the uniqueness and incorporeality of the First Being.

Thus the existence, uniqueness, and incorporeality of God can be established on the provisional hypothesis that the world is eternal. Now additional considerations show that on any hypothesis God is one and incorporeal; hence, on any hypothesis (i.e., whether or not the world has always existed), the existence of God, together with His unity and incorporeality, are assured.

Since the eternity of the world has not been proved, if we can find any positive grounds for creation, it will be better to accept this hypothesis. Now the world gives evidence of having been the result of an intelligent plan, and, therefore, presupposes a Designer who preceded and caused the realization of that design. The situation, then, is this: As neither eternity nor temporal finitude of the world can be demonstrated and as there are considerations favoring creation we should accept the latter. Moreover, the latter agrees with the obvious meaning of Genesis.

It is important to notice to what extent Maimonides adopts, and to what extent he rejects, the doctrine of emanation. In the *Guide*, he makes it clear that nine Intelligences account (more or less satisfactorily) for the heavenly movements, and that the tenth Intelligence (the Active Intellect) must be assumed to explain how the human intellect passes from potentiality to actuality.[35] He also holds that the soul or form of each sphere originated in the Intelligence corresponding to it, and more generally, that the Intelligences must be *emanated*, because there is no matter which would individuate them. He then points out that a number of points of the emanation doctrine are agreed to by the Scriptures and the Sages (i.e., the Rabbis whose teachings are found in Talmud, Midrash, etc.). Thus the Scriptures and Sages agree that the spheres are animated, that the spheres exercise influences on terrestrial phenomena, that angels (i.e., intelligences) are intermediaries between God and man. But, whereas Aristotle, Neoplatonically interpreted, of course, believed the Intelligences to be co-eternal with God, we [Maimonides speaking for the Jews] believe that God *created* the Intelligences and spheres, and

---

[35] *Guide*, II, 4.

endowed them with the powers they exercise.[36] Thus ". . . the creative act of the Almighty in giving existence to pure Intelligences, endows the first of them with the power of giving existence to another, and so on down to the active Intellect, the lowest, which is the sphere of the moon. After the latter follows this transient world, i.e., the *materia prima* and all that has been formed of it. In this manner the elements receive certain properties from each sphere, and a succession of genesis and destruction is produced. We have already mentioned that these theories are not opposed to anything taught by our Prophets and Sages."[37] The important difference here between Maimonides and his Islamic sources (especially Al-Farabi and Avicenna) is the insistence that the first Intelligence was created *ex nihilo* by God, and that the universe as a whole is of finite temporal duration.[38]

A few words must be devoted to Maimonides' doctrine of divine Attributes. That God is one and incorporeal, he never stops insisting. He also states that God is an Intellect and a Providence. But, since a plurality of attributes would violate the unity and indivisibility of the divine Nature, Maimonides insists with equal vigor that God's attributes must be conceived negatively. We can only state what God is not, not what He is. This is the doctrine of negative theology and Maimonides carries it to the limit. God transcends, and is utterly incomparable with, anything in the created universe. The things said of God are, therefore, only "attributes of action," i.e., they express God's effects on and in the world but in no way describe His own being.

[36] *Ibid.*, chs. 5, 6.

[37] *Ibid.*, ch. 11, p. 168. See also G. Vajda, *Introduction à la pensée juive du moyen âge*, Paris 1947, pp. 137-138.

[38] From *Guide*, II, 2. It is clear that Maimonides follows Avicenna in a number of other particulars, viz., in maintaining (1) the necessity of a *Giver of Forms* (the Active Intellect) both to things and to human minds; (2) that matter must be "prepared" to receive forms and likewise that the human mind requires preparation; (3) that prophetic inspiration comes from the active Intellect and affects the imagination as well as the intellect of man.

With regard to God's knowledge, Maimonides maintains that God, because He exercises a particular providence, knows all individual things. In other words, God's knowledge is not limited to a general knowledge of things by way of their universal or general causes. He must hold this doctrine because he insists on the free will of man and, therefore, on the element of contingency in the world of men. We cannot conceive how God can know particulars, but must be content to say that, by knowing Himself, He knows all that results from His creative activity.

In his psychological theory, Maimonides is largely dependent on his predecessors, Al-Farabi and Avicenna (in details he follows Al-Farabi). In particular, as already noticed, he accepts the doctrine that the Active Intellect is necessary for human cognition to take place; and he adopts their views in order to explain prophecy. He is also indebted to the same sources for his explanation of immortality. Here his rationalism carried him so far that he held that only the acquired intellect is immortal, i.e., the only part of consciousness which survives bodily death is the thesaurus of knowledge that is acquired during earthly existence. This puts the cultivation of intellectual virtues above that of the moral virtues (which, however, are indispensable means to the intellectual virtues; but only means, since even the ideal of earthly life is to know God). Thus knowledge is a necessary condition of survival after death.[39] This explains why Maimonides insists on informing all people about the existence, uniqueness, and incorporeality of God, and why he formulated a creed which comprises the intellectual minimum of belief. The least among the people are thus guaranteed a portion of the world to come after death if they accept a minimum of correct philosophical principles. In this respect Maimonides differs from his great

[39] *Guide*, III, 51, 54. See Guttmann, *Die Philosophie des Judentums*, p. 200; and Vajda, *Introduction à la pensée juive du moyen âge*, p. 143. See also Maimonides, *Mishnah Torah*, Yesode ha-Torah IV, 9. (The passage is translated in H. A. Wolfson, *Philosophy of Spinoza*, II, 290-291).

contemporary Ibn Rushd. The latter had prohibited any philosophical teaching to the masses, whereas Maimonides, in order to amass a measure of immortality to the least philosophical of men, insists that all have a correct idea of the nature of God even if they cannot master the philosophical proofs.

Maimonides had considerable influence, not only on the subsequent development of Jewish philosophy in the Middle Ages, but also on Christendom. Although he is severely censured in the *Errors of Philosophers* of Giles of Rome, Aquinas follows him on a number of important points and always quotes him with respect.

Two other philosophers among the medieval Jews deserve some mention here: Levi ben Gerson and Hasdai Crescas. The former is of especial interest as an example of a more extreme Aristotelian than most of the other Jewish philosophers, the latter as an avowed critic of Aristotle and his medieval Jewish followers.

Levi ben Gerson (1288-1344) was famous, not only as a religious philosopher, but also as a scientist.[40] His commentaries on part of Aristotle's *Organon*, in Latin translation, were included in the Latin editions of Aristotle of the sixteenth century. Like many of the other religious philosophers, ben Gerson believes in the essential harmony between the revealed Scriptures and philosophy.

[40] His book on an astronomical instrument was translated into Latin in 1377 on the instructions of Pope Clement VI.

CHAPTER VIII · PHILOSOPHY IN THIRTEENTH-CENTURY CHRISTENDOM

 N THE thirteenth century in Christian Europe, the two great developments for philosophy are the consolidation of the great universities and the gradual acceptance of the main works of Aristotle in the curriculum of studies. The faculties of arts and theology both found need and use for Aristotle's writings, but it was a long time before all his major writings were officially permitted to be studied, and various decrees of the Arts Faculty at Paris and Oxford attest to the suspicion and alarm which the apparent or real incompatibility of Aristotle's opinions with Christian dogma occasioned. And before the century had run its course, some of the essential doctrines of Aristotle were officially condemned by the Bishop of Paris.

By the middle of the century, as we are informed by a Statute of the Faculty of Arts (March 19, 1255), the following treatises were read: *The Old Logic* (*Logica Vetus*) consisting of the *Introduction* of Porphyry, *Categories*, and *On Interpretation*, as well as the *Divisions* and *Topics* of Boethius; *The New Logic* (*Logica Nova*) consisting of Aristotle's *Topics*, *Sophistical Refutations*, and *Prior* and *Posterior Analytics*; the *Nicomachean Ethics*, *Physics*, *Metaphysics*, *On Animals*, *On the Heaven*, *The Meteorology* (Book 1), the *Short Natural Treatises* (*On Sense*, *On Memory*, *On Sleeping and Waking*).

In addition to Aristotle, Porphyry, and Boethius, the Pseudo-Aristotelian *De Causis*, Costa ben Luca's *On the Difference of Spirit and Soul*, as well as Priscian and Donatus, were also regularly read.

There were regulations fixing the age and condition required for teaching, and the various grades in the faculties of bachelor, licentiate, and master were determined. The various methods of teaching are reflected in the types of books which have come down to us. The two main forms of teaching were the lesson (*lectio*) and the disputation. The courses in the works of Aristotle, for example, were, in the first place, expositions of each work in which a close elucidation of each part of the text was undertaken. But these works were also studies sometimes in the form of a series of questions on the main topics of a given work, say, the *Physics* or the *Posterior Analytics*. Such *Quaestiones* reflect the disputations method, in which various objections to the thesis to be defended on a given point were expounded and refuted. This was sometimes followed by the resolution of the question, but more often the objections were followed by the resolution which was, in turn, followed by replies to objections.

The main public disputations were held twice a year before Easter and Christmas. In these public disputations, the master propounded the question, then objections pro and con were propounded by the bachelors, and finally the master determined (resolved) the question.

In the Faculty of Theology, the standard textbook was the *Sentences* of Peter Lombard. This treatise in four books was composed around 1150 and dealt successively with: God as Unity and Trinity; Creation; Sin and Redemption; the Sacraments and Human Beatitude. The various Commentaries and Questions on the *Sentences*, while primarily concerned with elucidating and resolving theological problems, often contain much of purely or largely philosophical interest.

Another form of treatise, sometimes theological in content, sometimes philosophical, is the *Summa*. We may cite an example of the former type of *Summa*, the theological *Summae* of Alexander of Hales, of Albert the Great, and of Thomas Aquinas, and of the latter, the *Summa Philosophiae* of Pseudo-Grosseteste, the *Summa de Creaturis* of Albert the Great, and the *Summulae Logicales* of Peter of Spain.

The study of philosophy in thirteenth-century Christendom was greatly influenced by the translation of the works of Muslim and Jewish philosophical authors. Among the most important of these works may be mentioned the following: the *Metaphysica, Sufficientia* (Physical Writings), and the *De Anima* of Avicenna; the *Fons Vitae* of Ibn Gabirol; the *Dux Neutrorum* (*Guide to the Perplexed*) of Maimonides; Averroes' *Commentaries on Aristotle*; the *De Intellectu* of Al-Farabi; and the *Logica, Metaphysica,* and *Physica* of Al-Ghazali (his *Makasid*, i.e., *Tendencies of Philosophers*).

There is no simple way to classify the main divergencies in the philosophies of the thirteenth century, but one thing seems fairly clear. There was an attempt to develop philosophical doctrines which, while benefiting from the new perspectives which the recently translated works of Aristotle and the Muslims and Jews opened up, maintained some kind of consistency with the essentially Augustinian viewpoints of the twelfth century. This was made easier for some by the fact that there are enough parallels between, say, Augustine and Avicenna, to afford the possibility of developing the new ideas and resolving the new problems along ostensibly traditional lines. We find several examples of this tendency which Gilson has called avicennicizing Augustinianism. In a work of this kind I cannot attempt to do more than indicate by a few examples some of the main forms of what remains essentially Augustinian philosophy (in contradistinction to the more completely Aristotelian thought of Aquinas and the radical Aristotelianism of Siger of Brabant).

Robert Grosseteste (1175-1253), who, because he was Bishop of Lincoln, was often later referred to as the "Lincolnian," can be taken as a good example of Scholasticism of the earlier thirteenth century. He wrote a commentary on Aristotle's *Posterior Analytics* (which was much used throughout the thirteenth and fourteenth centuries) in which the tendencies of Augustinian Platonism and the Aristotelian views of the treatise on which he is commenting repose together in a specious harmony. This commentary as well as his various essays on natural philosophy attest to his great interest in the natural sciences. And his concentration on the study of light and optics constitute a parallel to his interest in the theory of knowledge. For, just as physical light is the basis of all material forms, so the light of divine illumination is the foundation of our knowledge of intelligible things.

In his theory of knowledge Robert Grosseteste, explaining Aristotle's insistence that sensation is an indispensable condition of knowledge, points out that knowledge is possible without sensation. For in God's mind there is eternal knowledge both of universals and of singular things and God does not know by sensing things. Furthermore the Intelligences, who know by radiations from the Primary Light, know both universals and singulars in the Primary Light. Now the highest part of the human soul acts without any need of a corporeal instrument, and, if it were not obscured and burdened by the body, would be able to receive the knowledge of all things by the radiations which illuminate the celestial Intelligences. As things are, however, the human mind must, in the present state, be stimulated by the senses from the stupor which it suffers from being in the body; hence, it must abstract the various forms from the data of the senses in which these forms are confused. By induction of the universal from repeated observation and by the analysis of the confused data of the senses, the mind eventually arrives at the principles of knowledge. His account of the inductive process is perhaps the first important discussion of this subject in the West although it depends considerably on Avicenna.

In his discussion of the sources of our knowledge, the Lincolnian combines Augustinian and Avicennian elements. His metaphysics also shows the influence of older forms of thought. His views of the nature of truth go back to Anselm and Augustine. There is, he allows, a truth of propositions, but, because the ultimate basis of this truth is the conformity of things to their exemplars (archetypes) in the divine Word, there is need of divine illumination. We may trust Roger Bacon's report[1] that Robert Grosseteste accepted a form of the Avicennian doctrine that illumination comes from the active Intellect and that this active Intellect is to be identified with God.

Grosseteste finds a parallel to divine illumination of our minds in the way in which physical light is the primary form of corporeal matter and in the manner in which light, by multiplying itself outward from a center of radiation, produces the physical world. His theory of the evolution of the cosmos from this radiation of light is elaborated in terms of the characteristic behavior of light, and this interest carries him into the study of optics and related subjects. The interest in mathematics which is indispensable to the exposition of such a theory is brought out more clearly in the work of his successor, Roger Bacon.

In his *Opus Majus*, a lengthy exposition of the need to improve philosophical study, Roger Bacon (born about 1214 or a little later; died after 1292) expresses points of view which link him to Avicenna and the older Augustinian doctrines and at the same time reveal his intense interest in the development of mathematics and experimental science.

The eternal light of Wisdom, he tells us, directs the Church, regulates the Commonwealth of the Faithful, brings about the conversion of infidels, and curbs evil men. But many things prevent men from receiving the benefits of divine Wisdom. There are four such hindrances to understanding: following unsuited authority, the bad effects of custom, the acceptance of the opinions of the uninformed masses, and the concealment of ignorance in the display of apparent wisdom. Bacon does not refrain from including some of the best intellects of his time within the scope of his scorn.

[1] *Opus Majus*, ed. J. H. Bridges, London 1900, I, 33-34; III, 36-53.

161

Theology is the one supreme science and it must be explained by philosophy and Canon law. The reasons for this preeminence of theology are as follows: All truth comes from Christ, and so all the truths which philosophers have discovered come from the divine Light.[2] The doctrines of Al-Farabi and Avicenna and of Aristotle concerning the active Intellect must be interpreted in this way. Augustine supports this doctrine. And Bacon tells us that William of Auvergne as well as Robert of Lincoln were of the same opinion. This active Intellect from which all illumination comes is God.

Scripture attests to the same view: all philosophy is reducible to divine Wisdom. And it was necessary that the fundamental truths which philosophers discovered be revealed to man from the beginning.

The whole aim of philosophy amounts to this, that through a knowledge of creatures, men be led to a knowledge of the Creator. In the *Opus Majus* there is an argument to establish the existence of God. It is a postulate for every reasonable person that there can be no infinite regression of causes, for an actual infinity is inconceivable and, indeed, impossible; hence, we must stop at some cause to which no other cause is antecedent. This ultimate cause cannot be its own cause since nothing can bring itself into existence; hence, the first cause had no cause and therefore always existed and will always exist. Such a thing will not be capable of nonexistence.

But though this argument be cogent, the full understanding of all that is involved requires a knowledge of mathematics and physical science, for a knowledge of the physical world requires a study of the category of quantity which is involved in all kinds of change. Mathematics, moreover, should be studied before other sciences because it is the easiest, it is more knowable both for the human mind and in itself. It is the most certain of the sciences, for while the other sciences—meta-

---

[2] This is plainly an allusion to John 1: 9 about the Light which enlightens every man who comes into this world.

physics, physics, and moral science—use the demonstration which proceeds from the fact that something is the case (*demonstratio quia*), mathematics uses demonstrations which proceed from the definitions of essences (*demonstratio propter quid*).[3]

In his discussion of experimental science, Bacon argues that of the two ways of knowing, by argumentation and by experience, experience is more fundamental. And he goes so far as to suggest that, even in mathematical demonstrations, the experience of the conclusion is more certain than the mere demonstration without experience. Experience, however, is of two kinds: one derived by way of external senses, the other through interior illumination. The former, although indispensable to acquiring knowledge, human and philosophical, is not sufficient even for gaining full certainty regarding corporeal things; hence, even in natural philosophy, interior illumination is necessary. Interior illumination has seven degrees: the barely scientific, the illumination which instills the virtues, the Gifts of the Holy Ghost "which Isaiah enumerates," the beatitudes, the spiritual senses, the peace of God, and, finally, raptures. Bacon concentrates much of his attention on the experimental sciences which are acquired by external experience and the first degree of interior illumination.

The last part of the *Opus Majus* is devoted to moral philosophy. In this part, Bacon discusses the existence and attributes of God, God's creative and providential function, the celestial Intelligences and angels, the immortality of the human soul, and the beatitude of man. This beatitude is the highest good of which man is capable, and morality and revelation are indispensable to its acquisition.

As the continuator of his teacher Robert Grosseteste, Bacon

[3] The distinction here is, roughly, this: *demonstratio quia* is argument from observed effects to their causes; *demonstratio propter quid* is argument which proceeds from a definition which, as it includes the nature of the cause of observed effects or consequences, explains such effects or consequences.

exhibits the characteristic tendencies and interests of a point of view which combines elements of Augustinian illumination with an interest in physical and especially optical studies. This combination of ideas is to be explained, in the most general terms, by the parallel which Grosseteste found between God as the Light which illumines men's minds and physical light which is the physical counterpart of the divine Light and the first material creation of God.

Another illustration of the essentially Augustinian trend of thought in the thirteenth century can be found in the work of St. Bonaventure. St. Bonaventure,[4] while he allows philosophy a limited autonomy, subordinates it to theology insofar as philosophy is a stage on the way to a knowledge which is superior to philosophy. Strictly speaking, philosophy is concerned with things which are in nature or in the soul in the form of knowledge that is placed in the soul or acquired by the soul *naturally*.[5] Now if we were limited to philosophical knowledge, i.e., to knowledge of sensibles, the possibility would not occur to us that there were anything higher than this. Indeed, Aristotle fell into this error. Since he did not know about man's Fall from grace and the consequent limitation of human cognition, he denied the existence of Ideas. From this, all the errors of the strict Aristotelians of St. Bonaventure's time followed: The denial of God's foreknowledge is entailed by the rejection of exemplars and this, in turn, involved the denial of creation. Hence follow the strict determinism, the eternity of the world, and the other views of the radical Aristotelians of the thirteenth century. Thus, although Aristotle had the doctrine of *knowledge*, he lacked the doctrine of *wisdom*. Plato, insofar as he acknowledges the Ideas, had something of the doctrine of wisdom, but lacked the doctrine of knowledge. St. Augustine had both and we must follow his lead in our metaphysics.

[4] Born John of Fidanza in 1221, taught at Paris from 1248 to 1255, General Minister of the Order of Friars Minor, died 1274.
[5] *Breviloquium*, Prol. 3, 2.

St. Bonaventure's attitude is nowhere better presented than in his *Journey of the Soul to God* (*Itinerarium Mentis in Deum*). In this little work we can see clearly the position of philosophy in the gradual ascent of the soul from sensory cognition to the highest reaches of mystical experience. The great speculative mystics of the twelfth century, Hugh and Richard of St. Victor, doubtless contributed much to St. Bonaventure's account of the mystical ascent, and the medieval mystics owe perhaps most of all to Pseudo-Dionysius.

In this *Journey* the soul begins by contemplating the visible world. For the human soul and the visible world are both so constituted that the soul can see the material universe as a ladder by which we can begin the ascent to God. For some things are footprints of God, others are images of God; the subhuman parts are footprints, man is an image.

In order to see how this ascent can be accomplished, we must realize the ascending degrees of the powers of the soul: sense, imagination, reason, intellect, intelligence, and finally at the apex of the mind, the spark of conscience.

We now turn to the visible world and the world within ourselves in order to see the correlates of the powers of the soul. The visible world reveals the traces of its Maker; it is, indeed, a *liber creaturae* or a *liber naturae*, a book of the creation, which is a living mirror of its Author. Our souls are, correspondingly, little worlds, microcosms through whose senses the Great World (the Macrocosm) enters.

The five exterior senses receive *species* of external sensible objects, from which, by reasoning from effects to causes, we obtain knowledge of the spiritual causes of physical events.

We obtain pleasure from the perception of the suitable proportions of sensible objects, and the power of judgment enables us to distinguish, among these sensibles, those which are useful and those which are harmful.

Our judgment, however, must be guided by reason which is the source of those laws by which we have certitude in our judgments about sensible objects. It is at this point that the Augustinian doctrine of illumination enters Bonaventure's thought in the *Itinerarium*. For although he accepts neither a doctrine of innate ideas nor a view according to which we contemplate the divine exemplars in this life, he holds that it is the *eternal reason* by which our mind is guided when it judges of things.[6]

When we turn from the material world into ourselves, since the previous steps have naturally led us eventually into our own minds, we recognize that our own self-love would be impossible unless we could know ourselves. The knowledge which the soul eventually has of itself is a *direct* knowledge.[7] But such self-knowledge would be impossible unless the soul aroused itself to remembering, for we cannot grasp anything by our intelligence which is not present in memory.[8] Hence, when each knows himself by "the eye of reason"[9] he also knows the three powers of the soul: memory, the power of intellection, and the power of volition. And, further, the functions of these powers become clear.

Memory has a rôle in foresight, it serves to retain and to perceive, and, in its retentive capacity, enables us to retain principles as well as simple ideas. This is necessary especially since some simple forms come to us from above which could not have been derived from sensation. The intellective power grasps the meaning of the terms, the propositions, and the inferences of discourse. This power is especially important, for unless the ultimate terms are understood, other terms will

---

[6] *In Hexaëmeron*, 12.

[7] Cf. St. Bonaventure, *De Mysterio Trinitatis*, I, 1, 10.

[8] Note that *memory* has the same general sense that was given by St. Augustine, *De Trinitate*, XV, 40.

[9] According to St. Bonaventure, *Breviloquium* II, 12, we see the physical world by the *eye of the body*, we see the soul and what is in the soul by the *eye of reason*, and by the *eye of contemplation* (also called *the eye of the mind* and *the eye of intelligence*) we see God and the things in God. This is all derived from Hugh of St. Victor, *De Sacramentis*, I, 10, 3.

not be understood. This is particularly true of the term "being" (*ens*), for unless one knows what "being" *per se* (*ens per se*) is, he cannot completely understand the definition of any substance. The comprehension of the meaning of "being" includes what St. Bonaventure calls its conditions, namely, *one*, *true*, and *good*.[10] But in understanding being we must also understand the so-called disjunctive transcendentals: being is either *diminished* or *complete*, *imperfect* or *perfect*, *in potency* or *in act*, etc. In his *Mystery of the Trinity*, Bonaventure uses the concept of being together with these disjunctive transcendentals to prove the existence of God.

We do not have a complete analysis of any created being without a knowledge of the absolute Being which is God. Our knowledge of truth is possible only in the Light of Eternal Truth, and our understanding of the necessity of inference depends on the eternal exemplars in God.

When we turn to the power of volition, the elective faculty, we know that it presupposes a knowledge of the *good*.

These three faculties of memory, intellection, and volition which we discern in ourselves lead us to the Blessed Trinity. For as man is made in the Image of God, the Image of the Trinity is found in these three powers of the soul.

Thus far man has considered God insofar as he has beheld Him in His traces and image in the visible world and in Himself. In order to proceed further man looks above his soul and first beholds the divine Unity through the concept of being (*esse*). Now we are dependent especially on the divine Light which illuminates the mind from above.

If, then, we concentrate attention on Being Itself (*Ipsum Esse*) we can see that Being Itself is so certain that it cannot fail to exist and cannot be conceived save as existing. St. Bonaventure formulates this cognition of the divine existence in

[10] These terms, together with *being*, comprise the so-called transcendental terms, i.e., the broadest terms of metaphysics which go beyond the ordinary categorical terms.

several ways. In the *Mystery of the Trinity*[11] he says: "If God is God, God is." This plainly is the positive form of the argument of Anselm: If that than which no greater can be conceived does not exist, then that than which no greater can be conceived is not that than which no greater can be conceived. Bonaventure simply puts this argument positively: if that than which no greater can be conceived is that than which no greater can be conceived, then that than which no greater can be conceived exists. In his *Commentary on the Sentences*, Bonaventure argues that anyone who would deny that God exists would be ignorant of the meaning of the term "God."[12] Again the truth "God exists" is one the predicate of which is included in the subject so that its denial would be logically absurd, i.e., self-contradictory.[13]

It is by means of the concept of *Being* that we know the divine Unity. By means of the term *good*, however, we are led to the contemplation of the Trinity of Persons. At this point in the *Journey of the Soul to God* we leave philosophy and enter the domain of theology. For the triune nature of the Godhead cannot be proved by natural reason, however illuminated by the divine Light it may be. The argument which follows, therefore, is not intended as a proof but rather as an elucidation of the suitability of the Trinity. The highest Being is also the highest Good: That than which a *better* cannot be conceived. Now this Good cannot be correctly conceived save as a Trinity. For, "the good diffuses itself."[14] Now the highest degree to which the divine Goodness can diffuse Itself is the generation of Another to which the Good communicates Its whole essence. An eternal generation of the Son and the

[11] *De Mysterio Trinitatis*, I, 1, 29. The argument can be made clearer in the following way: If God is God, then God is: But *"God is God"* is so true that it cannot be conceived not to be. Hence that God exists is indubitable.

[12] *Sent.*, I, 8, 1, 1, 2, fund. 4.

[13] *Ibid.*, Conclusion.

[14] This is the doctrine of Pseudo-Dionysius (*The Celestial Hierarchy*, 4) and the *Liber de Causis*.

procession of the Spirit from the Father and the Son is thus the highest degree of diffusion of Goodness and Love.

The *Journey* is now almost complete as far as the present life is concerned. Nothing remains now but for the soul to repose in the mystical transport in which our understanding and affection go entirely over to God. This is the highest approach to God, and St. Bonaventure describes it in terms of the Learned Ignorance or of the wisdom of the mystical union or as the experimental cognition of God. This must not be confused with the Vision of God vouchsafed the blessed souls in Paradise. It is rather a union of the soul with God in darkness.[15]

This outline of the *Journey of the Soul* provides us with the central themes of St. Bonaventure's thought. He follows generally the older forms of Christian thought which had been laid down by Augustine and Anselm and the mysticism of Hugh and Richard of St. Victor. At the same time, writing as he did in the thirteenth century and therefore after Aristotle and the Islamic philosophers had become a part of the intellectual thesaurus of Christian Europe, he has to deal with many of the philosophical issues which the study of Aristotle, Avicenna, and Averroes had introduced.

Thus he denied the possibility that the world is eternal and so opposed the views of Aristotle, Avicenna, and Averroes on this matter. He accepted a form of the doctrine of Gabirol that in all creatures, including the angels, there is a composition of matter and form, although we must remind ourselves that the matter in the angelic nature is not corporeal matter but rather the element of potentiality which distinguishes the creature from the Creator.

He also holds the Augustinian doctrine that seminal reasons are the source of living things, and he employs the "light-metaphysics" of the Oxford Franciscans to explain the fundamental constitution of the material world.

[15] *Itinerarium*, ch. 7. See also *Sent.*, II, d. 23, a. 2, q. 3.

I have already mentioned his adherence to the Augustinian doctrine of exemplarism, and the *Journey of the Soul* makes clear a basic theme which we find throughout his writings: that the world is full of symbols and analogues of its Maker. His theory of cognition is essentially one of illumination in the Augustinian sense. All these themes link St. Bonaventure with the main currents of Franciscan thought and differentiate him from both the so-called Averroists, such as Siger of Brabant, and the moderate Aristotelians, such as St. Thomas.

No account of the character of thirteenth century thought can omit the so-called Averroists. This term must be used with caution, because recent researchers have shown that it is very doubtful that there were many express followers of the interpretation of Aristotle which is to be found, e.g., in the Latin translations of Averroes' commentaries. But some facts which cannot be discounted may be stated.

In the first place, there were some teachers in the Faculty of Arts at Paris who insisted on what they regarded as the correct interpretation of Aristotle, especially those points where Aristotle's philosophy is in obvious disagreement with some of the main dogmatic principles of the Christian faith: the denial of exemplarism, the eternity of the world, the absolute dependence of accidents on their appropriate material substrata, the unalterability of the routines of natural process, and the denial of personal immortality. Christian dogma is in conflict with Aristotle (and certainly with Aristotle as he is presented in Averroes' commentaries).

In the second place, some insisted that *according* to Aristotle the eternity of the world, the unalterable regularity of nature, and the unity of the intellect (i.e., one intellect for all men) could be *demonstrated* conclusively by natural reason. Now those who insisted on this added that *they* themselves do not *affirm* that Aristotle was correct in holding to the strict demonstrability of these propositions. Nevertheless it was suspected that they were dissembling here. In a sermon delivered to the

University of Paris,[16] St. Thomas attacks these "expounders" of Aristotle to the following effect: Some people in philosophy say that natural reason can demonstrate propositions the opposite of which is asserted by faith. Now since one can only demonstrate that which is necessarily true, this means that faith asserts impossibilities which not even God can accomplish, for the power of God, although absolutely infinite, does not include doing what is logically self-contradictory. Hence, according to St. Thomas, such people are teaching that what is true in philosophy is false in theology. But this is absurd because truth cannot contradict truth.

Thirdly there is the evidence of the condemnations of 1270 and 1277 issued by Stephen Tempier against philosophical views incompatible with Christian dogma. Not all the condemned propositions were "Averroistic." But some certainly were: that there is numerically one intellect for all men; that man's will elects by necessity; that the world is eternal (87); that there was not a first man (9); that God does not act immediately in the changes which occur in the sublunar realm; that an accident, properly speaking, cannot exist apart from a subject, i.e., substratum (139).[17] Moreover, some of the condemned propositions clearly assert that some of the propositions of philosophy (which are incompatible with faith) are demonstrable: that it is impossible to refute the arguments of Aristotle on the eternity of the world unless we say that the will of the First [being] implies mutually incompatible things (89); that to make an accident exist without a subject . . . implies contradiction (141). There are other propositions included in the condemnation of 1277 that have Averroes as their target; e.g., that God cannot produce the effect of a secondary cause (that is, the natural operation of a natural

[16] This sermon is quoted, in part, in E. Gilson, *History of Christian Philosophy in the Middle Ages*, New York 1955, p. 398.

[17] *Chartularium Universitatis Parisiensis*, Denifle and Chatelain, Paris 1889, I, 534ff. The numbers in parentheses in text here indicate the numeration of the condemned articles in Bishop Tempier's decree.

agent) without this secondary cause (69). In all these propositions the important thing that stands out is the allegation that there are some propositions which are demonstrable in natural philosophy the opposites of which are held by faith.

When we attempt to discover who were the Christian teachers who held such views it is not difficult to single out at least two authors known to have been among the targets of the condemnation: Siger of Brabant and Boethius of Dacia (Boethius of Sweden). Yet when we examine exactly what they said it is difficult to convict them of holding explicitly to the doctrine that there are two mutually opposed bodies of truth, one of philosophy and one of revealed theology. It is more accurate to say that Siger of Brabant, as an expositor of Aristotle, was at pains to insist that Aristotle's views should not be twisted into conformity with Christian doctrine. Thus on the questions of the eternity of motion and of the world, Siger held that Aristotle believed his arguments for the eternity of motion and of the world to be demonstrative. As for his own opinions, aside from his repeated insistence that he is only expounding the views of Aristotle, Siger states that he is expounding the contents of philosophy (i.e., Aristotle) considered apart from revelation. It would be fair to say that he held that some philosophical views contrary to faith cannot be refuted by natural reason. In some cases this would mean that it would be impossible to show by natural reason wherein the allegedly philosophical demonstration of a proposition against a principle of faith is inconclusive. Thus, arguing by natural reason, one could produce irrefutable proofs of what is, according to the truth of faith, false. From this one who held to faith could only conclude that human reason is not ultimately dependable. There is no reason to suspect that Siger was insincere.

In a treatise *On the Eternity of the World* which is almost certainly authentic there is a clear statement of the position of Boethius of Dacia. The Faculty of Arts passed a decree forbidding any bachelor or master of arts to determine or even to dispute any purely theological question, and further prohibiting any bachelor or master to determine any question (which seems to concern both faith and philosophy) contrary to the faith.[18] In the aforementioned tract, Boethius of Dacia states that philosophy and the Christian faith are consistent with one another. The philosopher ought to dispute and determine any question about things by arguments and insofar as human reason can comprehend such matters. Philosophers in their proper rôle take no account of revelations or miracles. The natural philosopher, therefore, ought to deny whatever is incompatible with his principles, for he admits only what is possible through natural causes. From this limited viewpoint which the natural philosopher must take, a temporal beginning of the world, the resurrection of the dead, and the making of something without generation are all excluded. The Christian admits these to be possible by the action of a Superior Cause which is the cause of all nature. The philosopher is arguing within the limits of human understanding and arguing from the principles of physics. The Christian bases his views on the belief in a God who is not limited by the principles of nature; hence, there is no conflict. Faith is not science, but, if the contents of faith state something to be true, the truth or possibility of which is rejected by philosophy, philosophy contains falsehood to that extent. But the methods of philosophy must not, on this account, be given up or altered. Philosophy argues about things using reason alone. It reasons from principles which have been taken from things as we perceive them undergoing changes. And the philosopher speaks the truth when he says that certain events are excluded from occurring, granted the principles of physics. But the Christian also speaks the truth when, rising above these principles, he asserts the

---

[18] *Chartularium Universitatis Parisiensis*, I, 499, translated in L. Thorndike, *University Records and Life in the Middle Ages*, New York 1944, p. 86. The decree was issued on April 1, 1272.

possibility and actuality of those events from the standpoint of faith. This is the closest Boethius comes to asserting a doctrine of two truths. But two things must be noted: In the first place Boethius does not assert that natural philosophy can demonstrate that the world is eternal but only that the possibility of a temporal beginning *cannot* be shown by natural philosophy. In the second place, he does not assert that the conclusions of philosophy are true but only that it is true that such conclusions follow from the principles which the natural philosopher perforce adopts.

It is, however, easy to see that such a position is unsatisfactory not only from the standpoint of the theologians and the Faculty of Arts but also in itself. The status of the principles of natural philosophy must be decided. Either they are certainly and necessarily true, in which case there is a conflict between reason and revelation; or, they are only probable, in which case natural philosophy is dialectical and not demonstrative.[19]

On the other hand, such a view would naturally be opposed by Christian philosophers and theologians who believed in the power of reason and the unity of all truth, whether naturally acquired or revealed supernaturally. It is difficult to believe that the attack on the strict Aristotelians was solely on the ground of their interpretation of Aristotle. There would have been nothing unusual in saying merely that Aristotle *thought* that he had conclusively proved a proposition which, in fact, he had not proved conclusively. The real trouble must have been rather in the assertions that natural reason could produce irrefutable arguments for propositions the falsity of which were explicitly stated by the official teaching of the Church.

It is, of course, possible that some teachers went much

[19] For all this see: Géza Sajó, *Un traité recemment découvert de Boèce de Dacie*, Budapest 1954, [which contains an edition of *de Aeternitate Mundi* and an analysis] and Armand Maurer, "Boetius of Dacia and the Double Truth," *Medieval Studies*, XVII (1955), 232-239. Maurer's interpretation is unquestionably sounder than Sajó's.

further than Siger and Boethius and hinted that the Christian teachings were fables which the wise and the prudent could see for what they were. Indeed, some of the propositions condemned in 1277 suggest as much. But we cannot identify members of the universities who explicitly held such views.

Among the philosophers who opposed the radical Aristotelianism of Siger we can certainly count St. Thomas Aquinas, Albert the Great, and Giles of Rome, for several of their writings are explicitly directed against views of Siger and Averroes. In the case of St. Thomas, his tract *On the Unity of the Intellect against Averroists* attests to this. It is equally clear that St. Thomas and Albert are among those whom Siger criticized as misinterpreting Aristotle.

The development of thought in the later thirteenth century and throughout the fourteenth century shows the effects of the reaction against radical Aristotelianism or "Averroism." This is clear to some extent in the writings of St. Thomas even though he wrote before the condemnation of 1277, but it is very plain in the cases of Scotus, Ockham, and Nicolas of Autrecourt.

Although the high point in the development of medieval logic was not achieved until the fourteenth century, the beginnings of this development must be traced back at least to the twelfth century, as far as Christian philosophers are concerned, and earlier for the contributions of Muslim and Jewish philosophers. Medieval logic is the result of a confluence of Peripatetic and Stoic logic. There are many Stoic elements in the logical writings of Galen and Boethius, and we find distinct traces of Stoic logic in the writings of such Muslim authors as Avicenna.[20] The Stoic logic, while it owes something to the logical investigations of the Peripatetics, was developed in more or less conscious opposition to Aristotle and his followers. The nominalistic tendencies of the Stoics turned them away

[20] See *Ibn Sina, Le Livre des directives et remarques*, trans. A. M. Goichon, Paris 1951, pp. 57, 219; Avicenna, *Le Livre de Science*, Paris 1955, p. 32.

from a consideration of forms and their internal connections (which are among the concerns of the Aristotelian syllogistic) and toward a consideration of the logic of propositions. Furthermore, since the Stoics described demonstration as argument inferring the lesser known from the better known[21] and dialectic as the study of the relations between signs and things signified,[22] it was natural for them to develop that branch of the study of inference which is especially concerned with the hypothetical and disjunctive propositional forms. The medieval concern about the nature of implication (*consequentia*) has its prototype, if not its ancestor, in these Stoic discussions of implication. It is almost certain that Chrysippus adopted the following definition of the relation between antecedent and consequent in a conditional proposition: "If p then q" is true provided that *p* is incompatible with the denial of *q*. This definition, with some refinements, is the one which is adopted by most medieval writers. The Stoics formulated most of the basic rules of propositional inference, such as *modus ponendo ponens, tollendo tollens, ponendo tollens, tollendo ponens*.[23] Another important contribution of Stoic logic is their doctrine of the "*lecta*" of propositions which is concerned with what statements are about.[24] These contributions are all developed again in the Middle Ages, although it is sometimes difficult to ascertain whether or how the ancient doctrines found their way to medieval authors.

Boethius, in his commentaries on Porphyry's *Isagòge*, on Aristotle's *De Interpretatione*, and in his treatises on the Categorical and the Hypothetical Syllogism communicated a considerable portion of ancient logic, both Peripatetic and Stoic,

---

[21] Diogenes Laertius, VII, 45, 52.

[22] *Ibid.*, ch. 62.

[23] *Ibid.*, chs. 80-81; the best general account is that of Benson Mates, *Stoic Logic*, University of California Publications in Philosophy, Berkeley 1953.

[24] However, it is worth noting that the problem about what is the referent of a statement is already discussed by Aristotle in the *Categories*, 12[b]5-15.

although his account of the hypothetical syllogism suffers from ambiguities.[25] The doctrine, important in the medieval conception of semantics, that some words signify things (or, more exactly, thoughts of things) while other words signify words, i.e., the division of words into words of *first* and *second imposition*, is due to Boethius. Finally, the problem of the truth of propositions about future contingent events (which Aristotle introduced) was thoroughly discussed by Boethius and the medieval discussions of this problem all start from Boethius.

According to William Kneale, Abelard made the first important advances in logic after Boethius. We have already discussed his theory of the *dictum* of a proposition, which has doctrinal if not historical affinities with Stoic "*lecta*." Abelard was certainly interested in the nature of implication (*consequentia*) and distinguished between purely formal implications and those whose validity requires "supplementation from the nature of things."[26] This distinction is clearly the prototype of the later distinction of medieval logicians between *formal consequence* and *material consequence*.

Abelard also anticipated the later discussion of the so-called paradoxes of implication. He distinguished, that is, between implications which hold simply because they have a false or impossible antecedent and those which hold in virtue of a connection between the meanings of antecedent and consequent. He was also responsible for formulating many of the rules of implication.

When the entire *Organon* of Aristotle became available (sometime during the twelfth century), the Scholastic writers extended their interests in and their use of logic. It must be remembered that the subjects to which logic could be applied were greatly increased by the Latin translations of the works

[25] See Martha and William Kneale, *The Development of Logic*, London 1962, p. 191.
[26] M. and W. Kneale, *op.cit.*, p. 216; Abelard, *Dialectica*, p. 256.

of Aristotle, of the Muslim philosophers and scientists, and the translations of works of ancient science and mathematics. Moreover, some of the writings of Muslim philosophers contained logical doctrines new to the Latin West. Such were Avicenna's doctrine of primary and secondary intentions. This is parallel to the distinction of Boethius between words of primary and of secondary imposition. Thus the first intentions are thoughts about things outside the soul while second intentions are thoughts about thoughts. In terms of this distinction, logic may be characterized as a science of second intentions.

There are several important logical treatises of the thirteenth century such as those of William Shyreswood and Peter of Spain. The best and most systematic treatments, as far as is yet known, are those of the fourteenth century. Yet it is very probable that many of the doctrines expounded in the fourteenth-century treatises were well known in the previous century. The logical writings of Albertus Magnus comprise commentaries on all parts of Aristotle's *Organon* but there is no treatise on the logic of propositions.[27]

The most important contributions, in addition to the doctrines of the *Organon*, which are to be found in medieval logical treatises are most conveniently treated under the following heads: (1) The syncategorematic terms; (2) the doctrines of supposition of terms; (3) the theory of implication (consequence); and (4) the discussion of the "insolubles" (i.e., *puzzles difficult to solve*, particularly the problem of the "liar" paradox).

The distinction between syncategorematic and categorematic terms probably goes back to the Stoics (although there is some disagreement about this). It is first mentioned by the grammarian Priscian in the sixth century. The distinction roughly corresponds to our distinction between logical and descriptive terms. Categorematic terms stand for some things in the extradiscursive world and can be subjects or predicates

[27] See P. Boehner, *Medieval Logic*, Chicago 1952, p. 5.

in propositions. Syncategorematic terms, on the other hand, cannot signify anything by themselves, although, when they are taken together with other terms they aid in the signification of other terms. Thus "all," by itself, signifies nothing, but taken together with "man" in the proposition "all men are mortal" it serves the function of determining the *extent* of the application of "man" in the proposition in question.

The significance of this distinction for the medieval philosophers was manifold. One of the most important uses of the distinction is that it makes possible a definition of formally valid arguments. Thus, in the argument: "All men are mortal, and all Greeks are men, therefore, all Greeks are mortal," the validity depends on the *form* of the argument alone. The form consists in what is invariant in the order of syncategorematic terms when "men," "Greeks," and "mental" are replaced by any other term one pleases. As long as this order is retained, the argument will be valid whatever terms replace those in the original argument.[28]

The doctrine of supposition of terms was an attempt to develop a semantics. There is a considerable variety of meanings attached to the word "supposition" in different authors. The main concern here is that the doctrine enabled medieval philosophers and logicians to distinguish between mentioning and using a term. Thus when a term such as "man" occurs in the proposition "A man runs," the term stands for something in the world, namely, a human being. In the proposition "Man is a monosyllable" the term "man" stands for a word, namely, the word "man" itself. However, when the term "man" occurs in the proposition "Man is a species," some authors take it to stand for the universal nature, while others, especially some of the nominalists of the fourteenth century

[28] The lists of syncategorematic terms differ from one author to another. William of Shyreswood, *Syncategorematica*, ed. J. R. O'Donnell, *Medieval Studies*, III (1941), 46-93, gives *all, whole, either, none, nothing, neither, beyond, only, merely, is, not, necessarily, contingently, begins, ends, if, unless, and, or,* (and some other terms). Cf. Ockham, *Summa Logicae*, I, 4.

take it to stand for a specific concept in the mind. The first of these suppositions was called *personal*, the second, *material*, and the third, *simple*.

In the theory of implication (or *consequentia* as the medieval logicians called it) we have a continuation of Abelard's attempt to characterize the logical connection between antecedent and consequent in a logical thesis or a logically valid inference. Again there is a considerable variety of description of implication. In Albert of Saxony we have the following characterizations:[29]

One proposition, A, is said to be the antecedent of another, B, when A is so related to B that it is impossible for what A signifies to be the case and what B signifies not to be the case. The statements of Walter Burleigh[30] about implication (*consequentia*) make clearer what is involved. "In every valid implication, the opposite of the consequent is incompatible with (*repugnat*) the antecedent . . . but all incompatibility (*repugnantia*) exists in virtue of contradiction which is the primary incompatibility." Raymond Lullus,[31] the Pseudo-Scotus,[32] Albert of Saxony,[33] and many other logicians of the thirteenth and fourteenth centuries characterize implication in similar ways. These descriptions correspond, in principle, to the ancient Stoic definition.

Implication (*consequentia*) was subdivided into *formal* implication and *material* implication. An implication A is formally valid (or formal) if and only if every other argument B (which differs from A only in containing different categorematic terms) is valid.[34] In other words, an implication is formally valid when its antecedent is incompatible with the

---

[29] *Perutilis Logica*, Tract. 4, cap. 1.

[30] *Commentaria in libros physicorum*, Venetiis Apud Michaelem Berniam Bononiensem, 1589. In Septimum, fol. 838c.

[31] In C. Prantl, *Geschichte der Logik in Abenlande*, Leipsig 1855, III, 17, n. 623.

[32] John of Cornubia, *Opera Omnia Scoti*, Lyon 1639, I, 286B-289A.

[33] *Op.cit.*

[34] Albert of Saxony, *op.cit.*

denial of its consequent no matter how the nonlogical terms are replaced by other nonlogical terms. A material implication, however, is valid only for certain fixed terms. For example, if the antecedent is self-contradictory or if the consequent is logically necessary, the implication will be materially valid. It is sometimes thought that some of the medieval logicians recognized what we *now* call "material implication" or, more exactly, a "material conditional" proposition. But there is no convincing evidence that this is so. In this respect their logic was incomplete. But, despite this and other defects of their description of implication, the medieval logicians achieved a clarity about logical necessity that is superior to anything in ancient logic and, in some ways at least, equal to anything that was said on the subject until very recent times.

CHAPTER IX · THE PHILOSOPHY
OF AQUINAS

HOMAS AQUINAS is the single most significant philosopher-theologian of the latter part of the thirteenth century. He was regarded, even by opponents such as Siger of Brabant, as one of the outstanding philosophers of the time. The assignment to him of the task of composing the *Summa Contra Gentiles* by the General of the Dominican Order, the *Opuscula* written for Pope Urban IV, the letters in answer to requests from theologians and laymen—all attest to high regard for his person and authority. To this must certainly be added the most important fact that his main theological *Summae* are perhaps the most successful attempts made in the Middle Ages to produce an integrated system of Christian philosophical theology.

Though we are here interested only in his philosophy, it cannot be too strongly emphasized that Aquinas was first and foremost a theologian, and although he was as successful as any in differentiating between philosophy proper and Sacred Doctrine, his main purpose in his constructive works was theological. He states very clearly the relations between philosophy and theology: Philosophy can prove (by means of human reason unaided by any special illumination) some of the truths which are proposed by the Christian faith, it can *elucidate* truth which cannot be proved, and finally it can defend the principles of Christian faith against their detractors. But it is true at the same time that the subjects with which the philosophical theologian is principally concerned are already proposed by Sacred Doctrine. Moreover, although there can be no conflict between the truth obtainable by unaided reason and that divinely revealed, philosophy "falls short of faith."[1] Therefore, although the existence of God as prime mover and as efficient and exemplary cause of the world can be established by reason alone, the full meaning of "God" can come only from faith.

It is necessary, however, to emphasize Aquinas' firm adherence to reason and experience when he is writing on a matter he regards as decidable by human reason alone. Here he allows himself to be guided by pagan, Jewish, or Muslim philosophers whenever he finds them sound as philosophers. It is misleading to call him a Christian Aristotelian (indeed this is a contradiction in terms), but he goes as far in accepting Aristotelian views about the world and human action as it was possible for a Christian of the thirteenth century to do. Perhaps a more straight-forward characterization of his attitude toward the use of human reason would be this: The Creator has endowed all of his creatures with some measure of causal efficacy and some of them with that particular form of causal efficacy which is the exercise of reason. Such an endowment implies that reason has a function to perform and it implies that this function can be successfully performed. It is the duty of man to perfect himself in the exercise of this function, of the philosopher in particular to do this, and it is the duty of the theologian to set the just limits within which philosophy can accomplish its task.

The possibility of a Christian *philosophy* depends on whether there is a natural world the substantial constituents of which have, and regularly exercise, their own causal efficacy. At the same time, the possibility of a *Christian* philosophy depends on whether the world of creatures is radically dependent for its existence, its continuance, and its operation on a God who freely creates, conserves, and continually cooperates with His creatures. The causal efficacy of creatures has a twofold importance in considering whether a Christian philosophy

[1] In Boethius' *On the Trinity*, q. 2, a. 3, cited at length in *On the Truth of the Catholic Faith, Summa Contra Gentiles*, trans. Anton C. Pegis, New York 1955, I, 25.

is possible. On the one hand, since philosophy is concerned with the existence, nature, and activities of things, there must be a natural world in which such natures and activities exist. On the other hand, since philosophy is the knowledge of such a world, there must be intelligent beings capable of understanding such a world by their own cognitive powers. Thus, just as the doctrine of the real distinction of essence and existence preserves the radical contingency of things and requires that the world result from a Creator, so the doctrine that creatures have their own efficacy preserves the existence of a natural world and of creatures in the world capable of understanding it.

Before stating the views of Thomas Aquinas concerning God, the world, and man, it is necessary to be as clear as possible about these two main theses. First, then, I shall consider the distinction between essence and existence. The distinction, as far as the medieval Christian philosophers were concerned, was to be found in Avicenna.[2] According to Étienne Gilson, Thomas transformed the doctrine of this Islamic philosopher into a view which, in considering existence prior to essence, is the precursor of an existentialism. Existence, for Avicenna (at least as he was read in the thirteenth century) is not a constituent of the essence of anything, for we cannot infer from the knowledge of *what* a thing is the fact of its existence. Hence existence is an accessory accident which must be conferred upon a thing by an external cause in order that it may exist.

For St. Thomas, a part of this doctrine is correct and another part radically mistaken. It is true that we can and must distinguish, in any finite being, *what* it is and *that* it is. Moreover, this distinction is not created by the human mind and, so to speak, imposed on things; in each thing there is a nature or essence which is actualized by the ultimate reality

[2] As the Christians of the thirteenth century read Al-Ghazali and Avicenna, the distinction was to be found there.

or act of being. Such a nature or essence is distinct from its actualization. However, this distinction does not mean that there are essences without existence. It simply means that there is a feature of a thing, namely its essence, which can be understood without knowing whether such an essence has being in the universe of things. In the case, then, of those things whose essences are not the same as their act of existing, the act of existing must be derived from something other than themselves. We must be careful, however, to notice that this act of existing which is derived from something other than the thing which thus exists is not a sharing of existence in the sense that the existence of finite things is a part of divine existence. In other words, the existence of creatures through God does not mean that God is literally in all creatures as constituting their formal being. It means only that the efficient cause of the existence of finite things is a Being whose existence is the same as His nature or essence.

St. Thomas uses the language of participation here but it must not be misunderstood. The being or existence of creatures is derived from, but is not a particle of, the Being which is God. Being is the actuality of every form or nature. The essence or nature is a potentiality whose actuality is the act of existing. An essence is merely a way in which the divine nature *can* be imitated in the created world. For the plurality of essences in God (who is absolutely simple) amounts only to God's knowledge of the plurality of ways in which the Divine nature can be imitated. As such, an essence is a potentiality. The actualization of an essence is its act of being. In the case of a spiritual creature without any matter, there is a distinction of its nature and its existence; hence, even in purely spiritual creatures (angels) free from matter, there is a distinction between essence and the act of being. In all creatures the essence is *that which is*, and being is *that by which the essence is*. It is true that in things composed of matter and form we can, so to speak, regard the form as the actuality of which the matter is potentiality. But here we must distinguish a twofold composition. For a composite substance is composed *both* of matter and form *and* of essence and existence. The essence here comprises both form and matter. The existence of such an essence, therefore, is the ultimate actuality of the essence, and so is, as it were, the actualization of both the form and the matter. For the existence of a composite substance is the actualization, not simply of the matter, but of the whole substance.[3]

Some further light can be thrown on the doctrine if we consider St. Thomas' view of the relation between the world and man's cognition. Here St. Thomas follows Aristotle closely. The action of bodies on the senses of a human perceiver depends on the fact that the natures of physical things are literally in these things. This is directed against Plato who, as the medievals read him, had held that the natures are separate from the flux which is physical reality. Moreover, these immanent natures enable things to exercise their own causal efficacy, to project their likenesses into other objects and, specifically for the present discussion, to produce likenesses of themselves in perceivers appropriately situated. But such perceivers receive only the forms of outer things without their matter; hence, the first action of human intelligence is to receive the essences of things by way of abstraction. Only secondarily does the human mind know such things as existences and as singular things; hence, although essence is known primarily and existence secondarily and only through a judgment that such and such an essence exists in the singular thing, the singular thing is first in the order of being. Moreover, its existence is the primary actuality from which the essence can be abstracted. Because the human mind is an immaterial thing whose activity must be the abstraction of the immaterial aspects of physical reality, it first receives the essence of things. But this exigency of human cognition must not prevent us

[3] See especially Thomas Aquinas, SCG, II, 50-54.

from seeing that essences are only aspects of singular things each having its own act-of-being. This act-of-being can be expressed only by a judgment that such and such as essence *is*. The primary judgment is, therefore, that of existence.

The first concern of Aquinas in his two *Summae* is the existence and nature of God. Can the existence of God be proved conclusively, i.e., demonstrated? Some theologians had held that this is out of the question either because it is a matter of faith merely or because God's existence is self-evident (*per se nota*). Now a proposition is self-evident if its truth is immediately and ineluctably clear to anyone who grasps the meaning of the terms of which it is composed, i.e., if I understand the meaning of "S" and "P," I see that "S is P," if "S is P" is self-evident, because I see that "S" contains the meaning of "P" or because I see that "P" contains the meaning of "S."[4]

Thomas replies that the existence of God is not an Article of Faith but a "preamble" to the Articles of Faith. It is true that one can and should accept this preamble of faith if he does not know, or is incapable of grasping the demonstration. Secondly, he grants that the existence of God is self-evident in one sense: if the meaning of "God" and "is" is fully known, the proposition "God is" is known to be true. However, while "God is" is self-evident in itself, it is not self-evident to us (i.e., to human minds). For the human intellect gains all its concepts by abstraction from the data of sensation, and, because a wholly immaterial being, such as God or an angel, does not affect human sense-organs, we have no way of coming to a proper concept of God by way of abstraction. Hence, while we may have some description that corresponds to the meaning of "God" we have no definition of the Divine

---

[4] E.g., "Every whole is greater than its parts." These meanings of "self-evident" (namely, that the subject of the proposition plainly includes in its meaning the predicate or that the predicate plainly includes in its meaning the subject) go back to Aristotle, *Posterior Analytics*, I, 73[a]35.

nature; hence we do not know the meaning of "God" in this precise and full sense. Therefore, "God is" is not self-evident for us.[5]

There are two kinds of demonstration. One, demonstration *propter quid*, argues from the knowledge of an essence to some property of the essence. This is unavailable to us here since we do not know the essence of God in this life. Another, demonstration *quia*, argues from the existence of some sensible effects to the existence of a cause of these effects. By such a demonstration we can be brought to know *that* such and such a cause exists but not *what* the cause is. This sort of demonstration is available to the human intellect attempting to establish that God exists.

Accordingly, St. Thomas sets forth five ways in which God's existence can be proved. These five ways have two main features in common: (1) They all start out from some sensible events or facts, and (2) they all contain some form of a principle of causality. This is characteristic of Thomas' general view of philosophy and of nature. There are causal connections in the natural world and the human mind is naturally capable of discerning them. All these proofs, moreover, while each by itself is assumed to be logically complete, exhibit different features of the being whose existence is established. Thus the proof from motion establishes a prime mover, the proof from efficient causation shows that there is an ultimate cause for all change, the proof from possibility shows that there is a necessary being, the proof from degrees of perfection shows that there is a most perfect being, and the proof from the governance of things shows that the universe has a final cause or ultimate purpose and, therefore, an intelligent director.

The proof from motion, which is taken from Aristotle, runs as follows: The senses reveal that there are things in motion in the world. Now whatever is in motion is moved by another thing. For *to move* is to lead something from potency to act.

[5] See *S.th.*, I, q. 13; *On the Names of God*, q. 2, a. 1; SCG, I, 10-12.

Now, as nothing is, in the same respect and at the same time, both in potency and in act, nothing can move itself. Now we can ask, concerning the mover of any given object undergoing motion, whether the mover has been moved or not. If not, it is an unmoved mover, i.e., something which produces motion in other things without undergoing motion. On the other hand, if the mover of a given object in motion has itself undergone motion, we can ask the same question about the mover of the mover. There cannot be an infinite regression in movers which produce motion only by undergoing motion. For, if so, all movers would be potential movers and no actual motion would ever occur. Now we already know that this is not the case because sense has testified to the occurrence of motion; hence, after a finite number of regressive steps from any actual motion, we must assume an unmoved mover. And this, Aquinas asserts, is what men call God.

The second proof from efficient causation is, fundamentally, a restatement of the first argument but not limited to motion but extended to all sorts of causal efficacy. There is an order of efficient causes observed, nothing can be its own efficient cause, and a regressive infinity of efficient causes is impossible, so that we finally arrive at a first efficient cause.

The third way of proving the existence of God, "from possibility," was derived directly from Maimonides but indirectly from Avicenna. We observe that some things in nature come into existence and pass away after a time. From this we can immediately conclude that such things are merely possible beings in the sense that they can either be or not be. And that which is possible must at some time come to an end, assuming that it exists. If this had happened to all such possible beings a moment would ultimately arrive at which nothing of the sort exists. But then, since all these beings were merely possible, nothing could come into existence. Now if all beings were merely possible nothing would exist. But we see that some possible beings exist, and so we must conclude that not all beings are possible, i.e., that there is a necessary being. There cannot be a sequence of necessary beings which owe their existence to other necessary beings *ad infinitum*; hence, there must be a necessary being which is unqualifiedly necessary, i.e., a necessary being which is the cause of all being.[6]

The fourth argument appears at first sight to be quite Augustinian, and there is little doubt that the Augustinian tradition had always cherished this way of proving the existence of the greatest Being. But it is also clear that Thomas expounds it in his own way, and supports it with the authority of Aristotle. We find degrees of the good, true, noble, etc. among things. Now greater or less are asserted of several things only according as they are closer or further from some absolute standard; hence, if any degree of a characteristic exists in something, this implies that there is something which possesses the maximum degree of the characteristic. Moreover, that which possesses the maximum degree is the cause of all other things possessing any lower degree. Now as any essence achieves existence only from a being which is the perfection of existence, the existence of anything possessing any degree of a characteristic implies the existence of a most perfect being. The argument "from degrees" is thus a causal argument and can only be so interpreted as Thomas expounds it.

The fifth way, "from the governance" of things is a form of

[6] This form of the argument, which occurs in the *S.th.*, I, q. 2, a. 3, is somewhat puzzling. A more straight-forward argument occurs in the SCG, I, 15, 5: If possible beings exist, they must have a cause and we cannot proceed to infinity through the causes of things. Hence, we must assume that there is something which is a necessary being. If this necessary being owes its necessity of existence to something else, as there can be no infinite regression of necessary beings, we must finally assume that there is a necessary being which is necessary through itself. This is God. The idea of a series of necessary beings is, of course, not something to which St. Thomas himself actually subscribes. Since he has taken this proof from Avicenna and Maimonides he has adopted their language. Now Avicenna had, of course, allowed that some beings are necessary, not in themselves but through their ultimate cause. This was a part of the doctrine of the series of emanated Intelligences.

the argument from design. It is presented in two different forms. In the *Summa Contra Gentiles*, where the argument is attributed to St. John Damascene,[7] the argument is this: Things of diverse and discordant natures can be parts of one order only under the governance of one being which directs them to a definite end. Now we see in the world about us that diverse things are, always or for the most part, ordered to definite ends and in fact are coordinated into a harmonious system. Hence, there must be some being which providentially rules the world. In the *Summa Theologica*[8] the argument is stated differently. We observe that things which lack intelligence act always or for the most part in the same way and that they act so as to achieve the best result. Now whatever achieves an end and lacks intelligence must be directed toward that end by a being which possesses intelligence; hence, an intelligent director of all natural things must be assumed. In other words, the goal-directed activity of unintelligent things presupposes an intelligent being. These proofs bring out clearly the dual aspect of a teleological conception of nature: each thing of nature tends toward its peculiar perfection and all these tend toward one systematic and harmonious order. Both aspects of order presuppose an intelligence directing nature toward its perfection.

The plausibility of these arguments was to be questioned, not only by modern philosophers, but also by some of the medievals themselves. Al-Ghazali had already doubted these alleged discernings of the causal efficacy of natural things, and the fourteenth century provides more criticism along the same line. We may ask why St. Thomas accepted the fact of motion as indubitably presented to the senses. It seems fairly plain that Aquinas supposed that the concept of motion as "the realization of a potentiality" was, as all other naturally known concepts, derived by abstraction from observation. And

[7] SCG, I, 13, 35. Cf. St. John Damascene, *De Fide Orthodoxa*, I, 3.
[8] *S.th.*, I, q. 2, a. 3.

if this was the source of the concept there was no doubt that the concept applied to the objects from it had been abstracted. His arguments are demonstrations only if each of the premises are unquestionably known. The main question will be whether we can know definitely that there is motion in the sense required for Thomas' argument to proceed. The same consideration applies to the third argument: the reader must always remember that St. Thomas has in mind the Aristotelian conception of a *possible* being according to which every *possible* being (in this sense) can exist only for a limited time.[9] There is, no doubt, some confusion here, because, if we adopt Aristotle's view, necessity and eternity are mutually equivalent just as possibility is coextensive with limited temporal existence. The latter equivalence is really inconsistent with Christian doctrine; for, in one sense, some things must be regarded as possible which God will never create.

Having established the existence of God in these five ways, St. Thomas proceeds to derive some propositions concerning the divine nature (so far as this can be determined by natural reason). Before the details of these deductions are set forth it is necessary to say something about his doctrine of analogy. Likeness or resemblance has many forms: (1) One thing may be exactly like another; (2) there is also an imperfect likeness in, e.g., degrees of a quality; (3) there is generic likeness of things different in species; and (4) there is analogy. Now according to St. Thomas, it is only predication by analogy which is involved when we attempt to apply to God terms derived from creatures.

The human intellect derives all its knowledge from sense-perception, and so has no direct knowledge of anything not accessible to the senses. Hence, in its description of any non-material being it must have recourse to the material things with which it is acquainted by sense-perception. The terms applied to God, in particular, will be at best analogical, for

[9] Cf. Aristotle, *Metaphysics*, Book 14, 2, 1088^b23.

God and creatures do not resemble by way of exact likeness, degrees of quality, or generic likeness (since God is included in none of the genera of created things).

In one of his earlier writings, *De Veritate* (composed between 1256 and 1259), St. Thomas distinguished between the analogy of proportion and the analogy of proportionality. The former occurs when a term is applied to several things because they are all related to a given thing in various ways (e.g., *healthy* is applied to an animal primarily but to urine in a certain condition because it is a sign of health in the animal and to medicine because it is a cause of such health) or, a term is applied to two or more things because some are causally dependent upon one of them (as an accident is called a being and a substance is called a being, though the former usage is appropriate only because accidents are dependent on substances). The analogy of proportionality occurs when a term is applied to two things, say a and b, because a is to b as something c is to something d. Thus we may explain the relation of a to b by saying that a is to b as c is to d.

Now in this early work St. Thomas favors the analogy of proportionality as the explanation of the term analogically applied to God and creatures. But in his later works, the *Summa Contra Gentiles* (about 1260), the *De Potentia Dei* (1265-1268), the *Summa Theologica* (1265-1272), and the *Compendium Theologiae* (1273), he consistently holds that only the analogy of proportion is the appropriate analogy for predication of terms to God and to creatures.[10] This means, I think, that the terms applied to creatures can be applied analogically to God because God is the cause of the perfection of the creatures and because the character in the creature from which the analogy is taken exists eminently (i.e., in a higher degree) in God.[11]

[10] I am deeply indebted to H. A. Wolfson for this information. See his "St. Thomas on Divine Attributes," in *Mélanges offerts à Étienne Gilson*, Paris 1959, pp. 673-700.

[11] *S.th.*, I, q. 13, a. 2.

Now while this argument is entirely in general conformity with the medieval view that the character of things depends upon their eminent and archetypal existence in God, it must be also said that it is somewhat curious. The propriety of applying certain terms to God depends upon our understanding of those terms as applied to creatures. At the same time the propriety of applying these terms to creatures depends upon the eminent existence of the referents of these terms to God. Hence, although our understanding of God depends upon our understanding of creatures, the fundamental features of the material world derive their true meaning from the nature of a Being which, in itself, is not really comprehensible to us.

The existence of God has been established by causal arguments from the existence of the physical world as revealed to our senses. Yet the existence of the world, as these arguments show, depends on the existence of God. Though in the order of knowing we must progress from physical things to their ultimate cause, in the order of existence the progression is in the reverse order. How can the Being whose essence *is* its act of being produce the world?

The first thing which we must notice here is that Aquinas' Aristotelianism at once makes an adjustment to Augustine's doctrine of exemplars (divine ideas), an idea foreign to Aristotle himself but essential, in one form or another, to a Christian philosophy. A God who is not merely an efficient and final cause of the regular changes which characterize nature, but also a creator and a providence, must be conceived as an Intelligence whose creative activities follow a plan. Hence in some sense there must be ideas in God.

There are other considerations which lead us to the same conclusion. The plan of nature involves the intricate harmony of all its parts, and this must preexist in the divine conception of the world God is to create. This requires a plurality of ideas in God.[12] Again as cause of the world, the multiplicity of

[12] *S.th.*, I, q. 15, a. 1 and a. 2.

things in the effect must somehow exist in its cause. For in all causation, the nature as well as the existence of the effect must depend on the nature and existence of the cause. In univocal causation, this resemblance of cause and effect is obvious: here the agent produces something ostensibly like itself. In equivocal causes, the resemblance is not obvious, but the nature of the effect nonetheless depends on that of the cause. Again this requires some kind of preexistence of the effect in the cause and, in the case of God, the preexistence of things is the multiplicity of divine ideas.

According to Aquinas, this neither entails a multiplicity in God inconsistent with His unity and simplicity nor does it mean that God is numerically one with His creatures. For the multiplicity of ideas in God is simply God's simple knowledge of the multiplicity of ways in which the divine nature can be imitated by creatures.[13] Again, to say that things of the world preexist in God is to say that creatures are imitations of the divine essence and are participants of the divine essence but this does not mean that they are united with God. To imitate or to participate, for Aquinas, implies a numerical difference between God and the creatures.[14]

Although Aquinas sometimes employs the language of the Islamic, and ultimately of Neoplatonic, philosophers in saying that the divine goodness naturally diffuses itself, it is his express intention that the creation is a free act of God and is in no way necessitated by the divine nature. God could have refrained from creating altogether; moreover, He could have created differently than He in fact did. But given that there are things dependent on God, it is necessary to suppose that they have been created. For from the fact that there are beings by participation (i.e., things whose existences do not follow

[13] *S.th.*, I, q. 15, a. 2. This explanation of the resemblance between God and creatures is encountered frequently in other Scholastics.

[14] *S.th.*, I, q. 75, a. 5 ad 1um, ad 4um. Cf. also and especially *S.th.*, I, q. 3, a. 8, where it is expressly stated that an effect is *not* numerically identical with its efficient cause.

from their essences), it follows that they received their being
from God.[15]

The creation of everything in the world must be ascribed
to God. This includes the creation of primary matter.[16] But
this does not mean that a primary matter was first brought
into being without form of any kind, for, according to Aquinas, matter can exist only with some distinct form. Indeed,
it is a contradiction in terms to say that a being exists actually
but without any act.[17] Prime matter, in fact, does not exist
in the nature of things by itself because, as such, it is only
potential being, and so it is more accurate to say that primary
matter was concreated than to say that it was created simply.[18]
As a consequence, Thomas rejects the notion that matter has
any independent reality of its own (although some later
Scholastics, e.g., Scotus and Ockham, were to hold such a
view). It goes without saying that Aquinas rejected the doctrine of Ibn Gabirol that numerically one matter underlies
all things.[19]

It cannot be demonstrated that the world is eternal[20] any
more than it can be demonstrated that the world had a temporal beginning.[21] Aristotle's arguments refuted only erroneous views about the beginning of things. On the other hand
there is nothing about the concept of a *creature* from which
it ineluctably follows that there must have been a first member of any given species of creature. Arguments from efficient
causation are equally impotent for proving that the world
came into existence finitely many years ago. Nor does the
argument to a temporal creation from the impossibility of
an actually infinite sequence (which was used by some of the
Christian Scholastics as well as orthodox Muslim theologians)

[15] *De Ente et Essentia*, ch. 6; *S.th.*, I, q. 75, a. 5 ad 1um et ad 4um.
[16] *S.th.*, I, q. 44, a. 2.
[17] *S.th.*, I, q. 66, a. 1.
[18] *S.th.*, I, q. 7, a. 2 ad 3um.
[19] *S.th.*, I, q. 66, a. 2.
[20] *S.th.*, I, q. 46, a. 1.
[21] *S.th.*, I, q. 46, a. 2.

avail us here. For Aquinas allows that an infinity of temporally successive beings which are only accidentally ordered is logically possible. Consequently, the newness of the world must be accepted on faith alone as revealed by Scripture. It is always wrong for a theologian to claim to demonstrate what in fact is indemonstrable, and such a claim only exposes the faith to derision when it is discredited.[22]

After Thomas has decided on these questions, he asks whether the distinction of things in the created world is due to God directly, or whether this is due to some secondary agents. Plato in the *Timaeus* had taken the latter view, and so did some Muslim philosophers. Avicenna had argued that an Absolute Unity can produce but one being so that plurality cannot arise directly from God. But Thomas opposes all this and attributes the distinction and multiplicity of things to God acting directly.[23] The *reason* for the multiplicity of things is taken from the old doctrine of the plenitude of being. God alone is absolutely perfect and He created a world in order to communicate His perfection to something other than Himself. Now no one created being could adequately represent divine perfection, so that, in order that the divine perfection be imitated as fully as possible, it was necessary to create a hierarchy of beings that would exhibit, in as many different degrees as possible, the ways in which absolute perfection can be imitated. Hence, the plurality of things must be due to God directly. "For the universe would not be perfect if only one grade of goodness were found in things."[24]

St. Thomas' teleological conception of the creation requires him to maintain that there is but one world (*mundus*),[25] and that this world is hierarchically arranged. His teleology (taken from Aristotle as well as from revelation) is really

[22] This is St. Augustine's famous statement to the same effect in his *Literal Commentary on Genesis.*
[23] *S.th.,* I, q. 47, a. 1.
[24] *S.th.,* I, q. 47, a. 2.
[25] *S.th.,* I, q. 47, a. 3.

threefold. The parts of any creature exist for the sake of the whole creature, the several creatures are ordered to one another in the hierarchy, and the entire universe is ordered to God Who is the end and the ultimate good of the whole creation.[26]

In such a hierarchy there must be incorporeal as well as corporeal beings. For, in order that God be imitated as completely as possible in His creation, there must be some creatures that act as much like God as is possible for something which is not absolutely perfect. And as God acts by intellect and will (i.e., without corporeal instruments) there must be some purely intellectual (= spiritual and incorporeal) creatures.

Some earlier Scholastics, following the view of Ibn Gabirol, had maintained that the distinction of matter and form obtains for the whole hierarchy of created being, and had consequently maintained that even the angels are composed of matter and form. Such a universal hylomorphism (as this doctrine is called) is rejected by Thomas. It is true, he holds, that in spiritual creatures (e.g., the angels) there is a distinction between essence and existence, since in God alone essence and existence are identical. This distinction between the essence of a spiritual creature and its existence is enough to safeguard the dependence of all creatures upon God, and there is therefore no need to postulate a spiritual matter for incorporeal creatures.[27]

Creation, then, does not necessarily involve matter. At the same time the principle of plenitude requires that there be corporeal creatures as well as spiritual ones. Now in corporeal beings there is a twofold composition: not only is there the distinction between essence and existence but there is also a distinction between matter and form. The latter distinction is less fundamental. In a corporeal being its essence involves matter as well as form because matter is included in its def-

[26] *S.th.*, I, q. 65, a. 3.
[27] *S.th.*, I, q. 50, a. 1.

inition.[28] But a composite of matter and form considered as essence is a potentiality which must be actualized by an act of existence. Hence, the most pervasive sort of composition to be found in the whole creation is that of essence and existence, while the composition of matter and form belongs only to the corporeal part of creation.

The head of the corporeal part of the hierarchy of creation is man. Now in man and all other animate corporeal beings the soul is the form of the body. But man has a soul capable of existence after the dissolution of the body. The problem had already arisen whether, as a consequence, there might not be several substantial forms in such a being as man, and some Scholastics both before and after St. Thomas had held such a view. Their doctrine, known as "the plurality of substantial forms" was maintained by St. Bonaventure and other Franciscans (others, too, such as Kilwardby accepted it) on the ground that the form of rationality cannot be supposed to inform prime matter directly but only a matter already possessing substantial forms. At least the form of *corporeity* must already exist in prime matter in order that it be prepared to receive the higher form of the rational soul. Thomas rejects this and maintains steadfastly that there can be only one substantial form in any corporeal being. If there were several substantial forms in any being it would not have the essential unity required in order that it be *one* thing. One substantial form is necessary and sufficient for the unity of a single individual.[29]

In man there is but one soul which is the substantial form of the body. But while the soul is the act of the body, a man's soul is not the same as the man,[30] for the whole man essentially includes his body. In this respect man is like the rest of the corporeal animate world. Yet man differs from the brutes

---

[28] The *concept* of matter, *we* would say, is part of the *concept* of any corporeal being.

[29] SCG, IV, 81; *S.th.*, I, q. 76, a. 3 resp.

[30] *S.th.*, I, q. 75, a. 4; SCG, II, 57; *De Ente et Essentia*, ch. 2.

in the following respect: man's soul is capable of existence independent of the body whereas the souls of brutes are not thus subsistent.[31] Thus the human soul is unique in being incorruptible.

The human soul is an intellect which is directly united to the body[32] and it is present as a whole in each part of the body with which it is united.[33] As an intellect, it operates without using a corporeal organ of the body as its instrument (although bodily functions are indispensable in providing the materials of knowledge). Now some of the Muslim philosophers, especially Averroes, had argued that the purely intellectual operations required the assumption that there is but one intellect for all men. But Thomas, for both theological and philosophical reasons, opposes this view vigorously. Many human individuals cannot have numerically one and the same form. Moreover, if all men shared in one intellect, they would share in their phantasms and thoughts which is patently false.[34] Hence each man has his own intellect, and the integrity and individuality of each human soul is safeguarded. This is essential for individual moral responsibility and immortality.

Now although there is but one soul in each man, the individual soul must be distinguished from its powers, because the soul is actual even when its powers are not being exercised. Moreover, there must be several distinct powers of the soul, for the soul is both a subsistent being and also the form of the body and thus must be capable of exercising distinct capacities.[35] Thus some of these powers are in the soul as their subject, while other powers are powers of the composite of soul and body, yet as powers of the soul, all the powers flow from the essence of the soul.[36] And the purely intellectual

[31] *S.th.*, I, q. 75, a. 3; SCG, II, 82.
[32] SCG, II, 71.
[33] SCG, II, 72.
[34] SCG, II, 73, 75; *De Unitate Intellectus contra Averroistas.*
[35] *S.th.*, I, q. 54, a. 3.
[36] *De Spiritualibus Creaturis*, 4 ad 3.

and volitional powers remain with the soul after its separation from the body, whereas those powers which depend on the composition of soul and body do not remain in it after bodily death.[37]

St. Thomas enumerates five genera of such powers, namely, vegetative, sensitive, appetitive, locomotive, and intellectual. The vegetative powers comprise the functions of nutrition, growth, and generation; the sensitive include the functions of the five exterior senses (sight, hearing, smell, taste, and touch) as well as the functions of the interior senses of the common sense, the phantasy, the imagination, the estimative (or cogitative) capacity, and memory.[38]

As far as the intellect is concerned it is a passive and an active power. We are obliged to suppose that each man has his own agent intellect and that it is *in* the soul.[39] (As usual St. Thomas has in mind the Averroistic view and never fails to combat it at every turn.)

The various powers of the soul constitute a hierarchy with the intellectual powers at the head. We must now see how these intellectual powers operate so as to produce human knowledge. The basic operations of human thought are as follows:

First there is the understanding of indivisible forms of being, the forms subsumed under the Categories, namely, substances, quantities, qualities, relations, etc. This is simple apprehension. Then there is compounding and dividing, that is, the formation of affirmative and negative judgments. Finally, there is the process of proceeding from what is known in the search for the unknown, which is inference.[40]

---

[37] SCG, II, 81.

[38] SCG, IV, 58.

[39] SCG, II, 77, 76, 78; *S.th.*, I, q. 79; *De Spiritualibus Creaturis*, 10.

[40] *Exposition of Aristotle's de Interpretatione*, Book I, 1. Notice that the characterization of *inference*, proceeding from the known to the unknown, is Stoic rather than Aristotelian. Aristotle's description of the function of

Now the question arises to what extent the intellect of man is capable of error. According to Thomas it cannot err in understanding simple essences: here either it understands truly or it does not understand at all. Again, the human intellect can grasp certain propositions without possibility of error: a self-evident principle is one which is unerringly known provided we understand the meanings of the terms of which it is composed. For in these self-evident principles, either the predicate is included explicitly in the meaning of the subject or the subject is included in the meaning of the predicate. If we understand the meanings of subject and predicate in these cases, we see that it would be self-contradictory to deny that the subject has that predicate or that the predicate belongs to the subject.[41]

The human mind does not have simple essences and self-evident principles in it actually at the outset of the development of knowledge. As a composite being man depends on his bodily organs of sense in order to get knowledge of things. Though knowledge always involves universal concepts, and some knowledge consists of universal propositions, the source of such concepts and universal propositions, for man at least, is the senses. Consequently two problems confront us: What are universal concepts and how are they derived from the data of the senses?

The *knowledge* of a universal conception comes to us by a process which St. Thomas describes as the abstraction of forms from the images which things produce in the phantasy. We shall discuss this process presently. Our present concern is what is the nature and status of a universal. Most Scholastics,

---

inference *could* be so characterized, but there would be some falsification of Aristotle in so doing: Scientific inference for Aristotle is really the search for the *reason* for facts already known.

[41] *S.th.*, I, q. 17, a. 3; *S.th.*, I, qq. 9, 25, a. 3; f.19, a. 3, resp. See especially P. Wilpert, *Das Problem der Wahrheitssicherung bei Thomas von Aquin*, BGPM, Münster 1931, Band 33, Heft 3, pp. 174ff. See also Thomas Aquinas, *De Interpretatione*, I, lect. 13; *Posterior Analytics*, I, lect. 5.

as we have seen earlier, discussed this problem bequeathed them from Boethius' translation of Porphyry's *Isagoge*. St. Thomas' solution depends on a clue he took from Avicenna: The *nature* of any determinate thing (whether a substance, a quality, or any other categorical being) is neither one nor many. For example, *humanity* (what it is to be a man) or *whiteness* (what it is for a thing to be white) when it is considered as such (i.e., without reference to its extracognitive existence in nature and without reference to its intracognitive existence in any intellect, whether the human, the angelic, or the divine intellect is in question) is neither one nor many. For when such a nature is considered absolutely, nothing can be truly asserted of it save what belongs to it just insofar as it is such a nature. Hence, it is false to say of *humanity* that it is one or that it is many because each of these "notes" falls outside *humanity* as such. "If plurality were included in the concept of humanity, it could never be one, although it is one inasmuch as it is present in Socrates. Similarly, if unity were contained in the concept of humanity, then the nature of Socrates and the nature of Plato would be one, and as a consequence, [human] nature could not be multiplied in many individuals."[42] Considered as such, human nature neither includes nor excludes unity or multiplicity. As such it is indifferent either to being one or being multiplied as in many individuals. Hence the problem: how can *one* nature be in many numerically distinct individuals without being separated from itself?—a problem which had disturbed philosophers ever since Plato had propounded it in his *Parmenides*—is resolved. The nature, e.g., of *man* or *whiteness* is neither universal nor singular. Of course such a nature may be considered in its actual existence in individual things outside the mind or in the existence it has within human (or other) consciousness. It is only as existing in a mind that such a nature has the character of a universal. For

[42] Aquinas, *On Being and Essence*, trans. A. A. Maurer, Toronto 1949, p. 40 (I have slightly modified the translation).

when the nature exists as a concept in the mind it can be attributed to a number of individuals having that nature in the external world. Since, as we shall see presently, the concept which is abstracted from individuals in the world bears a likeness to those individuals, it represents each of them naturally.[43]

The unity of the nature of all individuals of the same species is not a numerical unity but only specific sameness or specific identity,[44] which, in the light of the immediately foregoing discussion, is presumably the same as the nature absolutely considered. The question arises, then, how such a nature is multiplied and individuated in the several individuals having a common nature. That this must be so is clear from the fact that Thomas holds along with Avicenna as well as the majority of other Scholastics, that everything existing in the world is an individual substance or an individual accident of such a substance. Numerically one and the same form, whether it be an accidental or a substantial form, can exist in but one individual. In his little essay *On Being and Essence*, Thomas holds that matter existing under determined dimensions and as located (he calls this "designated matter") is the principle of individuation. Designated matter determines that an essence exists in this or that case. Later, in his commentary on Boethius' *De Trinitate* this formulation is altered, but he returns to the original statement in his later works.[45] One material thing of a given kind is differentiated from another of the same kind by its matter existing in determined dimensions, place, and time. The essence of a non-material thing, on the other hand, cannot be communicated to any-

[43] *Ibid.*, pp. 41-42.

[44] Thomas Aquinas, *Expositio in Analytica Posteriora*, II, lect. 20. The difference between *numerical*, *specific*, and *generic* identity is derived from Aristotle, *Topics*, I, 7, 103ª6ff. It is frequently repeated in later authors, e.g., Boethius, *De Trinitate*, c. i.; John of Salisbury, *Metalogicon*, III, 9.

[45] See M. D. Roland-Gosselin, *Le "de Ente et Essentia" de St. Thomas d'Aquin*, Kain (Belgique) 1926, pp. 105-106.

thing else (i.e., cannot be an individuation of the common essence of many individuals numerically distinct from each other). Hence there is no possibility of diverse individuals of the same species in incorporeal beings, so that each spiritual creature (e.g., angel or demon) is different in its essence from every other.

We turn now to the question how the nature and the existence of individual things is known. In order to understand Thomas' answer we must keep several things in mind some of which have already been noticed. In the first place, Thomas insists that all knowledge comes originally from the senses stimulated to activity by outer objects. The natural object of the human intellect in this life is the essence or quiddity ("whatness") of a material thing. In the second place, everything in nature is individual so that universality must be achieved by the activity of consciousness. Thirdly, the causal efficacy of natural things must be maintained: Things in nature exert their effects upon each other, and the effect of things on the human organism is no exception to this rule. There would be no purpose in the existence of man's sensitive powers were they not essentially involved in the cognitive process.

As a consequence, there is no problem for Thomas as to how human knowledge is possible. There is only the question how human knowledge is achieved. Things in material nature are naturally capable of affecting each other and the human organism; on the other side, the human organism is naturally capable of being affected by the stimulation of things, and subsequently, naturally capable of acting on such effects as it receives from objects so as to abstract their natures and thus to obtain concepts of their natures and powers.

Some philosophers have held that natural objects cannot be the objects of genuine knowledge because genuine knowledge is universal, necessary, and immutable, whereas the material world is radically particular, contingent, and in unceasing change (Heraclitus). Plato, in order to save genuine knowledge, held that the object of knowledge was never a material thing in the world of change but rather a form existing apart from matter. But this will not do, for if it were true it would follow that we have no *physical* knowledge at all. In fact, Plato supposed that, because forms in consciousness exist immaterially and immutably, they exist thus in reality. It is possible that forms exist as individuated by matter in the world of change and that their universality and immutability are features of forms only as they exist in consciousness.[46]

Many philosophers (Plato, in particular) have supposed that the soul knows things by its own essence.[47] But this is true only of God. It is true that God knows all things by knowing His own essence. Human minds, however, plainly do not know things in this way. Another view (also attributed to Plato) is that the soul knows things by certain "innate species," i.e., by certain concepts which are in the soul from birth.[48] But experience seems to refute this view. Still another view is that of Avicenna to the effect that the soul derives its knowledge from certain "separate forms" (this means here, from an Intelligence, namely, the Agent Intellect).[49] But this view is false because it provides no reason why the soul should be united to the body. It is not a satisfactory reply to say that sensation "prepares" the soul to receive the radiations coming from the Agent Intellect. For if the soul, by its very nature, is capable of receiving the power of things from the Agent Intellect, it could dispense with the "preparation" provided by the senses. Hence, a blind man could receive the "species" (form) of color. But experience is against this.

St. Thomas does not fail to mention the Augustinian view that the soul knows material things by means of the divine

[46] *S.th.*, I, q. 84, a. 1.
[47] *S.th.*, I, q. 84, a. 2.
[48] *S.th.*, I, q. 84, a. 3.
[49] *S.th.*, I, q. 84, a. 4.

exemplars (Ideas in the divine mind).[50] In *one* sense this view can be said to be true. For the soul knows things in their exemplars but only by knowing their reflections in nature and further by virtue of the fact that *our* intellectual light exists by participation in the divine and eternal light.

Having thus disposed of views which he regards as false or true only as carefully "interpreted," St. Thomas concludes that intellectual knowledge is derived from sensible things by way of sensation.[51] Here he is obliged to explain, as against St. Augustine, how the mind can perceive things without being affected by their materiality. And he adopts Aristotle's doctrine that the perception of physical objects does not imply that anything material enters the soul. For the soul receives the forms of things into itself without their matters. The explanation of this process is something like the following: An object external to the human organism causes the medium between the object and the sense-organ to have duplicates of the forms of the object. In turn, the medium communicates forms to the sense-organs and thence to the faculties of sense. These various forms thus received are brought together (by the internal senses) into a common image or phantasm. The active intellect then abstracts the form from this image and thus produces in the possible intellect a form (species) by means of which an understanding of the object can be repeatedly obtained.

The active intellect, then, abstracts the intelligible species from the phantasms produced in the soul by the action of outer objects. But this explanation raises several questions. Does not this process of abstraction inevitably produce a falsification? The forms of material things do not exist in nature apart from their matters. Yet the intellect by its abstractive operation possesses only the forms without the matter. Will it not therefore misunderstand the natures of the things from

[50] *S.th.*, I, q. 84, a. 5.
[51] *S.th.*, I, q. 84, a. 6.

which these forms have been derived? In answering these questions St. Thomas points out several things. In the first place, for the intellect to abstract things from one another which cannot exist separately in nature would only imply falsehood if the intellect understands forms as existing separated from their matters. This it does not necessarily do. Although understanding requires that the forms of things exist in the intellect apart from matter, this does not mean that the intellect understands that they exist thus separated in the external world.[52] In the second place, the form in the intellect (the intelligible species) is *not* that which is understood, but rather it is that *by means of which* the object existing externally is understood.[53] Moreover, in the actual understanding of an object, the intellect must turn toward the phantasm of the object,[54] and thus indirectly recognizes that it is perceiving a singular thing by its awareness of the phantasm of that thing.[55]

We must notice another feature of St. Thomas' explanation of perception to have anything like an adequate understanding of it. To understand the nature of a thing by means of an intelligible species of that thing existing in the mind is to understand it in its *universal* aspect. In this sense, we understand the universal before we understand the singular. Moreover, in this sense we understand the universal directly and the singular only indirectly. What is more, we understand the more universal before we understand the less universal features of things.[56]

This does not mean that what we understand are the universal concepts themselves taken as universal. It simply means that the more generic characteristics of the objects present to the percipient are grasped before the more specific determina-

[52] *S.th.*, I, q. 85, a. 1.
[53] *S.th.*, I, q. 85, a. 2.
[54] *S.th.*, I, q. 84, a. 7.
[55] *S.th.*, I, q. 86, a. 1.
[56] *S.th.*, I, q. 85, a. 3.

tions (of these generic characteristics) are grasped. Thus it is that we understand the animal-character of, say, a human being before further analysis reveals the specific kind of animal, the human animal, which is the object of our perception.

Thus it remains true that the singular thing, the individual object, is the referent of the intelligible species by means of which the intellect knows. But as an intelligible species is the form of that object as it exists in consciousness, the universal aspect is known first and the singular thing existing outside the soul is recognized when we notice the concrete phantasm from which the active intellect has abstracted this species.

The knowledge of a singular and individual thing precedes the knowledge of the universal as far as human cognition is concerned. But the more generic features of the individual are known before the less generic, i.e., we know it as a thing before we know it as, say, an animal, and as an animal before we know it as, say, a man.

If we raise the question how the universal is known as being a universal we must introduce other considerations. The form of an external thing that is abstracted from an object is the intelligible species *by means of which* the object is known. As the vehicle of cognition, however, we are not aware of it, but rather of the object by means of it. But in understanding a thing, the intellect forms within itself a *concept* of the thing which is different from the intelligible species, although both the intelligible species and the concept are likenesses of the external object from which, ultimately, they were derived.[57]

Conceptual knowledge and knowledge of universals thus

---

[57] SCG, I, 53; *De Potentia Dei*, IX, 5; SCG, IV, 11; *S.th.*, I, q. 27, a. 1, *De Natura Verbi Intellectus*. Despite Gilson's attempt to expound these passages in a way which makes them mutually consistent, I find them very puzzling: *De Potentia Dei*, IX, 5 seems to identify the *species* with the *Concept*, whereas SCG, I, 53 and other passages explicitly deny this. But see E. Gilson, *The Christian Philosophy of Thomas Aquinas*, New York 1956, pp. 230ff.

arise. The universal concept is a concept that can be predicated of many things, and it is this that makes possible the act of judgment.

The direct knowledge of material things is, then, to St. Thomas' satisfaction, vindicated. And with this foundation, the propositions of natural philosophy are secured. Knowledge of incorporeal realities, however, can be obtained only indirectly. The soul of a man is not directly known. It is only by reflecting on one's own intellectual acts of knowing things that one knows that he exists and that he exists as an intellectual being.[58] In this sense, a man cannot deny his own existence.[59] But this knowledge of self is indirect and is quite different from the doctrine of direct self-knowledge which the more Augustinian Scholastics, e.g., St. Bonaventure, were prepared to defend.

The existences of other incorporeal beings, e.g., angels, demons, or God, are known, though very imperfectly in the present life, by inference from our knowledge of material things. We cannot arrive at such knowledge by abstraction from material things because the natures of these immaterial things are altogether different from those of material things.[60] In the afterlife, we shall have a direct knowledge both of our own souls and of the angels.[61] But our knowledge of singular material things will be general and confused in the beatified state,[62] and we will know only some singular things.[63]

It must be confessed that there are some serious difficulties of interpretation which arise when we inquire more closely into St. Thomas' views about our knowledge of material things. For, although the account of abstraction of the essence (quiddity) of material things that is given in the *Summa Theo-*

[58] *S.th.*, I, q. 87, a. 1.
[59] *De Veritate*, X, 12, ad 7um.
[60] *S.th.*, I, q. 88, a. 2.
[61] *S.th.*, I, q. 84, a. 2.
[62] *S.th.*, I, q. 89, a. 3.
[63] *S.th.*, I, q. 89, a. 4.

logica[64] makes it appear as if the relation between knowledge and its object is quite direct, a careful study of other passages in the same and other writings quickly dissipates this impression.

In one place,[65] it is true, we are told that the properties and accidents of material things adequately exhibit their natures and that all natural things which are limited to sensible matter are of this kind. But elsewhere Thomas maintains that the powers of material things are made manifest to us by the operations of these powers. Such operations can be discerned and, by induction from many particular observations of the exercise of such powers, we come to know them as powers,[66] and thus we arrive at the principles of natural science. Moreover, from the powers of things we eventually arrive at their essences. Many passages emphasize that the knowledge of the essence must be preceded by a knowledge of accidents,[67] that we acquire knowledge of part of the essence before knowing the whole,[68] and in some places St. Thomas explicitly says that we are not able fully to comprehend the natures of things whose properties we perceive by our senses.[69]

In order to know a part of the essence of, e.g., a man, we first apprehend the man as an animal. Now in order to know even this much we must have observed this and other men or animals exhibiting those characteristic modes of action which manifest the powers which define the animate. The essence of "being animate" is therefore derived from a number of observations of recognizable material things exhibiting characteristic nutritive, sensitive, and reproductive behavior.

[64] *S.th.*, I, qq. 84-85.
[65] In Boethius' *De Trinitate*, q. 6, a. 2.
[66] *Exposition of Posterior Analytics*, II, lect. 20; *ibid.*, I, lect. 4.
[67] *Ibid.*, II, lect. 13.
[68] *Ibid.*, II, lect. 7; cf. *S.th.*, I, q. 18, a. 2; *S.th.*, I, q. 85, a. 5; SCG, III, 69; *S.th.*, I, q. 77, a. 1 ad 7um.
[69] SCG, IV, 1, 5. See Hans Meyer, *Philosophy of St. Thomas Aquinas*, St. Louis 1946, p. 333.

And this surely is a complicated business that is a far cry from the speciously simple account of abstraction with which we were earlier concerned.

In a work of this kind it is possible only to give some of the characterstic doctrines of a philosopher limited to selected topics of his metaphysics and his theory of knowledge. And, in the case of St. Thomas in particular, this gives an impression that is unavoidably distorted. His theological Summae, as has often been remarked, have an architectural quality that is impressive in its systematic order and completeness. And while his philosophy is imbedded in this vast theological structure in such a way that the character of the whole system cannot escape distortion when the philosophy or, worse, a part of the philosophy, is extracted, it still seems possible to have discussed an important part of that philosophy without ineluctably falsifying it beyond recognition. That this is so depends in large part on the following facts. St. Thomas did distinguish between philosophy as an autonomous discipline and philosophy in the service of theology. Moreover, even as the handmaid of theology, philosophy serves several tasks, one of which is to demonstrate, by natural reason alone, propositions which are proposed as true by faith. Philosophy, acting to this degree of independence from revealed theology, can be expounded as philosophy and must be judged according to the tests of observation and reason. And St. Thomas, it may be fairly said, intended that his own philosophy should be judged according to such criteria.

CHAPTER X · DUNS SCOTUS

T HAS BEEN convincingly argued that the philosophy and theology of the fourteenth century can best be understood in the light of the Averroist controversy and the condemnation of 1277 (the so-called Articles of Paris). The effect of this is, I think, already evident in the work of Duns Scotus. Though many of his views have antecedents in earlier thirteenth-century theologians, the care with which he attempts to establish his main positions depends, to a great extent, on the crisis in philosophical theology brought about by the Averroist controversy.

He was born in 1266 in the county of Roxburgh, entered the order of Friars Minor in 1277, and entered Oxford before 1290. He lectured at Oxford and Paris between 1291 and 1300 and in Paris again in 1304. He died in 1308. The works which are generally agreed to be genuine are the *Opus Oxoniense*, most of the *Reportata Parisiensia* (both are Questions on the Four Books of the *Sentences* of Peter the Lombard), most of the *Quodlibetal Questions*, the *Questions on Metaphysics*, and the *De Primo Principio*. Many older studies of Scotus are very limited in value because they were based, in part, on works which subsequent research has shown to be unauthentic.[1] A number of works remain of doubtful authenticity such as the *De Anima* and the *Theoremata*. It is possible, however, to give a reasonably consistent account of the philosophy of Duns Scotus based only on works unquestionably genuine. All authorities emphasize the theological basis of Duns Scotus' philosophy, but this has been interpreted differently by different students of his thought. Gilson, for example, can be said to accuse Scotus of an exaggerated "theol-

---

[1] The *De Rerum Principio*, e.g., has been assigned to Cardinal Vital du Four, the *Grammatica Speculativa* to Thomas of Erfurt, the *Questions on the Analytics* to John of Cornubia, etc.

ogism," that is, of making revealed theology somehow logically prior to all natural theology. Other scholars, e.g., Fr. Allan Wolter, would qualify this severely. In the following account, the views of Fr. Wolter will be generally followed.

In the Prologue to his *Commentary on the Sentences*, Scotus asks whether philosophy alone can declare what is man's ultimate purpose and the means of attaining it, and he makes it clear that theology alone can assure man of his purpose and the means of its achievement. Scotus takes it that man's end is beatitude, the face to face confrontation of the human soul with God by a simple apprehension of the intellect. This is the state of the blessed souls in Paradise. Now by natural reason alone man could not know that such an end is possible. Aristotle, who may be taken as the representative of natural reason unaided by faith, has argued that all human cognition is derived in some way from the sensation of singular things of the physical world. The objects of human cognition, thus conceived, are the essences or quiddities of physical things. These are derived by abstraction from the data of sensation. Avicenna, of course, had argued that the primary object of our understanding is *Being*, considered as indeterminate. Now Duns Scotus recognizes that Avicenna held such a view, but he explains it by the fact that Avicenna had obtained from his religion the idea of something beyond sensation as the object of human understanding. As a Muslim, Avicenna accepted the immortality of the soul, and hence he believed in a non-sensible cognition of things other than the objects in the physical world. Therefore, Scotus denies that we can naturally know that Being is the first object of our intellect in the sense in which Being is wholly indifferent to the distinction of the sensible from the non-sensible. In an important sense still to be elucidated, the theologian, and not the natural philosopher, informs man of the possibility of a cognition of which man is incapable now (i.e., in this life, after the Fall of Adam).

We must now determine what Scotus means by saying we cannot, by natural reason as we possess it in our present state (i.e., that of human nature in its Fall from original innocence), know that "being is the primary object of the intellect" when being is considered without any restrictions. Scotus does not mean to deny that man can naturally obtain a univocal concept of being, for this would be inconsistent with his explicit and emphatic view that (1) truths certain and free from any admixture of error can be had by human beings in the present state, and (2) that we can demonstrate the existence of God from the consideration of *being*, and finally (3) that man has a single univocal concept [sc. of Being] which it takes from creatures but which is applicable to God. What is intended is rather this: The assurance that the human intellect is capable of knowing by simple apprehension whatever exists or whatever is capable of existing is something which is given by Revelation, for the Testament (Paul: Epistle to the Corinthians) states explicitly that the beatific vision will be a face to face confrontation of God, and this Scotus interprets as a simple apprehension or intuitive cognition of the divine essence. The natural reason of man in his present lapsed state provides no clue that an intuition of anything nonmaterial (e.g., God and the angels) is possible. Aristotle, whom Scotus takes as the spokesman for human reason in its lapsed condition, has argued that human knowledge depends on sense-experience and is limited to what may be abstracted from our sense-encounters with material things. Revelation assures us that we are capable of cognizing other than merely material objects and their actions. But this does not mean that we cannot now in this lapsed state form a concept of being which, though derived from creatures, is applicable univocally to God and creatures. In fact, the metaphysics and the theory of knowledge which Scotus skillfully designed are nicely adapted to his theology without being in any way dominated by it. On the one hand, faith alone can assure us that cognition can rise higher than the level of the material world, i.e., that were it not for our present limitations (which Scotus usually intimates are due to the Fall of Adam), we could now perceive any being. On the other hand, even in the present state man can form the concept of Being free from any limitations. Again, although human knowledge, in man's present state, arises from sensation and the inner experience of his psychic acts, the data thus obtained are not ineluctably dependent on their sensitive source. For the certainties of human cognition require sensation only as an occasion. The knowledge of fundamental principles, for example, is guaranteed by the necessary connection of the terms of which these principles are composed, and, even though such terms were derived from our sometimes erring senses, once we have such terms, the cognition of their mutual and necessary connections is immediate and unerring. In this way, the certitude of human natural knowledge is protected against the scepticism which an overemphasis on theology is almost certain to suggest.

Scotus sides with Avicenna against Averroes in holding that Being is the highest object of metaphysics. If we hold that God is the object of metaphysics, we would be obliged to admit that the physical proof from observed motion is the only demonstration of the existence of God, as Averroes held. This would not only subordinate metaphysics to physics, but also would expose this proof to certain criticisms which would be ineffectual against a metaphysical argument. Hence Scotus chooses to prove the existence of God in metaphysics, and because a science does not prove its principles but rather begins with them, *being* (and not God) is the highest object of metaphysics.

The question now arises whether we do have a concept of Being which is univocal and distinct from other concepts. Now we know that we have a distinct concept of being for we experience in ourselves[2] that we can conceive being without conceiving it as either *being in itself* or *being in another thing*, because when we conceive *being* we may doubt whether it is *being in itself* or *being in another thing*. Hence we know that we can conceive being as such. Now although *being* (*ens*) is predicated analogously or equivocally when it is taken as a perfect and proper concept, *being* (*ens*) as an imperfect and common concept is univocal to God and creatures and to substance and accident, etc. Scotus insists that *being* is one of many concepts which must be unequivocal because otherwise we could not reason at all, because otherwise we could not (at least in our present state) have any idea of substance, and because otherwise, in the present state, we could not reason at all about God.[3]

Being can be conceived distinctly only because it is an unqualifiedly simple concept. Such a concept is wholly unknown unless it is simply grasped as a whole and in itself, i.e., apart from other concepts. (Other concepts, however, cannot be grasped without the concept of being.) It follows, of course, that *being* cannot be defined or explained by any other concept.[4] We can explain "being" (*ens*) only by saying that it applies to that "to which it is not repugnant to be." I take this to mean that the concept "being" refers to whatever can exist, i.e., it applies to anything, the assumption of whose existence contains no contradiction.[5]

We now must raise the question concerning the distinction of essence and existence. Scotus recognizes a distinction between the being of essence and the being of existence. But he is insistent on the following: that *to be* is not something added

[2] *Quaestiones in Metaphysicam*, IV, q. 1, no. 6; *Rep. Par.*, IV, d. 49, q. 7, no. 5.
[3] *Op. Oxon.*, I, d. 3, q. 2, a. 4, no. 5.
[4] *Op. Oxon.*, I, d. 3, q. 2, no. 24; *ibid.*, q. 3, no. 12; *ibid.*, d. 2, q. 2, no. 31.
[5] *Op. Oxon.*, IV, d. 8, q. 1, no. 1; *ibid.*, I, d. 2, q. 7, no. 10.

to essence,[6] and that *to be* does not differ *really* from essence.[7] There are several reasons for this. In the first place, we cannot maintain that the being of existence has differentiating characteristics which are different from the differentiating characteristics of essence. The differences of things must be made out in terms of the categories. Furthermore, if existence were something added to essence, the existing individual would be an accidental unity, i.e., not a genuine individual but an accidental composite of several things. Yet we know that an individual is an essential unity. For these reasons, essence and existence are not *really* distinct things. They are, however, *formally* distinct. This means that in a single individual, the *nature* of the individual differs from its existence even though it is logically impossible for the nature and the existence to be separated even by divine power. Also the difference between nature (or essence) and existence in the individual is there before any activity of a mind which discovers and contemplates the difference. In other words, the formal distinction[8] is in the thing prior to any operation of the human (or other) intellect.

An important reason why this formal distinction between essence and existence must be maintained is that a nature or essence insofar as it is such does not include its existence. From the fact that I know *what man* is I cannot infer that a man exists. This applies, not merely to *man* as a common nature, but to *this man* as well. In every individual man there is a formal feature peculiar to each individual which constitutes its individuality. Since this individuating trait is a part of the *formal* nature of the individual, it does not contain or imply the existence of the individual; hence, neither the common

---

[6] *Op. Oxon.*, IV, d. 11, q. 3, no. 46.

[7] *Rep. Par.*, IV, d. 43, q. 2, no. 18.

[8] Scotus uses this concept, not only to account for the distinction between essence and existence, but also to account for the difference between the common nature, which an individual shares with other individuals of the same kind, and the individual difference or *haecceitas* which is peculiar to an individual.

nature *man* nor the peculiar nature *this man* contains existence in such a way that the existence can be inferred from the nature. Therefore, existence and essence must be distinguished. In sum, while existence and essence are only formally distinct, they are distinct to the extent that the existence of any created or caused thing cannot be deduced from its nature or essence.

All these reflections are important for the understanding of Scotus' proof for the existence of God. For, as already noticed, Scotus wishes to produce a proof that moves wholly within the realm of concepts. This will satisfy the strictest demands of demonstration: the premisses are to be necessary and freed from any essential dependence on the evidence of the senses. The concept of being in its complete indeterminacy is our point of departure.

According to Scotus, *being* is one of the transcendental terms, that is, *being* is one of those terms "which cannot be contained under any genus."[9] The medieval philosophers generally classed the metaphysical terms "being," "one," "thing," "good," "true" as transcendental, since such terms are in no way restricted in application to things or kinds of things falling under the Aristotelian categories. Scotus calls transcendental, not only such a term as *being*, but also whatever terms pertain to *being* as long as it is indifferent whether being is finite or infinite. Anything which is common to God and creatures (such as wisdom) is therefore to be regarded as transcendental. *Being* is the first of the transcendental terms, then come the terms which are unqualifiedly convertible with *being* such as *one*, *true*, *good*, and the like. In the third class of transcendentals we encounter the important disjunctive attributes of *being*, especially, "infinite or finite," "substance or accident," "necessary or contingent." Finally, we have what Scotus calls the pure perfections such as omnipotence and omniscience (which are predicable of God alone)

[9] *Op. Oxon.*, I, d. 8, q. 3, no. 19.

and wisdom, knowledge, freedom (which are predicable both of God and of certain creatures).

Now Scotus formulates his proof for the existence of God in terms of *being* and the disjunctive attributes of *being*. It has been reasonably conjectured that Scotus owes his proof to St. Bonaventure.[10] The statement that something is an effect formally implies that it has been effected by something capable of producing such an effect. Now, while Scotus allows that this is a legitimate way of beginning a proof for the existence of God, he prefers to begin in a slightly different way, namely, to start from the concept of an effectible thing.[11] For *being* can be divided disjunctively into the transcendental disjunctive "finite-infinite," or "effectible-effective," so that all being is either effectible (capable of being caused) or effective (capable of causing). These terms "effectible," "effective" must, at the start, be thought of in the order of possibility. In other words, to say that "something is effectible" is merely to say "it is possible that something may be caused." Such a proposition is, according to Scotus, logically necessary and hence may be taken as a premiss of demonstration in the strict sense of demonstration. It is then free from contingency and independent of sensation. For, as we shall see later in the discussion of Scotus' theory of knowledge, we know evidently that such a proposition is necessarily true even though its terms were originally obtained from senses capable of error. The senses were only the occasion for the acquisition of these concepts and thus they are not dependent on sensation for the evident truth of some propositions into which they enter.

[10] A. Wolter (*The Transcendentals and their Function in the Metaphysics of Duns Scotus*, St. Bonaventure, N.Y. 1946, pp. 132ff.), traces Scotus' proof to St. Bonaventure, *De Mysterio Trinitate*, q. 1, a. 1, *Itinerarium Mentis*, ch. 5, n.5.

[11] Scotus, *Lectura Prima*, Vienna cod. 1449, fol. 8 b (quoted by A. Wolter, "Duns Scotus and the Existence and Nature of God," Proceedings of the American Catholic Philosophical Association, Catholic University of America, Washington, D.C. 1954, p. 103). See now *Scoti Opera Omnia*, Vatican City 1950, Tome 16.

Something, *a*, is effectible. Either it is effectible by itself or by nothing or by another. Now two of these alternatives are at once excluded: nothing can produce itself, and a thing cannot be effected by nothing at all; hence, it must be effected by something other than itself. The question now arises about the other thing, *b*, by which it was effected. Either *b* is the first unqualifiedly effective being, in which case the *possibility* of a first effective being has been proved, or *b* is also an effectible being and hence requires an effective being in its turn. As there can be no infinite regress in effective beings which are effective only by virtue of being effected by something else, we must come eventually to a first effective being. This proves that a first effective being is a *possibility*. In order to prove that it is also an actuality, we must consider that *if a being does not exist by virtue of itself it cannot exist by virtue of itself*. Now we have proved that a being can exist by virtue of itself (the possibility of a first effective being); hence, by *tollendo tollens*, there is a being which does exist by virtue of itself.[12] This, in essence, is Scotus' proof for the actual existence of a first effective being. It moves from the order of possibilities to the order of actualities. The main purpose of this procedure (in contrast, e.g., to that of Aquinas) was to avoid any contingent or empirical premisses in a strict demonstration.

Scotus is here clearly in the tradition of Anselm and Bonaventure. By tracing his way through the concatenation of pure concepts he believes that he can prove something about what is actually the case. In fact, Scotus thinks that the argument of Anselm can be "touched up" in such a way as to avoid the usual criticisms.[13] For "God is that which, when conceived

---

[12] I.e., If not A then not B
But B

Therefore, A.

[13] *Opus Oxon.*, 1, d. 2, part 1, qq. 1-2; *Opera Omnia Scoti*, Tome 2, pp. 208ff.; cf. *The De Primo Principio of John Duns Scotus*, Franciscan

without contradiction, a greater cannot be conceived without contradiction." The addition to Anselm's argument is, for Scotus, essential because a contradictory concept is not thinkable. Here, perhaps, is one of the sources of Leibniz' similar treatment of the argument of Anselm.

The existence of God having been established, Scotus inquires as to His nature. That there is actually a first Being which is unqualifiedly effective means that there is actually an absolutely Infinite Being. This Infinite Being is simple in the highest degree. This means that God does not consist of different essential parts or of quantitative parts. Likewise God does not consist of substance and accident. For any of these forms of complexity would be inconsistent with God's being *first* in all the ways in which He is eminent as being absolutely primary. In this absolute simplicity, God differs radically from creatures. No creature is absolutely simple, for every creature has some potentiality and is capable of undergoing some addition. Even the incorporeal beings are capable of thinking and volition, and such powers are not identical with the nature of the incorporeal beings; hence, such beings are not absolutely simple.

Yet some concepts are unequivocally attributable to God and creatures. Whatever is suitable to *being*, when *being* is thought of as indifferent to the distinction of finite and infinite, is common to God and creature. For example *goodness* and *wisdom*, as transcendental terms, are applicable to God and some of His creatures.

Now as *wisdom* and *goodness* are "formally distinct,"[14] the question arises whether any such distinction of essential perfections is consistent with the divine simplicity. Scotus is

Institute Publications, Philosophy Series, No. 5, St. Bonaventure, N.Y. 1949, text and trans. Evan Roche, O.F.M., pp. 122-125.

[14] This important notion of Scotus will be dealt with later on. At present, this must suffice: two or more "realities" or "formalities" are formally distinct when there is not a complete identity among them, and this distinction obtains independently of, and prior to, the operation of any intellect.

at pains to argue that God is an Infinite Being and absolutely simple. His solution amounts to this: The divine attributes of goodness and wisdom, are formally distinct "on the side of the thing," i.e., there is a formal distinction of perfection in God not constructed by us in our thinking about the divine nature but existing in the divine nature before any operation of the human intellect. Now two such attributes as goodness and wisdom, as found in a creature, are both limited or finite characteristics. As such, neither has anything in common with the other. But these attributes in God are both infinite. As such, they can remain *formally* distinct from one another and yet really identical with one another and with the divine essence. But the reason for their identity with one another is not the fact that these attributes are both really identical with a third term (sc. the divine essence) but rather the fact that the attributes are both formally infinite.[15]

The exemplary ideas of the creatures preexist in some way in God. For "an idea in the divine thought is an eternal reason according to which something can be made in its own nature outside the divine thought."[16] And though the divine ideas have no reality other than in the divine intellect, they are not formally identical with the divine intellect.[17] Indeed, Scotus describes the existence of ideas in God as a "diminished," a "representative," and an "objective" being. Yet Scotus insists that the divine ideas are not the result of God's volition, indeed, they have their feeble diminished existence in the Divine mind prior to any action of the divine will.[18] It is important to emphasize this point because Scotus has often been (incorrectly) described as excessively voluntaristic in his view of the divine will. God in knowing his essence simultaneously knows all the ideas contained therein. This knowledge, then, precedes any divine volition. The nature of things and

[15] *Opus Oxon.*, I, d. 8, q. 4, a. 3, nos. 25, 26.
[16] *Opus Oxon.*, I, d. 35, q. 1, no. 12.
[17] *Opus Oxon.*, I, d. 36, q. 1, nos. 7, 10.
[18] *Opus Oxon.*, I, d. 39, q. 1, a. 2, no. 7.

their necessary connections are, therefore, not dependent on the divine will. The divine ideas include the ideas of all beings which is to say the ideas of all things "to which existence is not repugnant." Anything the supposition of whose existence contains no contradiction falls within the prospect of the divine intellect. The selection of those beings which are to be created as well as the creative act itself are the contingent acts of the divine volition: God freely chooses and causes the existence of things other than Himself. And because the creative act is a *free* act, it is *possible* that the world was created in time (and not from eternity as some of the Muslim philosophers, Avicenna and Averroes in particular, had taught). And Scotus is satisfied to argue for the metaphysical *possibility* of the Scriptural doctrine of temporal creation.

There are many doctrines of Scotus which differentiate him from some of his Franciscan predecessors on the one side and from St. Thomas on the other. Two of these concern the angelic nature but illustrate characteristic tendencies of his thought. Unlike St. Thomas, who maintained that, since matter is the principle of individuation, no two purely spiritual beings could be of the same species, Scotus maintains that there can be two or more spiritual creatures (e.g., angels) which are the same in species. Now because Scotus does not appear to have adopted the theory that there is some kind of spiritual matter in incorporeal beings (the doctrine of universal hylomorphism),[19] and, more importantly, because according to him, matter is not the principle of individuation, there is nothing to prevent the existence of a multiplicity of individuals of the same kind.[20] Again, Scotus rejects one of the explanations why an angelic intellect differs from a human intellect.

The essence of the angel is different from that of the human soul, not because the angelic intellect thinks intuitively and the human soul discursively, nor even because the human soul can

[19] See E. Gilson, *Jean Duns Scot*, Paris 1952, p. 392, n. 1.
[20] *Opus Oxon.*, II, d. 3, q. 7, nos. 3, 5.

be united to a material body as its form while the angelic nature does not admit of such a union, but rather because the angelic nature is a complete species whereas the soul of man is but a part of the (human) species.[21]

When we turn to Scotus' theory of the material world, we encounter other doctrines which are of considerable interest. The first of these is that Scotus holds matter to be some positive entity really different from the reality of form;[22] hence, although it is true that a form has a reality of higher degree than matter, matter does not exist simply in virtue of some form which determines it.[23] Matter must exist in its own right and distinct from form, because, although matter can receive a further determination from a form, this would be impossible if matter without form were nothing at all.[24] And so matter, in one sense of the word "actual," can be called a being in act.[25] In fact, Scotus goes so far as to say that it is a contradiction to say that matter is a part of a composite being and that it does not have some reality of its own.[26] It follows from all this that matter *can* exist without form and that matter is knowable apart from any form which informs it.[27] Hence, in virtue of His absolute power, God could create matter without any form, whether accidental or substantial.[28] Because it illustrates a tendency of which Scotus is one of the earlier illustrations, it is worthwhile to quote what he says on this point:

"Every absolute thing which God produces among creatures by the intermediary of a second cause, He can create without this second cause which is not a part of the effect [to be produced]. Now the form which confers existence on matter

[21] See *Quodlibetal Questions*, IX, no. 1; XIV, no. 13.

[22] *Opus Oxon.*, II, d. 12, q. 1, nos. 10, 13. And contrast the view of St. Thomas in *Quaestiones Metaphysicam*, VIII, lect. 1.

[23] *Opus Oxon.*, II, d. 12, q. 2, no. 10.

[24] *Opus Oxon.*, II, d. 12, q. 1, no. 11.

[25] *Opus Oxon.*, II, d. 12, q. 1, no. 15.

[26] *Opus Oxon.*, II, d. 12, q. 1, no. 16.

[27] *Opus Oxon.*, II, d. 12, q. 2, nos. 7, 10.

[28] *Opus Oxon.*, II, d. 12, q. 2.

is a second cause which is not of the essence of matter insofar as it is matter. Hence God can create the matter without the form."[29] This appeal to the divine omnipotence, conceived as limited only by the principle of contradiction, as a means of resolving metaphysical problems is to be encountered with ever increasing frequency in the scholastics of the fourteenth century.

It is now time to turn our attention to one of the distinctive theses of Scotus' philosophy, the doctrine of the formal distinction. This doctrine is important for the resolution of theological difficulties and especially important for Scotus' treatment of the problems of universals and individuation. I shall first attempt to explain the formal distinction and then go on to discuss its connection with these philosophical problems.

Some "things" differ from others really (*realiter*) and numerically. Two stones or two men are different *really* and numerically. They may exist at the same time and together. But it is logically possible for them to exist separated from one another or even possible for one of them to exist and the other not. Again there are distinctions which are made entirely by the mind to which there are no corresponding differences of any kind in the external world. Thus there are diverse ways in which the mind can consider the same thing.[30] But in addition to the *real* distinction of things and the rational distinction made by the mind, there is a distinction which exists in things but which does not admit even of a logically possible separation. In a thing there are several features distinct from one another which cannot be separated from one another even by divine power. These features Scotus describes as "formalities" or "realities," and often describes the difference between two *formalities* in a given thing as their formal non-identity.[31] Thus two such features of one thing are *really* identical (i.e.,

---

[29] *Loc.cit.*, P. Duhem, *Système du Monde*, Paris 1954, VI, 369, suggested that this thesis may have been derived from Henry of Ghent.

[30] *Quaestiones in Metaphysicam*, VII, q. 9, no. 4.

[31] Cf. *Rep. Par.*, I, d. 45, q. 2, no. 9; *ibid.*, d. 33, q. 2, no. 11.

are not two independent things) but *formally* distinct (or *formally* non-identical) provided that in the thing itself they are so different that the mind can think of one without thinking of the other even though the two formalities are inseparable even by divine power.[32] Thus in the nature of man, the formalities *animality* and *rationality* are formally distinct from one another. Indeed, they are formally distinct prior to and independent of our discovery of such a difference by the operation of our minds.[33] Again, that by which each individual of a given species is this particular individual rather than another, the formal feature which is the peculiar "thisness" (*haecceitas*) of the given individual, is formally distinct from the nature which it has in common with other individuals of the same species.

Let us see how Scotus employs the formal distinction to explain the principle of individuation and the nature of universality.

In the world there are only individuals. Yet certain individuals are in some essential ways exactly like one another so that there is some objective basis for our classifications of things together in species, genera, etc. This basis is the common nature, say, the "horseness" (*equinitas*) by virtue of which horses are alike and which is the objective correlate of the universal concept we can form of the species. Now Scotus here follows Avicenna and holds that the nature in itself is neither one nor many. The nature in itself is simply what it is, and its contraction into one individual or its existence in the mind as a universal concept requires further principles which are distinct from the nature as such. Sometimes Scotus says that this nature has a "less than numerical" unity in the several things of which it is the nature. This nature is in itself indifferent to being in one or another thing, but can be, and is, in

[32] See M. J. Grajewski, *The Formal Distinction of Duns Scotus*, Washington, D.C. 1944, p. 93; Scotus, *Opus Oxon.*, I, d. 2, q. 7, no. 41; *ibid.*, II, d. 3, q. 6, no. 15; *ibid.*, I, d. 2, q. 7, no. 44.

[33] *Opus Oxon.*, II, d. 1, q. 5, no. 5.

several numerically distinct things. Thus, *horseness* is the common nature of each of the things which are horses, but horseness is simply horseness and in itself is not universal or particular.

In order, then, for such a nature to be the nature of a particular individual something must be added to it which is not formally identical with it. In order, that is, for horseness to become *this horseness*, some individuating feature must be added, the "thisness" (*haecceity*) by which a nature becomes this nature, i.e., the nature of this individual. Hence, Scotus postulates an individuating principle in addition to the nature in order that a nature become contracted to a given individual.

It must be emphasized that, according to Scotus, this individuating principle, the "thisness," cannot be discerned by us (in the present life) and is for us only an indispensable requirement of theory.[34]

The nature can also be considered from the standpoint of universality. The universal exists by virtue of the intellect. But Scotus repudiates the suggestion that this implies that the universal is a "figment" of the mind. Strictly speaking, a figment is that to which nothing corresponds in things outside the mind. But the universal, although in actuality it exists only in the mind as one concept applicable to many things, has its objective basis in the specific nature which exists in external things.[35] If there were nothing in things outside the soul to which our universal concept refers, we would know nothing about the nature of things but would know only our own concept;[36] hence, although we can say that the universal concept is formed by the mind, its basis is to be found in the nature of things, viz., the specific nature existing in the several individuals of the same kind.

[34] *Rep. Par.*, II, d. 12, q. 8, no. 10; *ibid.*, d. 3, q. 3, no. 15. The main point is that we do not perceive the individuating differences in this life: the "thisness" is not sensed.

[35] *Super Universalia Porphyrii*, q. 4, no. 4; *Rep. Par.*, II, d. 2, q. 5, no. 12.

[36] *Quaestiones in Metaphysicam*, VII, q. 18, no. 10.

Scotus' theory of cognition must be considered in several different aspects, the first of which is directly related to his theory of the universal. It is necessary, according to Scotus, to suppose that there is an intelligible species, for the only way the universal can become an object of the mind is by an intelligible species.[37] Hence, we must assume both an active and a possible intellect in man in order to explain how the common nature is abstracted from the perception of singular things and presented to consciousness as a universal. But we must emphasize that the intelligible species, in its primary function, presents the external object to the mind.[38] Thus the active intellect of each man causes a form to exist in the possible intellect which represents the object (from which this form was derived) as universal which the sensible species represents as singular.[39] Thus the intellect sees the common nature in the singular thing and it is in virtue of this that universal cognition is possible. For "It is not included in the quiddity qua quiddity that it exist in the singular even though the quiddity only exists in the singular."[40] In other words, when the specific nature which exists externally only in the singular is made an object by the intellect, only that is contemplated which is essential to this nature as such. And since in the nature there is nothing pertaining to this or that individual, it can be taken as a universal in the mind.

With respect to single individuals, Scotus does not deny that we have an intuitive knowledge of them. We do not know a single individual in terms of its singularity, i.e., in the present life we do not perceive the individuating difference (the *haecceitas*), but we do cognize individuals.[41] Why we cannot in this life know the individual things in terms of their individual differences is not easy to say. Scotus is inclined

---

[37] *Opus Oxon.*, I, d. 3, q. 6.
[38] *Opus Oxon.*, I, d. 3, q. 6, no. 16.
[39] *Opus Oxon.*, I, d. 3, q. 6, no. 8; *Rep. Par.*, I, d. 3, q. 4, no. 4.
[40] *Opus Oxon.*, I, d. 3, q. 7, no. 28.
[41] *Rep. Par.*, II, d. 12, q. 8, no. 10.

to attribute this present deficiency in us to the Fall or to some requirement of harmony and order.[42]

It is in Scotus' defense of natural knowledge against sceptical criticisms that we find some quite original ideas which serve to explain his positions in natural theology that have already been indicated.

The human mind cannot err either with respect to the first principles of knowledge or with respect to conclusions which follow logically from these first principles in an evident way. For even if we assume that the senses sometimes err and that some of our concepts have been derived from erring senses, the necessary connection which we discern among those concepts are known in a way that precludes the possibility of error. For in such cases we see that some concepts include others or exclude others, so that to deny such conceptual connection or disconnection would be self-contradictory. Similarly, conclusions drawn syllogistically from such self-evident premisses are so related to the premisses that the denial of the conclusion with the acceptance of the premisses would amount to patent self-contradiction.[43] Not even God may be assumed to violate the principle of contradiction;[44] hence, in order to obtain certainty about first principles and the conclusions deducible from them, we need not assume innate ideas on the one hand[45] nor a special illumination on the other. Innate ideas are unnecessary because, however indispensable sensory cognition may be in given instances, the logical connection of the concepts derived from sensation is in no way dependent on sensation as a cause of our certainty. The certainty resides in the perception of necessary connection, however the concepts exhibiting such connection may have come to us. And

[42] *Opus Oxon.*, I, d. 3, q. 3, no. 24.
[43] *Opus Oxon.*, I, d. 3, q. 4.
[44] *Opus Oxon.*, I, d. 39, q. 1, a. 2, no. 7.
[45] *Rep. Par.*, II, q. 23, no. 3; *Opus Oxon.*, I, q. 3, a. 4, nos. 2-5.

we have no need here of a special illumination, for the general illumination of men in the possession of intellects with the natural power to know first principles is sufficient.

We are also able to know with complete evidence our own internal states and actions. That we are feeling, willing, judging—any of these states and activities in ourselves are immediately experienced and known in such a way as to preclude error or even the possibility of error. And although the propositions expressing such states are *contingent* propositions,[46] they are completely verified by our experience.[47]

Moreover, some of the propositions of natural science can be known with certainty. For we have reposing in the soul the proposition that "whatever happens as in many cases from a cause which is unfree (i.e., a natural cause and not a free volition) is the natural effect of that cause." Now if, with this self-evident proposition, we combine observations in which a natural cause is over and over again *accompanied* by some effect, we can conclude that the effect in question *resulted* from this cause. It is true that we cannot say that such an effect will ineluctably result from such a cause because either a natural impediment or a supernatural act of God (Who must cooperate with every natural cause in its productive activity) might prevent it. But what we can know with certainty is that such a natural cause has the *aptitude* to produce such an effect. In other words, natural knowledge of causal connection is limited to knowing that certain agents have the power to produce certain effects, and so will produce those effects in suitable circumstances if they are not impeded and if there are no miraculous interventions of God. This last qualification, of course, is generally understood by all the thirteenth-century Scholastics. But it begins to be emphasized in Scotus' time more than it was before the condemnations of

---

[46] I.e., propositions which express facts which might be otherwise.

[47] *Opus Oxon.*, I, d. 3, q. 4.

1277, and will assume an even greater importance in ᴊhe fourteenth century.

Scotus further holds that sensory cognition can be protected from sceptical doubts by the application of self-evident propositions reposing in the mind. Thus when there is a conflict of sense-reports, as in the case of the stick which visually appears to be bent or broken when part of it is submerged in water although it continues to feel straight and whole to our sense of touch, we can apply the principle that "nothing hard is broken by something soft which gives way before it."[48] Now this proposition is self-evident from the meaning of the very terms of which it is composed, and we have already explained how such self-evident propositions are beyond the effective reach of sceptical doubts; hence, the errors of sensation can be corrected by intellectual cognition of self-evident propositions. In such ways natural knowledge can be protected against scepticism.

From these considerations we can see one reason why Scotus preferred his proof for the existence of God to others. For even though we can argue from the sensible observation of actual motion to the necessity of a first mover, our knowledge of causal transactions is absolutely certain only when stated in terms of the natural aptitudes of things rather than in terms of our perception of their invariable performances.

The knowledge which we have of our own souls is limited in the present life and state. While it is true that I know that I exist, this does not mean that I have a cognition that is direct and intuitive of myself which reveals the *nature* of the soul or the individuating difference of my soul. For both as a result of the Fall and in terms of my natural powers in the present state, my soul is not naturally brought into activity save by the action on it of some sensible objects outside.[49]

[48] Cf. A. Wolter, *Duns Scotus, Philosophical Writings*, Edinburgh 1962, pp. 114-115.
[49] *Opus Oxon.*, II, d. 3, q. 8, no. 13.

As a consequence of this limitation of cognitive powers in the present life and state, we cannot know, but can only believe, that the soul is a subsistent form which can exist independently of the body.[50]

Unlike St. Thomas, Scotus allows only a formal distinction between the soul and its powers.[51] Thus the soul is only formally distinct from its several powers as they are from one another. The distinction of the soul from the body is another matter. For while Scotus admits that the total being is made one by a single form, this does not imply the suppression of other forms which it completes; hence, there may be several substantial forms together in individuals composed of matter and form. The form of body (*forma corporeitatis*) thus remains in the composite which is animate or human. And so Scotus maintains a plurality of substantial forms in man.[52]

The general impression that we receive from Scotus' philosophy when it is compared both to those of his predecessors and to those of his successors is this: His explanations of the character, extent, and limits of human thought are more completely determined by theological considerations than is the case with St. Thomas, although he makes more of an effort to deal with essentially philosophical difficulties than such a theologian as St. Bonaventure. His arguments are more complex and elaborated in greater detail than those of Aquinas and, aside from differences of temperament, this can be partly attributed to the greater care that was necessitated by the increasing critical tendencies of philosophical theologians after the 1277 condemnations.

When we compare his thought with that of later medieval philosophers we can see it as a transitional stage between the relatively high confidence of many thirteenth-century phi-

[50] *Rep. Par.*, IV, d. 43, q. 2, no. 17.
[51] *Opus Oxon.*, II, d. 16, q. 1, no. 15.
[52] *Opus Oxon.*, IV, d. 11, q. 3, no. 46.

losophers about natural theology and the increasing caution, reserve, and extreme critical attitudes of many fourteenth-century writers. It is not going too far, I think, to say that, after Scotus, the main works in natural theology and natural philosophy are remarkable rear-guard actions.

CHAPTER XI · WILLIAM OF OCKHAM

ILLIAM of Ockham was without any doubt the single most influential philosopher of the fourteenth century. This is true with respect to his immediate influence, which is well attested by the university decrees against his teachings of 1339 and 1340, and with respect to the controversies in which his views play an obvious role. As the most important nominalist his influence extends to the seventeenth century. Unwittingly, but nonetheless certainly, he contributed to the decline of the Scholastic attempt to provide a reasonable accord between philosophy and revelation by so severely limiting the uses of exact reasoning that it could no longer serve its accustomed function.

At the same time, it cannot be too strongly emphasized that Ockham had no such intention. He was primarily a theologian and the stormier part of his career was concerned with a struggle between his Order and the Papacy over the questions of Franciscan poverty and the extent and limits of Papal power. He was summoned to Avignon in 1324 to answer charges made against his theological and philosophical views, but the proceedings against him on this score were never concluded and the documents of censure which have come down to us are, relatively speaking, milder than usual. In any case, whether or not he was actually guilty of theological heresy, this was far from his intention. In order to see how he came to hold the views which have made him famous, we must look again back to the condemnations of strict Aristotelianism, issued in 1270 and 1277 by Étienne Tempier, Bishop of Paris.

While the religious philosophers of Islam and medieval Jewry had their problems in adjusting the claims of Revelation and Tradition to the philosophical views of man and the universe inherited from Plato, Aristotle, and Plotinus, and their ancient followers and commentators, the issues were always more acute and more precise in Christendom. This was due to the greater importance of a creed in Christendom than elsewhere, to the existence of an officially recognized body of ecclesiastics empowered to interpret and define the body of dogma contained in or implied by the accepted creeds, and, finally, to an official and accepted system by which the decisions of such an ecclesiastical body could be enforced. The readiness with which this whole system was accepted by those most immediately affected, the body of learned men, must be explained by the general acceptance of the view that theological orthodoxy is an indispensable condition of salvation.

The Christian philosopher or theologian of the thirteenth or fourteenth century had a twofold commitment: on the one hand to the dogmas of his religion and on the other to the evidence of experience and the arguments of reason. The condemnations of 1270 and 1277 made him more acutely aware than ever before of the difficulty of living up to these commitments. We can make this plainer by some reflections on the essential incompatibility between the philosophy of Aristotle and Christian dogma.

In Aristotle's system there is a place for contingent events although it is somewhat ambiguous. In one place, at least, Aristotle insists that propositions about singular events in the future are neither determinately true nor determinately false. His argument to this conclusion is apparently fallacious but his motives are clear enough. If there were nothing undetermined about the future it would be idle to give counsel or advice. But aside from the indeterminacy (real or apparent) of those events which issue from human volitions, there is another sense in which we cannot be sure about the future. First we cannot be sure, even in the case of regular natural processes, that they will always come out in the same way. Unknown influences may interfere with the usual action of a natural cause. Again, and perhaps this is only an aspect of the previous point, the matter of which an object is composed may not be entirely suitable to the complete realization of its form. For the rest, however, the events of the world, celestial and terrestrial, are determined by necessity. The heavenly bodies are never varied in their eternal movements, and the action of terrestrial causes is necessitated and only thwarted by impediments. So this is not a real exception to the deterministic conception of the world. In a word, with the possible exception of human volition, all events are determined.

The metaphysical and physical doctrines of Aristotle require that things be composed of substances and their accidents; furthermore, accidents cannot exist without inhering in a material substratum. To say that accidents *cannot* exist without such a substratum means that it is absolutely impossible, in other words, that it is a contradiction. Aristotle's physical theory requires that matter, motion, and time be eternal, but it also requires that space be finite and that there can be no vacuum either within or beyond the ultimate ramparts of the universe. Moreover, the theory excludes a plurality of worlds.

In his psychology, Aristotle speaks as if the human consciousness does not survive bodily death. There is but one active Intellect by and through which all men think, and this alone is eternal. The philosopher whose intellectual consciousness has been actualized by this active Intellect enjoys, in this life, the only true felicity, but there is no room in the system for survival of consciousness after the dissolution of the body. All these contentions of Aristotle were condemned by the "Articles of Paris" in 1277, because Christian dogma requires beliefs opposed to each of them.

The Creed of Nicaea begins with "I believe in God, the omnipotent Father, maker of heaven and earth and of all things visible and invisible," and this was always interpreted to mean that God can do anything which does not involve a contradiction in terms, i.e., the only limit to divine omnipotence is logical absurdity. God can produce or conserve a cause without its usual effects, or an effect without its usual cause. An accident can, by divine power, be produced without a material substratum to support it. The miracles of Scripture and the Sacraments require this; the doctrine of the absolute omnipotence of God allows for it. But these doctrines were excluded by the metaphysics and natural philosophy of Aristotle on grounds offered as logically conclusive. It follows that, if the Church is right, Aristotle's arguments must contain some flaws.

The condemnation of extreme Aristotelianism for the purpose of defending Christian belief against alleged demonstrations incompatible with it made theologians and philosophers in Christendom more wary than ever in accepting Aristotle's views. It is of great importance to notice that they did not, for the greater part at least, reject Aristotle's logic. On the contrary, accepting and developing the logic of Aristotle to a finer degree of precision than had been hitherto done, the theologians confronted Aristotle the natural philosopher with Aristotle the logician. The result of this confrontation was a thorough critique of the pretensions of Aristotle's philosophy. At first this did not involve a complete rejection of most of the arguments and conclusions of the Stagirite. They were modified and qualified and some were rejected. But the process of closely scrutinizing the doctrines of Aristotle led ultimately to their total rejection by the most radical among the fourteenth-century theologians, and this process got under way shortly after the condemnation of 1277. It may be an exaggeration to say, with Duhem, that this was the beginning of modern science, but it is not seriously in doubt that it was one of the contributing factors.

The more critical approach to philosophy can already be discerned in the works of Duns Scotus. Although Ockham opposes the Subtle Doctor on many central issues in philosophy, he follows closely his laboriously cautious method. Above all, his thought is guided by certain maxims—some theological; others, rules of method—which must be understood in part in terms of the attack on "Averroism" which culminated in the Articles of Paris.

Ockham's principal maxim about philosophizing, the principle of Parsimony, was not invented by him; indeed, it can be traced back to Aristotle.[1] But whereas in the case of Aristotle and others, it is difficult to separate the methodological principle from metaphysical assumptions about the simplicity of the world, Ockham is quite clear on the matter. For Ockham there is a principle of Parsimony which applies to human thought, not to the universe. In fact, he expressly stated that "God does many things by means of more which He could have done by means of fewer simply because He wishes it. No other cause [sc. of His action] must be sought for and from the very fact that God wishes, He wishes in a suitable way, and not vainly."[2] The principle of Parsimony applies only to our philosophizing, and it states that "what can be done with fewer [means] is done in vain with many," or "plurality is not to be assumed without necessity."[3] But we must recognize what the "necessities" here are, and we could put the principal maxim in a different way in order to bring this out: "Nothing is to be affirmed without a reason, unless it is known as self-evident or by experience or is proved on Scriptural authority," or again, "We must not assume anything as indispensable for explaining a certain event unless reason, experience, or revelation requires us to do so."[4] And

[1] See George Boas, *Some Assumptions of Aristotle*, American Philosophical Society Transactions, N.S., 1959, XL, Pt. 6, 22ff., who cites *De Caelo*, 302^{b}21; *Physics*, 259^{a}12; *Metaphysics*, 990^{a}34, 991^{a}9, etc., as instances of Aristotle's use of the principle.

[2] *Sent.* I, d. 14, q. 2, G.

[3] Ockham uses other variants, but the famous "Entia non sunt multiplicanda praeter [or *sine*] necessitate" does not appear, so far as is known, in Ockham's writings. Cf. W. M. Thorburn, "The Myth of Ockham's Razor," *Mind* (July 1918), pp. 345-353.

[4] See *De Sacramento Altaris*, ch. 28; *Sent.*, I, d. 30, q. 1, D.

this makes it clear that the principle of Parsimony is not to be applied to the interpretations of Scripture and Creed already decided by recognized ecclesiastical authority.

The main substantive theological principle to which Ockham repeatedly appeals is the divine omnipotence which he interprets thus: God can accomplish anything which can be done without contradiction. This means that his entire philosophy is embedded in a theology which, in emphasizing the absolute omnipotence of God, implies the radically contingent nature of all creatures.[4a] This, however, must not be misunderstood. It does not mean for Ockham what it meant for the Islamic Mutakallimun or for some Christian theologians of the thirteenth century (e.g., William of Auvergne), namely, that there is no causal efficacy in creatures. For Ockham states that God can do anything without second causes that He does with them, and this and other things He says about causality make it plain that He believes in the causal efficacy of creatures (i.e., second causes). The uses which Ockham makes of the principle of divine omnipotence are quite different. In order to understand this principle we must first speak of Ockham's views on logic, especially on the nature of reasoning and on the difference between demonstration and probable argument. At present, it is enough to say that the theological principle of divine omnipotence is often used by Ockham as a means of refuting views with which he disagrees. For example, in treating of relations, Ockham maintains that if relations were real things existing extramentally and distinct from their terms, God could create a relation without creating the terms of this relation. Since this seems absurd, it is concluded that relations are not such extramentally real things. (Ockham has other reasons, of course, for this conclusion.)

Again, in discussing causality, Ockham holds that definitive

[4a] See P. Vignaux, *Le Nominalisme au XIVᵉ Siècle*, Montreal 1948; P. Vignaux, *Philosophy in the Middle Ages*, New York 1959, pp. 171-172.

proof that anything in this world causes something else is out of the question, for "although combustion invariably follows approximation of fire to a combustible object, it is possible that the fire is not the cause, since God could have ordained that He alone would cause combustion whenever fire is brought near to the object to be consumed, etc.[5] We must be clear that, as Ockham uses it, the theological principle of divine omnipotence is used negatively to exhibit the limits of demonstrative reasoning. When it is used positively, since divine omnipotence is an article of faith and not something that can be demonstrated, the argument on which this principle depends will be probable or persuasive, not demonstrative strictly speaking. The application of these principles of Parsimony and divine omnipotence will be understood better after Ockham's views on logic have been set forth.

All the sciences are collections of habits.[6] The object or objects of science are propositions; the subject or subjects, however, are the subjects of such propositions. But as the subject of a proposition is a term of discourse, science is not about things but about terms. A *real* science, however, is about terms which stand for things; logic, on the other hand, is a science about terms which stand for other terms. In other words, logic is about mental contents (intentions) which stand for other mental contents. This view about the nature of sciences, real or logical, has led modern (and some medieval) critics of Ockham to believe that Ockham's view is sceptical insofar as our knowledge extends, not to things, but only to mental contents or meanings. Nothing could be further from the truth. As will be clear later, Ockham's views about *universals* led him to state that nothing universal exists extramentally in the nature of things. Whatever exists outside consciousness

---

[5] Ockham, *Sent.*, II, qq. 4, 5, R.

[6] In the Aristotelian sense, as interpreted by Ockham, a habit is "a quality generated after an act" (*Quodl.*, II, q. 18), which is difficult to lose and which differs from a disposition by being more stable (*Summa Logicae*, I, 55). See L. Baudry, *Lexique philosophique de Guillaume d'Ockham*, Paris 1958, pp. 107-108.

(*extra animam*) is individual or singular, so that any *common nature* postulated to explain the resemblance of members of the same species is to be emphatically denied. Hence, because sciences consist of propositions (usually universal and always containing universal terms), we are obliged to hold that science is about terms or concepts. A real science is about concepts which stand for real things *in rerum natura*; logic, however, is about concepts which stand for other concepts.[7]

In logic, which studies the kinds of terms and propositions of which discourse (as forms of statement and inference) is composed, we must distinguish the *signification* and the *supposition* of terms. Terms of discourse are either mental, spoken, or written. Mental terms are *natural* signs, the spoken or written terms are artificial signs instituted arbitrarily or by human custom. When a term of mental discourse makes something to be understood it can be said to signify it. However, terms of mental discourse sometimes signify things and sometimes signify concepts of the mind. A mental term or concept which signifies a non-mental thing is a term of *first intention*; whereas if such a term signifies a concept of the mind it is a term of *second intention*.

The *supposition* of a term is a characteristic which terms have only when they occur in propositions. When a term stands for its normal referent (significate) it has *personal* supposition. For example, in the statement "man is an animal," man stands for its normal referent. But in the proposition "Man is a species" the term *Man* (whether the concept *man* or the word "man") stands for a concept in consciousness, and is said to have *simple* supposition. Finally, when we have such a proposition as "Man is a word," *Man* has material supposition. This doctrine that concepts or words have different suppositions (i.e., ways of *standing for*) is used with great effectiveness by Ockham in his discussion of universals.

[7] See, for all this, the Prologue to the *Exposition of the Eight Books of Aristotle's Physics*, text edited and translated in P. Boehner, *Ockham: Philosophical Writings*, Edinburgh 1957, pp. 2-16.

It is also necessary to add some words here about the distinction between the syncategorematic and categorematic terms.[8] The latter kind of terms comprises all terms which fall under the categories of Aristotle, i.e., terms standing for substances, quantities, qualities, relations, etc. They are what recent and contemporary logicians call "descriptive" terms. Syncategorematic terms are such as *all, some, none, nothing, only, if, and, or, is,* etc. These terms do not have a meaning by themselves but serve a function in conjunction with categorematic terms. They are what recent and contemporary logicians call "logical constants." The syncategorematic terms cannot signify anything by themselves, but, taken in conjunction with categorematic terms, exercise a certain function with respect to the categorematic terms. For example, "all" does not by itself have a certain signification but, when added to "man," makes the latter term stand for all men.[9] It is fairly clear that Ockham and other logicians of the fourteenth century recognized that the syncategorematic terms are among the principal concerns of logic, and also that the forms of propositions are determined by the syncategorematic terms. In other words, they had the conception of a purely formal logic.

These distinctions are only a few of the complexities of Ockham's logic but they will serve for the purpose of discussing his views on universals. Not only is the doctrine about universals the one with which his name is usually associated, but it is also a central feature of his thought. There is no doubt that some terms are singular in meaning and others universal. The question is whether universal terms have significations peculiar and proper to themselves. As we know,

---

[8] Ockham did not invent this distinction nor the others just discussed. His description of categorematic and syncategorematic terms is standard for the thirteenth- and fourteenth-century treatises on logic. The distinction and terminology come from the grammarian Priscian (about A.D. 500) who attributed it to the "Dialecticians" who are commonly assumed to be the *Stoics*. The special meaning of the *suppositions* given above was not the explanation generally given.

[9] *Summa Logicae,* I, 4.

the medieval philosophers in Christendom in the thirteenth century, as well as most of the Islamic and Jewish philosophers, agreed that the singular thing is the primary reality, and that there is no universal thing outside the human mind existing *apart* from and independent of individuals.[10] Nevertheless, many of these philosophers held that there is a common nature in many individuals which, considered in itself, is neither one nor many, but simply what it is. We find variants of this view in Avicenna, Averroes, Aquinas, Scotus, and others. The universal is, they held, a concept abstracted from individuals of the same species (although "abstracted" must be taken *cum grano salis* in the case of Avicenna at least, since he held that the universal concepts are radiated into human minds from the Active Intellect when these minds were prepared by sense-experience to receive them). Such an abstraction, however, would amount to falsification if either of two things occurred:

a) if the mind took such abstractions for realities having independent extramental existence, i.e., for forms in the Platonic sense.

b) if there were no common nature distributed among the several instances in the world from which the abstraction was made. Hence they concluded that, although there are no universal things existing extramentally and independent of individuals, there is, in individuals of the same kind, a common nature which, considered by the mind in abstraction from these individuals, is universal. The universal concept in the mind must have a foundation in things outside the mind, and

[10] See Avicenne, *Le Livre de Science*, Paris 1955, p. 118; M. Horten, *Die Metaphysik Avicennas*, Halle 1907, pp. 284-302; or Avicenne, *La Métaphysique du Shifā*, Librairie Philosophique M. Doyan, pp. 725-735, Chemin Ste. Foy, Quebec 1952, pp. 21-27 of the 2nd fascicule. The translation is by M. Anawati. See also Thomas Aquinas, *Commentary on the Metaphysics*, I, lect. 10; *de Ente et essentia*, chs. 3, 4; Scotus, *Quaestiones in Metaphysicam Aristotelis*, I, 7, q. 13, n. 17s, n. 23; *Opus Oxon.*, I, 2, d. 42, no. 6, etc. Averroes, *Tahafut al-tahafut*, S. Van den Bergh, London 1955, I, 65, 203, 356.

this foundation can be only the nature common to things of the same kind. It is this view and all its variants which are rejected by Ockham.

In order to avoid misunderstanding occasioned by the term *nominalism* which has been applied to Ockham's doctrine during and since the Middle Ages, we must point out at once that, in a common interpretation of *nominalism*, Ockham cannot be called a nominalist. For some people mean by *nominalism* a view which holds that things called by the same common name (e.g., by a common noun) have only the name in common, that is, that there is no extramental basis for calling a number of things by the same general term.[11] Now, as we shall soon discover, Ockham holds no such view. For while he rejects the whole doctrine of common natures, he holds that the universal concept is appropriately applied to each of a set of individuals if and only if (1) they resemble one another, and (2) if the concept resembles each of the individuals. Before we develop his positive view further, it is best to state his attack on the doctrine of common natures. His positive view can best be called *conceptualism*, insofar as this term carries the implication that universals are concepts, and insofar as it is well understood that such concepts are properly applicable to singular things only insofar as these things resemble one another and insofar as the concept resembles each of them.

Ockham's attack on the doctrine of common natures depends on his rigorous application of the received maxim that *Being* and *One* are mutually convertible, i.e., that whatever exists is one and whatever is one exists. As Ockham understands this maxim, it means that whatever is is numerically one, or that every real thing is numerically distinct from every other real thing. All unity is numerical and all diversity is numerical. There is thus no room for a nature common to several numerically diverse individuals. For if there were a

[11] Cf. H. W. B. Joseph, *Introduction to Logic*, London 1916, p. 31, where this view is attributed to James Mill.

common nature in several numerically distinct individuals, God could not annihilate one individual without destroying all the other individuals of the same kind. Moreover, if a universal were one thing existing in many singular things, the universal or the singular thing could, by the absolute power of God,[12] exist without the other. This is absurd because the universal is supposed to be the essence of the singulars in which it exists.

Ockham's main thought about universals comes out clearly only when he attacks the view of Duns Scotus. According to Scotus, the common nature does exist in singulars, but in a special way. The common nature does not have numerical unity but a kind of unity "less than numerical unity." Now in each individual of a given kind, we find both the common nature (of the kind in question) and what Scotus calls the individuating difference or the *haecceity* (*thisness*). In Socrates, for example, there is the common human nature which is contracted to Socrates by an individual difference which is peculiar to Socrates. This is the principle by which the common nature is individuated. Between the common nature in any individual (for example, Socrates) and the individual difference there is what Scotus calls a formal distinction on the side of the thing. By this mode of expression, Scotus explains, we are to understand that there is a distinction in every individual between its common and its peculiar nature, which distinction exists prior to any operation of our intellect.

In other words, the formal distinction is not made by the discernments of the mind of the observer. It is there in the object before we discern it. Moreover, the distinction is said to be a formal distinction by way of contrast to a real distinction. If two things are really distinct, one can exist either in separation from the other, or one of them can exist without the other existing. But if there is a formal distinction of two formal parts of a given thing (Scotus calls these formal parts

---

[12] Note the use of the principle of divine omnipotence here.

formalities or *realities*), it is impossible, even by divine power, for one to exist without the other.

In sum, in an individual of a kind, the common nature and the individual difference are different from one another but not separable from one another. This was the important part of Scotus' solution of the problem of universals. The universal concept has a foundation in things outside the mind, namely, the common nature in the individuals. This common nature is not numerically one in the diverse individuals. It has a unity, but this unity is less than numerical. Each individual is numerically or really distinct from every other. Yet in order to account for the propriety of applying a universal concept to each of a set of things, Scotus is constrained to adopt Avicenna's notion that, considered in itself, the common nature is neither numerically one nor numerically many, whereas, considered as the common nature of diverse individuals, it has numerical unity with each of these individuals, though it retains its "less than numerical" unity.[13]

Now Ockham rejects this doctrine mainly on the following grounds: If a and b are really (i.e., numerically) identical, whatever is truly assertible of a is truly assertible of b and conversely.[14] Also "wherever there is any distinction or non-identity, contradictory predicates can be verified of the distinct things . . . [thus] if a and b are not the same in all ways then . . . 'a is the same as a in all ways' and 'b is not the same as a in all ways' are true; thus 'to be the same as a in all ways' and 'not to be the same as a in all ways' are verified of a and b.[15] Now it is impossible for a pair of contradictory predicates to be verified of any terms unless the things for which these

---

[13] For this account of Scotus' views see, e.g., M. J. Grajewski, *The Formal Distinction of Duns Scotus*, Washington, D.C. 1944, Catholic University of America Philosophy Series, XC, 93 ff.

[14] This definition of identity, often attributed to Leibniz, actually goes back to Aristotle's *Topics*, VII, 151^{b}1–152^{b}35. Cf. also Thomas Aquinas, *S.th.*, I, q. 40, a. 7 ad 7um. "Quaecumque sunt idem ita se habent quod quidquid praedicatur de uno, praedicatur de alio."

[15] *Sent.*, I, d. 2, q. 1, D.

terms stand are distinct (numerically)."[16] For all pairs of mutually contradictory predicates are on the same footing, that is, there are no degrees of contradictoriness. Soul and not-soul, body and not-body, donkey and not-donkey, God and not-God, being and not-being, all these are pairs of contradictory predicates and the repugnancy of any one pair is equal to that of any other. Moreover, if, in order to prove two things numerically distinct, it would not suffice to verify contradictory predicates of them, then "every way of proving a distinction of things in the creation would be destroyed, because contradiction is the most powerful way of proving a real distinction of things from one another."[17] From all this, Ockham concludes that if we can assert something of *a* which we must deny of *b*, we may conclude that *a* and *b* are really different things. Hence, the common nature must be really distinct from the individuating difference. From this it follows that Scotus' attempt to explain the basis of universal concepts fails. For Ockham, whatever things are discernible are different numerically, and therefore separable, at least by the absolute power of God.

The doctrine of common natures, according to Ockham, arises from three main sources. First, the wrong question has been asked. Instead of asking "How does the universal or common become singular or individuated?", we should ask "How can anything singular become universal?"[18] For, as everything in nature is radically and originally singular,[19] the problem is to explain how conception (which is a singular event of consciousness) can function as a universal term naturally capable of signifying a number of things. In the second place, it was always assumed that, in order to account for the resemblance of things, something distinct from those things

---

[16] *Ibid.*

[17] *Sent.*, I, d. 2, q. 6, E.

[18] *Sent.*, I, d. 2, q. 6, Q. Cf. *Tractatus de Principiis Theologiae*, attributed to Ockham, ed. L. Baudry, Paris 1936, p. 60.

[19] *Sent.*, I, d. 2, q. 6, O, P, Q; *Expositio Aurea*, lib. praedicab. proemium.

had to be invoked, whereas it is possible that this resemblance can be explained without any *tertium quid*.[20] Finally there is the doctrine of abstraction, derived from Aristotle and adopted by many of the medieval philosophers. According to this doctrine, universal concepts arise by abstracting a common nature from the observed resembling individuals. Although, so the doctrine goes on, this common nature cannot exist apart from the singular things of which it is the essential form, it can be *thought* apart from such individuals. According to Ockham, this is impossible: "That *a* and *b* are one thing, that *a* is not really distinguished from *b*, and yet that the intellect divides *a* from *b*, by thinking of *a* and not thinking of *b*, or conversely, is impossible."[21] Doubtless there are in nature many mutually distinct things which are united into one composite, such as matter and form, substance and accident, etc. Of such things we can truly say that the mind can separate or divide the composite into its constituents. For these constituents are really different things united into a composite.[22] Each can exist apart from the others, at least by divine power. For, since God's power is limited only by what is self-contradictory, whatever He *can* do is at least logically possible. We can conceive as separate what God can separate. The mind can abstract only what is capable of separate existence. And since the common nature of the abstractionist is, on his own hypothesis, not capable of separate existence, it cannot be conceived as separated. The idea that such was possible is one which contributed to the plausibility of the doctrine of a common nature.

Ockham's own solution to the problem of universals can now be understood. There are no common natures, but everything in nature or in the mind is individual or singular. The only absolute realities are, therefore, substances and their qualities. In terms of substances and qualities, we are able to

[20] *Sent.*, I, d. 2, q. 6, EE; *Summa Logicae*, I[a], 17; *Expositio Aurea*, lib. praedicab. proemium.
[21] *Sent.*, I, d. 2, q. 3, H.   [22] *Ibid.*

explain how individual things and individual qualities constitute a basis for the formation of universal concepts. The explanation of resemblance, given in several places in Ockham's writings, is very clearly stated in his *Commentary on the Sentences* and in his *Sum of Logic*. If two individuals are alike, say Socrates and Plato, it is not necessary, nor is it possible, to say that they are alike *in* something or *in* some things. For there is no universal thing, no common nature, *in* which they are alike. Socrates and Plato are alike (in some respects, exactly alike), but they are alike only by means of their own intrinsically individuated selves, as far as their substantive resemblance is concerned. Or they may be alike in virtue of one or more of their accidents. Yet both their substances and their accidents are radically individual. But here it is preferable to let the author speak for himself: "It must be allowed that [Socrates and Plato] are alike *by means of* some things because they are alike *by means of* their forms and their very *own selves*";[23] again, "Strictly speaking, it should not be admitted that Socrates and Plato are alike in something or in some things, but rather that they are alike by means of some things, because they are alike by means of themselves. Socrates is like Plato, not *in* something, but *by means of* something, because he is like Plato by means of himself."[24] It is true that Socrates and Plato are numerically different and specifically alike. But since there is no opposition at all between specific likeness and numerical difference, there is no reason why two individuals cannot resemble (specifically) and differ numerically.[25]

[23] *Summa Logicae*, I, 17.
[24] *Sent.*, I, d. 2, q. 6, EE. The text: "De virtute sermones non debet concedi, quod Socrates et Plato in aliquo conveniunt nec in aliquibus, sed quod conveniunt aliquibus, quia se ipsis; et quod Socrates convenit cum Platone non in aliquo, sed aliquo, quia se ipso." See, for an excellent discussion, P. Vignaux, *Dictionnaire de théologie Catholique*, Tome 11, Article *Nominalisme*.
[25] "Inter convenientiam specificam et differentiam numeralem nulla est penitus oppositio." *Summa Logicae*, I, 17 ad 7[um] (ed. P. Boehner, St. Bonaventure, N.Y. 1951, p. 53).

The basis of the universal concept in the mind is the resemblance which individual substances (or individual accidents) bear to one another. The detailed explanation of how this concept arises from experience is given by Ockham in many of his works. The problem is complicated by the fact that Ockham presented three different theories of the nature of universal concepts, among which he ultimately made a choice. The concept is either a "fictive" creation of the mind, or a quality of the mind distinct from the act of knowing, or finally the act of knowing itself. These alternatives need not concern us at present, but it is necessary to mention them because some of Ockham's detailed statements are in terms of the first theory which he later abandoned entirely. The mind notices intuitively a singular thing existing outside the mind and forms in itself, or receives in itself, something which is similar to the external object which is the object of this intuitive noticing. This similitude of the object can serve as a sign in consciousness of the object outside; and, if separated from the accidental features which *de facto* distinguish one object from another, this similitude can stand for all the objects which resemble the object which initially produced the similitude.

In other words, the universal concept, if it is specific (in contrast to generic) can theoretically be abstracted from a single individual of the species. In virtue of the fact that the concept resembles the individuals, just as they resemble one another, it can stand as a natural sign for those individuals. Universal terms of oral or written discourse are artificial signs introduced by custom or by arbitrary choice. But the natural universal in consciousness is produced there by the object without any activity (voluntary or involuntary) of the mind.[26] It is its *resemblance* to each of a number of singulars that provides the nonarbitrary element, that is, that relates the concept to its appropriate referents. Since there is nothing in a universal

[26] *Sent.*, II, q. 25, O.

concept which makes it more appropriate to one of a set of exactly resembling individuals than to another, Ockham says that it stands *indifferently* or *confusedly* for any of them.[27]

"Thus to have the confused intention [i.e., concept] of man is nothing other than to have an intention [i.e., concept] by which one man is no more understood than another, and this is nothing other than that such a cognition is no more a similitude of one man than of another man. Still by such a cognition a man is better understood than is a donkey. This is the case because such a cognition by some mode of assimilation is more assimilated to a man than to a donkey. Thus I say that an infinite number [sc. of men] can be understood by such a confused cognition. . . ."[28]

Universals, then, in the first instance, are not words but concepts. They are not arbitrarily imposed on things, but are natural signs existing as qualities of the mind, produced there by the natural operation of perception and thought, and contain only that feature of a particular individual which exactly resembles another individual. The resemblance of the concept to the individuals for which it stands makes it a natural sign, that is, renders it capable of standing *naturally* for its referents. The fact that the concept contains only one, indeed only the *essential* feature of the individual, renders it suitable to stand for any one of a set of resembling individuals rather than one in particular; hence, it is what Aristotle defined a universal to be: a sign naturally apt to be predicated of many.

Accordingly, we can say that *man* is common to men, pro-

---

[27] See *Sette Questioni inedite di Occam sul Concetto*, ed. Francesco Corvino, Rivista Critica di Storia della Filosofia, Anno x, Milan 1955, pp. 265-289. These are the questions on concepts from Ockham's *Quaestiones in Libros Physicorum*. See esp. pp. 284,[47]–285.[63] Note that Ockham has a special meaning for *confused* (as in *conceptus confusus* and similar expressions). A universal concept, since it is simple (not composed) is not cognized confusedly (*Expositio super Libros Physicorum*, I, ad textum 4, quoted by Boehner, *Traditio*, 1946, IX, 309, n. 6). His point is rather that "I call a concept confused by means of which the intellect does not distinguish one thing from another" (*Sent.*, I, d. 2, q. 7, P).

[28] *Sette Questioni inedite*, see above, n.27.

vided that we realize that *man* is taken in simple or material supposition. If we take *man* in personal supposition, *man* is not common. This is because *man*, when it supposits personally, stands for individual men. There is no common nature to which the term might refer. So that while it is true that the concept refers naturally and *confusedly* or *indifferently* to every, some, or any man, its referent or referents are always individuals.[29]

We may now turn to some further details of Ockham's logical theories. His conceptualism leads him to apply the principle of Parsimony to many of the concepts of science which, by other authors, had been viewed as referring to special realities. Although cognition of universals often achieves definitions of the essential natures of things, this is not always the case. We must distinguish between definitions which provide us with a *real essence*, a *quid rei*, and those which provide us only with a *nominal essence*, a *quid nominis*, for many terms of discourse are only convenient abbreviations for complexes of propositions.

Sometimes these compendious ways of speaking lead us to believe that the word stands for a single absolute thing. This supposition must be avoided. The abstractions of geometry and physics must not be mistaken for features of the world. Accordingly, Ockham provides analyses for the concepts of *motion*, *time*, *place*, etc., which, to his satisfaction at least, reduce the ultimate furniture of the world to substances and qualities, and thus he deliberately impoverishes ontology. The term *motion*, for example, does not stand for a reality distinct from individual substances or qualities, a sort of incomplete reality. It is only a convenient abbreviation for a complex of statements. The following, written by an unknown contemporary, summarizes Ockham's doctrine well: ". . . motion does not have a real definition but only a nominal one, and in its definition many affirmations and negations are posited.

[29] *Sent.*, I, d. 2, q. 6, EE.

For example, in local motion it is said that local motion is [simply] for a movable thing to be in some place and immediately before for it to have been in other infinitely many places such that it is never true to say of these places twice: 'the movable thing is in this place and immediately after this it will be in the same place.' "[30]

In a word, motion, place, time, etc., are reducible without remainder to absolute things, namely substance and quality, because the terms *motion, place, time* are abbreviations (introduced for embellishment or compendiousness) for complexes of statements. A complex of statements is "held together" only by syncategorematic expressions which by themselves signify nothing. It would not be too anachronistic to suggest that these terms of physical science are, for Ockham, logical constructions. But we must at once be on our guard against supposing that such logical constructions are based on what some of our contemporaries call sense-data. The ultimate constituents of reality for Ockham are substances and qualities which have an extramental existence and which are certainly not sense-data or merely sensible qualities, or anything of the sort. Ockham is a thoroughgoing realist in such questions, as will be seen from his discussion of the psychology of perception. His guiding principles in dealing with the abstractions of physics such as motion are simply these: (1) Whatever can be saved by supposing *motion* to be the name of an absolute form can be saved equally well or better by supposing that word to stand for a complex of statements involving substantive and qualitative terms and logical constants. This is another use of the principle of Parsimony. (2) If motion were an absolute thing, God could create and conserve it without creating or conserving anything else, which is absurd. This is an application of the doctrine of divine omnipotence.

The theory of demonstration which Ockham develops in his

[30] *Tractatus de Principiis Theologiae*, ed. L. Baudry, p. 93. Cf. Ockham, *Sent.*, II, q. 9, H.

logical writings and which he presupposes in his metaphysical discussions is based on Aristotle's logical works. Ockham takes the term "demonstration" very strictly, as do other Scholastics of the thirteenth and fourteenth centuries. "By demonstration all who speak correctly about the subject mean a syllogism composed of two necessary premisses which are known through themselves by means of which a conclusion is known which otherwise would have been unknown."[31] (In its most powerful form, a demonstration is one whose premisses are both universal and affirmative.) Consequently, a demonstration is to be radically distinguished from all other sorts of inference, even from formally valid inferences whose premisses are known for certain. It is necessary to add this for two reasons: First, in order to distinguish probable or persuasive arguments from those which are definitively and unqualifiedly conclusive; second, to differentiate demonstrations from the scientific arguments by which the premisses of demonstration are established. This second point can be illustrated by an account of the way in which the principles of science are acquired.

Taking up the somewhat concise and even obscure remarks of Aristotle on induction,[32] Ockham holds that some propositions can be known with certainty only through experience. Thus we want to know that one thing causes another in order to obtain a general causal principle. Suppose that we are trying to establish that all herbs of a given species are helpful to anyone who is feverish. This proposition cannot be syllogistically inferred from any better known propositions. The knowledge that it is true is derived from what Ockham calls intuitive cognition, i.e., from direct experience. Indeed, many such intuitive cognitions are required. For I observe that health is restored to a feverish person after he eats such an herb. Now if I have removed all other possible causes of his restoration

---

[31] *Summa Logicae*, III, II, I. Compare *Sent. Prol.*, q. 6, D.
[32] Aristotle, *Posterior Analytics*, II, 19, 99^{b}15–100^{b}17; *Metaphysics* A, 980^{b}25–981^{a}12.

to health, I can know with certainty that this herb caused the return of his health, and thus I have experimental knowledge of a cause. In order to proceed from this single case to the general proposition, I must also know with certainty that all individuals of the same kind have such a nature as to have a determinate and fixed effect on objects of a determinate kind. In other words, I must know that every agent of a given kind can produce an effect of the same kind. Now the two propositions—(1) This herb healed that sick person, (2) all things of the same kind are equally effective—suffice for establishing the proposition that all herbs of the kind can heal persons afflicted with fever. The argument is logically conclusive, but it is not a demonstration because (a) one of the premisses is contingent, and (b) the other premiss provides an *extrinsic middle term*, i.e., one so general that it does not especially pertain to the specific subject matter under discussion. In genuine demonstration, the middle term must be immediately pertinent to the predicate of the conclusion. Thus, while induction is a formal implication, it is not a demonstration. It is worth emphasizing that Ockham everywhere insists that the principles of natural science are not only indemonstrable, but are ultimately and ineluctably dependent on experience. The singular propositions on which natural science depends are evident, but are not self-evident.[33]

Science consists of demonstrations whose ultimate premisses (excepting mathematics) must be based on experience. But we must add some further qualifications about the character of these premisses. We cannot state them in categorical form for, strictly speaking, we cannot show conclusively that any finite cause brings about a finite effect. Since God can do anything, the accomplishment of which does not involve contra-

[33] This account is based on *Sent. Prol.*, q. 2, G-O; *Summa Logicae*, III, II, 10. See P. Vignaux, *Le Nominalisme au XIVe siècle*, Montreal 1948, pp. 65ff.; D. Webering, *Theory of Demonstration According to William Ockham*, St. Bonaventure, N.Y. 1953, p. 161; E. A. Moody, *The Logic of William of Ockham*, New York 1935, pp. 239ff.

diction, He could bring about any effect on the occasion of an event which we regard as its cause but without using the event as His cooperating instrument.[34] Hence we must always couch scientific principles thus: "All A's are effective of B," i.e., "All A's *can* produce B"; and not thus "All A's produce B." Of course Ockham does not suppose that all second causes are only occasions for the exercise of divine power. He simply holds that all natural scientific judgments presuppose the common course of nature (*suppositio communis cursus naturae*). But the qualification is crucial as we will see when we come to discuss the more sceptical views of Ockham's younger contemporaries.

Ockham's psychological theory is naturally introduced by the point just made, for in it the question arises whether God can cause evident knowledge of the nonexistence of a substance or quality. Although Ockham's answer to this question has been one of the main sources of the charge of scepticism which was brought against him,[35] it has usually been misunderstood. We must, therefore, begin by understanding the foundations of knowledge according to Ockham's teaching.

The grasp of, and assent to or dissent from, a proposition presupposes that the terms of the proposition are grasped and understood. According to Ockham, this requires that there be an intuitive cognition, both sensitive and intellectual, of a presently existing object. Normally, an object present to sense causes an act of perception which lasts as long as the object is present, for "Nothing can be known in itself naturally unless it is known intuitively."[36] As a result of such intuitive cognition, we can also have *abstractive* cognition. But because abstractive cognition abstracts from existence or nonexistence, it is not possible to know with evidence by abstractive knowledge that something exists or not.[37] Intuitive cognition can be

[34] *Sent.*, II, q. 5.

[35] Both by Luterell (then Chancellor of Oxford) and the *Magistri* of Avignon (and by modern and contemporary critics).

[36] *Sent.*, I, d. 3, q. 2.   [37] *Sent. Prol.*, q. 1.

had, not only of objects external to the mind, but also of one's own mental states. For I have an intuitive cognition of my own cognitions, volitions, delights and sorrows, etc., that is, of all that which a man can experience in himself.[38] One does not experience or cognize himself as being an intellectual substance. In other words, no one has an intuitive cognition of himself as an immortal soul which informs his body as a substantial form. The important point here is that knowledge of the contingent facts about the world or one's own states presupposes an intuitive grasp of things, for intuitive knowledge is that by which one is able to know whether or not a thing exists.

Now is it possible for a person to have an intuitive cognition of something if no such thing exists?[39] And, if so, does this in turn mean that I can have evident knowledge that such a thing exists when it does not exist? It is important to distinguish these questions. God can, by His absolute power, cause an intuitive cognition which would naturally be caused by an object, because whatever God can produce by the mediation of secondary causes, He can produce and conserve without the secondary causes. Moreover, God can cause a *belief* that an object exists which does not exist. But God cannot cause an *evident knowledge* that an object exists which does not exist, for this is a contradiction in terms, namely, that we have evident knowledge that something exists which does not exist. Hence, if God causes supernaturally the experience of an object which does not exist, and we are able to have any evident knowledge in this case, it will be that such an object does *not* exist. Hence, although God can produce experiences in us which normally are produced by objects, He cannot

[38] *Sent. Prol.*, q. 1.

[39] *Quodl.*, V, q. 5, and VI, q. 6 are translated in R. McKeon, *Selections from Medieval Philosophers*, New York 1930, II, 368-375; see also Boehner, The *Notitia Intuitiva* of Nonexistents according to William Ockham, *Traditio*, I, 223-275 (which includes an edition of *Sent.*, II, qq. 14-15); L. Baudry, *Lexique philosophique de Guillaume d'Ockham*, Paris 1958, article, *Notitia*; cf. Ockham, *Sent. Prol.*, q. 1.

make us *know* what does not exist, but only produce an act of belief. The fact that evident knowledge is naturally caused by an intuitive notice and *also* by the object causing this notice, does not imply that the intuitive notice, *by itself*, must cause such evident knowledge. The *notice* is only a partial cause and so, without the object, need not and cannot cause evident assent.

It must be admitted that Ockham has several lacunae in his account of perception which were certain to cause trouble, and, as a matter of fact, were partially responsible for the scepticism of some of his younger contemporaries. For the question arises, how do we distinguish an act of belief from an intuitive cognition? According to Ockham, intuitive cognition and all forms of abstractive cognitions are different from one another. Intuitive and abstractive cognitions differ intrinsically: *seipsis different*.[40] But, as Baudry has observed,[41] we are not told how we know that God has miraculously produced an act of belief in us and not an intuition of an object. Moreover, Ockham sometimes speaks as if the cognition of our inner states were more evident than any other cognition, which might be interpreted to mean that the cognition of objects external to ourselves is not beyond doubt. Perhaps, as Baudry suggests, a more careful analysis of texts will reduce or eliminate some of these difficulties. Or, perhaps, the immediate character of our cognition of psychic states puts them beyond question.

As matters stand, it would appear that the doctrine of divine omnipotence sometimes gets in the way of Ockham's insistence on the primacy of intuitive cognition. Ockham wanted to insist on the primacy of knowledge of the singular thing for at least two reasons: (1) It would provide support for his attack on common natures: if the only extramental realities are singular things and if universal concepts are

[40] *Sent. Prol.*, 9.1, GG; see, for this point, E. Hochstetter, *Studien zur Metaphysik und Erkenntnisehre Wilhelms von Ockham*, Berlin 1927, pp. 66-67.
[41] L. Baudry, *Lexique philosophique*, *op.cit.*, p. 177.

derived from singulars and refer only to singulars, it is necessary to insist on a direct and immediate knowledge of singular things. (2) A direct intuitive knowledge of external reality avoids any intermediary between objects and our cognition of them and so avoids the sceptical consequences Ockham saw lurking in the notion of intelligible species. However, the doctrine of divine omnipotence allows the possibility of creditive acts regarding objects when there are no such objects. This allows the possibility of a psychological certitude which is different from the certitude of evidence but which cannot be distinguished from it by any intrinsic marks.

There are other problems of a similar sort when we turn attention again to Ockham's views about the cognition of causal connection. We have to distinguish between the problem of discovering causal connection, assuming the *natural* course of events, and the same problem, assuming supernatural intervention. The first problem depends for its solution partly on the meaning of *cause*. The intrinsic causes of a physical thing are its matter and its form. The extrinsic causes, the efficient and the final causes, are conceived as follows:

Sometimes Ockham defines the efficient cause as follows: "all that which, being posited, another thing follows, is the cause of that other thing,"[42] or more precisely, "That is the cause of something which, not being posited, the thing does not exist, and, being posited, the thing exists."[43] If this were not a correct description of *cause*, there would be no way to know that something is the cause of another thing. In some passages, Ockham adds that the cause must be brought near to the object in which the effect is to be produced, and that the occurrence of the effect must be instantaneous.[44] Why does Ockham hold that this is the only way to discover that one thing causes another thing? Have not philosophers held

[42] *Sent.*, I, d. 11, q. 3, N.
[43] *Expositio in Libros Physicorum*, fol. 123c, 203a, quoted in L. Baudry, *Lexique philosophique, op.cit.*, p. 36. Cf. *Sent.*, I, d. 45, q. 1, D.
[44] *Sent.*, II, q. 2, G; q. 5, K; *Summulae in Libros Physicorum*, II, 9.

that a complete knowledge of a thing would comprise knowledge of its causes and effects? Does not Ockham's view amount to reducing efficient causation to regular succession? These are all questions which are suggested by Ockham's description of "cause," and we must attempt to answer them in order to place him in his proper historical perspective. Once again, it is necessary to keep in mind the theological doctrine of divine omnipotence which always casts its shadow over everything that Ockham says as a philosopher.

Ockham states that something is perfectly cognized if nothing that is predicable of it is unknown.[45] But there are two kinds of perfect cognition: in perfect nonpropositional cognition of a thing a knowledge of its intrinsic causes suffices, that is, a knowledge of its matter and form or its integral parts. In perfect propositional cognition of a thing, it is necessary to know from how many causes it arises and from what causes it arises and what are its first and proximate causes.[46] Now the simple (nonpropositional) knowledge of one thing never suffices in order to have a simple knowledge of another thing. We know this from experience; hence, to know a cause *as being a cause* (*sub ratione causae*) presupposes a knowledge of the thing which is its effect. For a cause, insofar as it is a cause, involves a relation, but a relation, as known, presupposes the knowledge of its terms. Hence, to know a cause *as a cause* is the result of knowing its effect; it does not provide that knowledge at the outset.[47]

There is certainly no evidence that Ockham regards causality as nothing but regular succession, though this charge has been made. But it is one thing to believe, as Ockham does, that causes are genuinely efficacious,[48] and another thing to believe that this efficacy is revealed to us in an observation of

[45] *Expositio in Libros Physicorum*, fol. 113a, in L. Baudry, *Lexique philosophique, op.cit.*

[46] *Prol. Sent.*, q. 9, F. [47] *Sent.*, II, qq. 14, 15, YY.

[48] *Quaestiones in Libros Physicorum*, q. 136, fol. 23 B, in L. Baudry, *Lexique philosophique, op.cit.*

causal processes which ineluctably inform us of that efficacy. And Ockham does not believe that any experience does or could yield this. For, speaking strictly, we cannot demonstrate that any secondary causes are efficacious. God could have ordained that He alone would produce combustion whenever a cloth was brought close to a flame, just as He has ordained that He will always infuse grace in the soul whenever certain words (i.e., of the Sacraments) are pronounced. We cannot even prove conclusively that anyone is a man from the fact that we observe that something in human form eats, drinks, etc., as is evident from the case of the angel which appeared to Tobias.[49] It is no wonder, then, that we cannot demonstrate that something is a cause or an effect.[50] All that observation can reveal is concomitance and sequence, and this suffices, assuming no miraculous intervention, to establish causal connection.

If we turn attention to Ockham's natural theology we find his conceptualism and his strict notion of demonstration at work. One of the subjects of metaphysics is *being*. For Ockham this must mean that metaphysics is concerned with the concept of *being*. This is true for several reasons. In the first place, Ockham returned to the doctrine of Averroes that there is no real distinction between existence and essence.[51] In the second place, Ockham maintains that, although *being* (*ens*) is equivocal when applied to objects belonging to different categories, there is a univocal *concept* common to God and creatures. For if there is any natural knowledge of God it must be in terms of a *concept* common to God and creature. Since we do not, in this life,[52] have an intuitive knowledge of God, we do not have an abstractive concept proper to God, for such abstractive knowledge of a proper concept must be derived from an intuitive notice of a thing; hence, if we are to have *any* concept at all in terms of which natural knowl-

---

[49] *Tobit*, ch. 12.   [50] *Sent.*, II, qq. 4, 5, R.   [51] *Quodl.*, 2, 7.
[52] *in statu isto*, as contrasted with the beatified state in after-life.

edge of God is to be possible, it must be in terms of a concept derived from creatures, but unequivocally common to God and creatures. This concept is abstracted by omitting the *imperfections* of the creature, and applies then to both God and creature. This is the univocal concept of *being*.[53]

It is often supposed that Ockham denied that the existence of God can be *demonstrated* (in the strict sense of this word). This is not the case. In his *Questions on the Sentences* (a relatively early work) as well as the *Questions on the Physics* (a later work), Ockham gives the same argument. The existence of *a* being which conserves that which is produced can be *sufficiently proved* (I take this to mean the same as *demonstrated* from the context of the discussion in *Quodlibet*, I, q. 1). For conservation of one being by another requires the sustained coexistence of both the conserver and conserved. There cannot be an actual infinity in a series of conservers each of which is conserved by another being; hence, there must be a first being, unconserved, but conserving other beings.[54] What cannot be proved conclusively is that there is only *one* such first conserver. If we mean by God "something more noble and better than anything other than Himself" we cannot prove conclusively that God exists; hence, we cannot prove that there is, in this sense, only one God. If we mean by God, "that than which nothing is better and more perfect," we can demonstrate that at least one such exists. But we cannot prove that there is but *one* such being.[55] This we must hold only by faith. Ockham adds many other limitations of our natural knowledge of God, for example,

[53] There are, says Ockham, three different sorts of univocal concept: (1) when the things to which the concept applies are exactly similar; (2) when the things to which the concept applies are partially similar and partially dissimilar; (3) when the things to which the concept applies are wholly dissimilar in intrinsic or extrinsic characteristics. Only this last form of univocation applies to the present case. See *Sent.*, III, q. 9, Q, R, S; *Sent.*, I, d. 2, q. 9, K, L, M.

[54] The proof can be found in *Sent.*, I, d. 2, q. 10; in *Quaestiones in Libros Physicorum*, q. 136; and in a discussion in *Quodl.*, I, q. 1.

[55] *Quodl.*, I, q. 1.

that we cannot prove conclusively that God is the efficient cause of all things outside Himself.[56] It is true that we can provide *persuasive* arguments for this proposition. But *persuasions* are dialectical, not demonstrative, arguments. This strict separation of *demonstration* from other forms of argument is characteristic of Ockham's thought.

The importance of probable arguments in medieval thought after 1277 cannot be overemphasized. The concept of a probability, as a precise philosophical notion, is derived from Aristotle, and is known and used by most of the medieval philosophers. But the range of propositions for which only probable arguments are available was considerably extended after 1277. We observe this in Duns Scotus, but it is a tendency which pervades the thought of Ockham. The emphasis on divine omnipotence makes this tendency inevitable. What is a probable argument for Ockham? He gives two definitions, one in his *Sum of Logic*[57] which runs as follows: Probable statements are those which are true and necessary but neither known through themselves, nor known by experience, nor deduced from propositions known through themselves or known by experience, but are such as appear to be true to all, or to the majority, or to the wisest. A probable or topical syllogism, therefore, begins with probable statements and concludes to probable statements. Because the premisses are true and necessary, the conclusion is true and necessary, even if not evident. In the (as yet unedited) *Exposition of the Sophistical Refutations*, we find another definition which is closer to the general usage we encounter in many fourteenth-century authors after Ockham. "The probable is taken in a two-fold sense. Strictly, a probable is something necessary to which the majority or the wise assent, but which is neither a premiss nor a conclusion of a demonstration. . . . Broadly speaking, the probable is said to be that which appears to the many or to the wise to be true, whether it be true or

[56] *Quodl.*, III, q. 3.   [57] *Summa Logicae*, III, I, I.

false. . . ."[58] Now from this second definition we can see that some propositions which are necessarily true can appear to be true while other necessary truths will not appear to be true. For example, certain articles of faith are probable and others (which seem to contain a contradiction) are not. Again, some false propositions can be probable, e.g., certain propositions which contradict some of the articles of faith. Finally, there are propositions which may be true, and which appear to be true, e.g., some undecided propositions in physics or astronomy.

The strict limitations which Ockham imposed on knowledge properly so-called initiated a period of sceptical and critical philosophy which went far beyond Ockham's intentions. This restriction of knowledge also introduced the widespread employment of probable arguments in matters which had hitherto been thought to be knowable in the strict sense. Thus, whereas Ockham follows Aristotle frequently and whenever he can, many of his fourteenth-century successors will attack Aristotle without giving any quarter. The question of Ockham's influence, therefore, is very complex. His conceptualism had a lasting influence into the seventeenth and eighteenth centuries; indeed, it is no exaggeration to say that the British Empirical philosophers from Hobbes to Hume owe their conceptualism to Ockham directly or indirectly. The negative influence, on the other hand, is hard to assess, for while many of the arguments and methods of the sceptical philosophers of the fourteenth century were supplied by Ockham, many of his substantive conclusions were explicitly rejected.

[58] From "Lectures on Ockham" (unpublished) which were delivered by the late P. Boehner; see also L. Baudry, *Lexique philosophique*, *op.cit.*, pp. 216-217.

CHAPTER XII · THE CRITICAL TENDENCIES OF THE FOURTEENTH CENTURY

HE ATTEMPT to use the philosophical concepts and techniques of Graeco-Roman antiquity in the service of a revealed religion was pronounced a failure by many of the philosophers of modern times from the seventeenth century onward. We tend to attribute this, in part at least, to the repudiation of Scholasticism by many of the Humanists of the Renaissance. In this there is a twofold misconception. On the one hand, while Erasmus satirizes the Scholastics unmercifully and Hermolaus Barbarus called them barbarians, we find outstanding Humanists, e.g., Pico della Mirandola, coming to their defense. It is equally clear that essentially Scholastic modes of thought persist among the so-called Paduan Averroists as well as among the Florentine Platonists. On the other hand, the repudiation of the substantive content of Aristotle, as well as a thoroughgoing critique of Aristotelian methods, is to be encountered among the Scholastics themselves. It is not too much to say that the intellectual foundations of medieval thought were undermined effectively by some of the fourteenth-century Schoolmen.

We know enough now, I believe, to say how and to what extent this was accomplished. There is little question that Ockham's influence here, though unintended, was almost decisive. But Ockham was neither the first nor the only philosophical theologian to introduce considerations which made it impossible to use philosophy any longer as the handmaiden of theology.

Once again, the insistence on the absolute power of God in order to make a place for miracles, the crucial point made by Al-Ghazali in the eleventh century, is both historically and logically the cause of the failure of philosophy to serve the interests of revealed religion. We must be on our guard, however, against supposing that there was a complete or general capitulation to criticism. On the contrary, compromises and resistance permitted the Scholastic method to last in the schools far into the seventeenth century.

The most extreme form of the criticism of Scholasticism is that of Nicolas of Autrecourt. He was at the Sorbonne in 1328, and he was undoubtedly one of those against whom the university decrees of 1339 and 1340 were directed. He was summoned to the Curia at Avignon to answer charges of error and heresy and was finally punished in 1347 by the public burning of his writings and the deprivation of his license to lecture.

The information on which we must base our account of his thought is fragmentary. The schedules of his errors contained in the documents of his trial (*The Articles of Cardinal Curty*; it was Curty who conducted the process against Autrecourt), three letters, and fragments of others in the schedules, a theological question about beatification, and part of a polemic against Aristotle, constitute his literary remains. Yet the information supplied by the writings of his contemporaries, including replies to his criticisms of Aristotle by John Buridan, Albert of Saxony, and Thomas of Strasburg, as well as the writings of those whom he positively influenced, enable us to reconstruct his thought with considerable accuracy.

The point of departure for Nicolas is the insistence that there are only two kinds of certitude: the certitude of faith and the certitude of evidence. Philosophy is concerned only with the latter. Now the certitude of evidence has no degrees: either we have this certitude completely or not at all. This certitude has two forms: the certitude about the incomplex and the certitude of the complex, which means the certitude concerning nonpropositional experience and the certitude concerning propositions. Incomplex certitude concerns sensation and inner experience.[1] In a sense to be explained, the basis of both forms of the certitude of evidence is the principle of contradiction: contradictories cannot be true at the same time.

This principle is the first principle, both because nothing is prior to it and because it is prior to everything else. For a proposition is absolutely first if all our certitude is reduced to it and it is not reducible to any more primitive propositions; this is known from the meaning of "first." That all our certitude depends on the principle is proved as follows: Take any proposition of which you say you are certain but which is not dependent on the principle of contradiction. It is possible (that is, no contradiction results from the assumption) that the proposition appears to you to be true and yet is not true;[2] hence, any proposition other than the principle of contradiction (and whatever is reducible to it) lacks the certitude of evidence.

It is true that we are certain of the objects of our senses and of our mental acts. It is also true that this sort of certitude is not propositional.[3] Still it can be justified by the principle of contradiction, for every cognition is a cognition of itself;[4] hence, I am certain of my own existence. That Nicolas thought that the certainty of one's own existence can somehow be established by the principle of contradiction he never states explicitly. All that he says on the subject can be comprehended under the following heads:

(1) every cognition is a cognition of itself; (2) it may be that the intellect has no other act than the act by which it

---

[1] Nicolas of Autrecourt, *Exigit Ordo Executionis*, ed. J. R. O'Donnell, *Medieval Studies*, I (1939), 235, lines 6-9.

[2] Nicolas of Autrecourt, *Epistola* 2ᵃ *ad Bernardum*, ed. J. Lappe, BGPM, Münster 1908, Band VI, Heft 2, p. 7*14-16. Cf. John of Mirecourt, *Questioni inedite di Giovanni di Mirecourt sulla cognoscenza*, Rivista Critica di Storia della Filosofia, Anno XIII (Florence 1958), p. 438, lines 18-21.

[3] O'Donnell, *op.cit.*, p. 235, lines 6-9; p. 280.

[4] Whether volitions were cognitions was discussed at this time, and Hugolin de Malabranca held that every volition is cognizant of itself though directed toward an object. See K. Michalski, *Le problème de la Volonté*, Studia Philosophica, II, Lemberg 1937, pp. 280-281.

comprehends itself and the content of the act; (3) somehow each of us knows that he exists. But the indirect evidence that this sort of certitude is somehow dependent on the principle of contradiction is considerable. In a letter of a certain Giles (Egidius) to Nicolas it is stated, "It is necessary that intuitive cognition be the same as the things cognized, for otherwise it would not follow logically that a thing exists because it appears intuitively."[5] In an anonymous commentary on the *Sentences*, the author, outlining a theory which in other respects sounds like Nicolas', states that one has a certitude, based upon the principle of contradiction, that something which appears to him exists. For it is a contradiction that something appears and does not exist. This means that every cognition is the certitude of its own existence, and that whatever is not its own condition is not known with certainty to exist.[6] John of Mirecourt (who was evidently influenced by Nicolas) includes the certitude of one's own existence under the certitude guaranteed by the principle of contradiction.[7] All this makes it very probable that Nicolas held that the principle of contradiction somehow guarantees the existence of even those nonpropositional experiences which we have. It goes without saying that the ultimate source of this idea, as far as Nicolas is concerned, is St. Augustine.[8] We must be careful not to assume at this stage of the argument that Nicolas thinks he has proved the existence of the soul as the substantial form of the body or as an independent substance. All that can be safely assumed is that cognition certainly exists.

The Scholastics generally divided cognition into three distinct kinds: simple apprehension, the cognition of propositions, and inference. We have seen how simple apprehension is guar-

<hr />

[5] Lappe, *op.cit.*, 18* 28-30.

[6] Anonymous, *Sent.*, II, q. 2. British Museum Harley MS 3243, fol. 123ᵣ, quoted by K. Michalski, *Le Scepticisme et le criticisme dans la philosophie au XIVᵉ siècle*, Cracow 1926.

[7] *Op.cit.*, p. 441, lines 150-166.

[8] Who, incidentally, is actually quoted for support by Nicolas: O'Donnell, *op.cit.*, p. 280, lines 5-8.

anteed. Propositions are cognized with certainty provided that their denials are self-contradictory. A first principle known through itself (that is, known as self-evident) is one the denial of which is recognized as self-contradictory without any knowledge other than the meaning of the terms of which the proposition is composed. In the case of inference (*discursus*), an inference is known with certainty provided that it can be reduced to the principle of contradiction. Thus, in any valid implication, whether syllogistic in form or not, the opposite of the consequent is logically incompatible with the antecedent. Indeed, this practically defines the meaning of valid implication. Now this means that the consequent is really identical with the antecedent or with a part of what is signified by the antecedent. For, if this were not the case, it would not be immediately evident that the antecedent is incompatible with the denial of the consequent. It makes no difference how many deductive steps may intervene between the antecedent and the consequent. In a sorites, the antecedent of the first proposition (or part of what is signified by the antecedent) is identical with the consequent of the last proposition. In a word, valid inference cannot lead the mind from one thing to another and different thing; hence, from the fact that one thing is known to exist, it cannot be inferred by evidence reduced to the principle of contradiction that another thing exists.[9]

Nicolas deduces from this that none of the propositions of Aristotle on natural philosophy are evidently certain. His main points of attack are (1) on the alleged knowledge of substances, both material and immaterial; (2) on the alleged knowledge of causes. Let us begin with substance. We are not immediately acquainted with anything that is indubitably a material substance in Aristotle's sense. It is assumed that "sub-

[9] Lappe, *op.cit.*, 9* 15-20; cf. John of Mirecourt, *op.cit.*, p. 445, 5[a] *Conclusio*. Cf. Anonymi 99, *Sent.*, 3[a] *Conclusio* (British Museum Harley MS 3243, quoted in Michalski, *op.cit.*).

stance" (in this sense) means something other than the objects of the five senses and other than our acts of experience, for substances thus understood do not appear intuitively. Nor can the existence of substance be inferred with certainty from anything which does appear intuitively, for the existence of one thing cannot be evidently inferred from that of another and different thing. Now if material substance cannot be inferred from the contents of intuition, so much the less can immaterial substances be inferred with certainty from that source. This is not all. It does not even appear possible to establish the existence of substance as a probability. For in the case of a probable inference of this kind, we say that *b* probably exists if *a* exists, because previous experience revealed something like *a* and *b* in conjunction or succession. Now since experience never reveals the indubitable conjunction of substance with anything appearing to our consciousness (since it never reveals substance at all), there can be no probable knowledge that there are substances based on anything which appears in our experience. The reader who is familiar with Hume's *Enquiry* or *Treatise* will recognize here an anticipation of the arguments that "reason" in either of the "proper" meanings cannot provide evidence for the existence of substances.[10]

Nicolas states that the argument that there is not even a probability of substances is one which he does not accept but does not know how to answer. He adds that an answer certainly exists, and this has been taken as ironical. Whether or not this is so, we shall observe that in a later writing, he holds that there is a probability that substances exist. We must notice that *probability* meant two different things for the medievals who followed Aristotle's usage here. The usual meaning of the term is applied to a proposition (or propositions) which is accepted by the wise or the majority but which is not obviously true. It is applied to propositions which can

[10] Hume, *Enquiry Concerning Human Understanding*, §xii, p. 12; *Treatise*, Book I, Part IV, §2.

be shown to follow from plausible or generally accepted premisses. It is, however, also used for what happens "for the most part." In other words, the logical meaning of probability as well as the frequency meaning are both employed, though in a primitive sense. We could say, in elucidating Nicolas' meaning, that there is no probability that substances exist in the sense in which probability means a generalization from an observed frequency.

It is important to notice that the dictum (on which all Nicolas' criticism is based) is not merely that the existence of one thing cannot be logically inferred from the existence of another thing. The full statement has come down to us in the fragments of his sixth letter to Bernard of Arezzo and from his introductory lecture on the *Sentences*: (1) The existence of one thing, *a* does not imply that of a different thing *b*; (2) the existence of *a* does not imply the nonexistence of *b*; (3) the nonexistence of *a* does not imply the nonexistence of *b*; (4) the nonexistence of *a* does not imply the existence of *b*.[11] From this we may conclude that it was not his intention to defend a phenomenalism. And, as we shall see presently, his defense of the atomistic doctrine that things may be eternal is based, in part, on the fact that, just as we cannot infer an existence different from appearances, so we cannot infer from experience that things, with which we are not directly acquainted, do not exist.

The critique of our alleged knowledge of substances is combined with a critique of our alleged knowledge of causal connection. Here, or so it seems to the present writer, Nicolas uses logical, theological, and empirical arguments. If an efficient or final cause is different from the effect it produces, the existence of causes cannot be logically inferred from that of their effects nor conversely.[12] This is an immediate conse-

---

[11] Lappe, *op.cit.*, 31* 10-32*3.

[12] See the notice of John of Mirecourt: "Autrecourt satisfactorily deduces the following: That no demonstration or investigation concerning any effects whatever, whence they come, or concerning natural causes what or what

quence of the principle that one thing cannot be logically inferred from another and different thing. Moreover, the fact that experience does not even reveal that there *can* be natural effects would seem to indicate that Nicolas also had in mind the empirical argument that natural causation cannot be directly observed. It is plausible to assume that such was his intention for several reasons. First his own statements in the reply to a critic,[13] second his statements to Bernard in the fifth letter,[14] and third because he probably was familiar with the Islamic doctrine to this effect and certainly must have read Ockham's very similar views on the subject. With all this it would indeed be implausible to think that he had neglected the empirical argument that experience does not exhibit unquestionable instances of causal efficacy. Of course, he appealed also to the theological doctrine that God could be the cause of every natural effect. This, as we have seen, was historically the origin of the whole critique. But it is always worth noticing that the logic of his position in no way depends on the theological argument.

In another work, Nicolas adds a further argument against the attempt to establish natural causation by an appeal to experience. The original form of this argument was perhaps Aristotle's discussion of *induction* of the basic premisses of the sciences.[15] But it was given by Scotus in this form: Whatever occurs in a great number of cases from an unfree cause is the natural effect of that case. Now if we observe in the case of an unfree cause A (i.e., a natural cause) that, however great the diversity of accidents, B attends it in many cases, we can conclude that B is the natural effect of A. This is essentially the *method of agreement* as used to determine the effect of

---

kind of effect they produce or will produce, is in any way evident or certain; to assert the opposite would contradict the divine liberty."

[13] Lappe, *op.cit.*, 29*9.

[14] See my reconstruction of this letter: *Journal of the History of Ideas*, Vol. 3, no. 2 (April 1942), pp. 220-227.

[15] *Posterior Analytics*, II, 19 and *Metaphysics*, I, 1.

a cause.[16] Nicolas observes that this method of argument either begs the question or produces a habit of conjecturing and not certitude. For it is not certain to begin with that a given object is a natural cause. Frequency of past association does not imply such association in the future;[17] hence, either we assume that a given object is a natural cause without proof and argue that something is its natural effect from observed frequency of association—in which case the important question at issue is begged—or we use observed frequencies to tell us both what the cause and the effect are. The latter method will not produce certainty since it depends on the uncertain proposition that what will happen in the future is decisively indicated by what has happened in the past. The affinities of the argument with Hume's will be obvious.

We cannot prove conclusively that any thing is the end for which another thing exists or toward which another thing tends, for God, in virtue of His absolute power, could have assumed the nature of any finite being, a donkey or even a stone.[18] The nobility or worthiness of a thing cannot be inferred from its appearance. The effect of this is, of course, to cut the ground from under the argument that there are evident degrees of worth and that, therefore, a highest degree of worth exists, i.e., God.[19]

It is necessary, in order to discredit the doctrine that man has unerring knowledge of causes or substances outside him-

[16] The formal argument is as follows: There is some characteristic K such that every case of A is a case of K. Assuming completely known instances, suppose x_1 and x_2 are given such that $ACBx_1$ and $ADBx_2$ where D and C are entirely different. It follows that B is the only possible value of K. Therefore, B is the effect of K.

[17] O'Donnell, op.cit., p. 237, lines 39-47.

[18] That no blasphemy was intended here is obvious: Similar statements can be found in St. Thomas, e.g., Sent., III, d. 2a, q. 1, a. 1 and Scotus, Sent., III, d. 3, q. 1, a. 2.

[19] Michalski, La Physique nouvelle, p. 139, "Dicit Petrus Guichart quod de creatura nescimus quanta sit perfectionis et per consequens nescimus, si sit infinitae perfectionis, sicut exemplificat de adamas, antequam visum fuit per experientiam, quod attraheret ferrum."

self, to reveal the fallacies lurking in the standard arguments for such knowledge. Nicolas does this in a number of cases of which I shall cite only a few. In his controversy with Bernard of Arezzo, Nicolas admitted the *formal* validity of the following argument: If an accident exists, a substratum exists. Now whiteness is an accident, therefore there is a substratum for whiteness. But such an argument accomplishes nothing, for to call something an accident means that it has a substratum. Neither experience nor logic can assure us that anything is in fact an accident. Indeed, anything could be proved by this method of argument. Suppose I say that the word *"homo"* means *"hominem esse cum asino."* Then *homo est* implies *asinus est.* Again, he argues that if you take away the word "transmutation" and simply accept the appearances you will see that transmutation cannot be inferred with logical necessity from the appearances. "The appearances are: a thing exists which did not previously exist." Those who interpret change as the transmutation of a substratum (i.e., the loss or acquisition of a quality in a substratum) admit as much. But even this is inferred, because all that appearance reveals is that something or some quality now appears which heretofore did not appear. In any case, a substratum cannot be inferred from the sequence of appearance and disappearance or of existence or nonexistence of items of experience. Thus generation and corruption, defined so as to cover only what is apparent, can mean only the existence after the nonexistence of some items of experience.[20] Hence, if the maxim *ex nihilo nihil fit* means merely the natural order which is found in reality of generation and corruption so that nothing is generated unless something precedes it in existence, it can be accepted. If it means something else, we are not bound to accept it.[21]

There is no doubt that the critique of causation and substance was intended to discredit, not only the natural philosophy of Aristotle, but also the natural theology of Aristotle

---

[20] O'Donnell, pp. 192, 34-193, 5.   [21] *Ibid.*

and the Schoolmen. If we cannot know physical substances and their causal characteristics, we certainly cannot know that there are any separate substances (i.e., God or intelligences or angels). Nicolas nowhere explicitly rejects the Anselmian argument or the causal arguments. But his philosophy implies such a rejection and the theologians who were his contemporaries and who were either influenced by him or who exerted influence on him are quite explicit about this. Holcot,[22] Mirecourt,[23] Jacques d'Eltville,[24] and other fourteenth-century theologians whom Michalski studied held that demonstrations of the existence of God (if "demonstration" is taken strictly) are out of the question. Their arguments were based on the same considerations as those with which Nicolas was concerned.

In some ways, however, Nicolas was more radical than most of his contemporaries as far as we can tell at the present stage of research. For we find a number of fourteenth-century theologians and philosophers who hold that, while demonstration in the strictest sense is not available for establishing natural philosophy, there is still some form of demonstration that will suffice for that purpose. Nicolas, on the other hand, holds that all forms of reasoning short of strict demonstration are merely probable. In his later work he appears to carry scepticism even further so that even demonstration and self-evidence are made to depend on an assumption which is only probable.

In his letters to Bernard and Giles, the discussion is almost exclusively concerned with what is self-evident or demonstrable. In his later *Exigit Ordo*, the question at issue is not merely whether Aristotelian philosophy is demonstrable, but

[22] *Quodl.*, I, MS Pembroke College, Cambridge 236, fol. 195ʳ (Michalski, *op.cit.*).

[23] *Prima apologia*, Johannes de Mirecuria (ed. Stegmüller, *Recherches de théologie ancienne et médiévale*, Vol. 5, 1933, pp. 66-67; *Questioni inedite, op.cit.*, p. 411, lines 167-178.

[24] MS Bruges 181, fol. 35ʳ, *Sent.*, I, d. 2, III, q. 2, quoted by Michalski, *op.cit.*

also whether it is the most *probable* account of natural appearances. The prologue of this work makes it plain that the value of an important part of medieval culture is at stake, as Vignaux has rightly said.[25] Men have spent the better part of their lives in the study of Aristotle and his commentator, Averroes, in which there are almost a thousand allegedly demonstrated conclusions. Now this study turns out to be a waste of time, first, because the demonstrations are defective, second, because the opposites of the conclusions are more probable, and third, because men can obtain what little knowledge is vouchsafed them by studying things according to natural appearances rather than books. Indeed, if the culture of the Scholastics were abandoned in favor of a study of things, men of good will would devote their time to moral matters and the good of the community.

In order to show that Aristotle's conclusions are not only indemonstrable but also less probable than some alternatives, Nicolas attempts to establish the radical thesis that all things are eternal. He does not maintain, of course, that this radical thesis is true, and so does not claim to demonstrate it. It is a matter here of showing that the eternity of all things is more probable than that there is generation and corruption of substances (as Aristotle and his followers maintained). We must therefore attempt to determine how "probable" is to be understood, and how probable arguments can be used to establish the eternity of things. There is an operation of mind distinct from faith (in the religious sense) and also from the certainty arising from experience, self-evident propositions, or propositions deducible from such evidence. This operation results in probable opinion. Such an opinion is probable in relation to our present stock of information, and so its probability can be altered by augmenting or diminishing this stock. Probable propositions may be false, for there is nothing to prevent a

[25] Article: Nicolas d'Autrecourt in Vol. XL of the *Dictionnaire de théologie Catholique*, pp. 569ff.

false proposition from being more probable than its contradictory. The relative probabilities of propositions and their contradictories can be assessed by an impartial judge. Finally, propositions are probable principally in terms of the conception of a final cause.[26] Because arguments from material, efficient, and formal causes have been largely discredited in his critique of Aristotle, Nicolas has recourse only to final causes.

Nicolas assumes along with his adversaries that there is some good in the universe and a conception of good in the mind of man. "The *good* is in the mind for a measure for quantifying beings, and universally for determining the contingent dispositions of things in order that it may be accepted that all entities in the universe are rightly disposed. That is to say, it may be accepted that those things exist if it is good that they exist, and those things do not exist, if it is bad that they exist."[27] Nicolas supposes that nature provides evidence that this principle of the good is true. The adaptation of animals reveals this. Moreover, unless we assume such a principle, no explanation of the world as it is is possible, because there is no reason why this world exists rather than an infinite number of alternative possible worlds.[28]

If, then, there is a principle of good, the universe is so constituted that each thing exists for the sake of others. There is a systematic arrangement of all things and their subordination to a single end. This means that nothing exists unless it contributes to the good of the whole universe. The universe, thus conceived, must always be equally perfect. From all this it follows that the idea of "a corruptible being which is part of a whole everywhere and always equally perfect" contains a contradiction; hence, the principle of good seems to involve the eternity of things.

In order to set up this view in opposition to its rival, it is necessary to show two things: first, that the beginning and

[26] For all this see O'Donnell, *op.cit.*, pp. 203, 204, 187, 184.
[27] O'Donnell, *op.cit.*, p. 185.   [28] Cf. Leibniz.

ceasing of things cannot be proved, and second, that natural appearances can be accounted for more economically on this view that on its rival. In particular, Nicolas will attempt to establish the eternity of infrasensible atoms, of sensible qualities, of imaginable qualities, etc. In a word, all objects must be eternal, even the contents of perception, imagination, and thought.

There are two ways of proving that sensible qualities are eternal: (1) to prove that they cannot begin or cease or (2) to show that all arguments for proving that sensible qualities are generated or corrupted are inconclusive. The latter is the only course open to Nicolas because we cannot infer unperceived continued existence from a presently perceived existence; hence, we need to show that cessation of appearance does not imply cessation of existence. Now it is plain that we cannot infer the nonexistence of whiteness from the fact that it ceases to be perceived. Moreover, a quality which we see and later do not see often reappears in our experience, and nothing prevents us from holding that it is numerically one and the same quality which has appeared, disappeared, and appeared again. We may simply assume with Plato that such qualities do not begin or cease to exist but simply are connected and disconnected with places at different times.[29]

The apparent generation and corruption of things can be explained very simply by the congregation and segregation of atomic particles. Indeed, all the phenomena of apparent change can be accounted for in terms of the motion of atomic particles. The eternity of the soul and its acts present special problems, among others, how the soul is connected with its acts.

Now every theory which attempts to explain the appearances in terms of unobserved entities must make statements about such entities which cannot be completely understood. This is as true of the atomic theory as of the Aristotelian

[29] This is probably derived from the *Phaedo*.

explanation of change in terms of matter, form, and privation. In both theories conditions are stated which are not, in principle, observable. And since of things which do not fall under the observation of the senses we do not have proper concepts and hence do not have demonstration, we must resort to explanation based on remote and extrinsic analogies. Thus, just as the Aristotelians cannot explain the *inherence* of their accidents in substances, so Nicolas cannot explain the connection and disconnection of mental acts with the soul in terms which reflect exactly and faithfully the nature of the connection. Both theories are, therefore, on a par as far as such difficulties are concerned. Both contain terms the meaning of which can be imperfectly grasped by superficial analogy with things with which we have some direct acquaintance.

Nicolas devotes many pages to the elaboration of the details of his atomism, especially to the defense of the vacuum, the constitution of the continuum, and the nature of motion. The most important question for him is the nature of motion, because the doctrine that all things are eternal has to be reconciled with the fact that change does occur. He adopts Ockham's account of motion because he believes that it is consistent with his own view that things are eternal, for if the term "motion" and its cognates have only a nominal definition, "motion" does not refer to any reality. Motion, taken as the name of something real, is unintelligible, for that which is composed of nonentities will be a nonentity. Now if motion were a thing, its parts would be real, but the parts of motion are past or future and so do not exist. If the term "motion" is, on the other hand, the abbreviation for a conjunction of propositions, such a difficulty does not arise, for to say that something moves is simply to say that an object is at one time remote from a given object and later not remote from the given object. Thus, that an object moves means only that it is successively in different positions at different times. Now if relations (including spatial relations) are not distinct from their terms, no new reality exists when an object moves, and no old reality ceases when an object moves; hence, the eternity of things is consistent with the facts of change.

It is hardly necessary to observe that this whole argument depends on the assumption that relations are reducible to their terms. In fact, Nicolas expressly stated as much early in the treatise *Exigit Ordo.*[30] Now this assumption was one of the more extreme views about relations which were held in the middle ages, and can be certainly traced to William of Ockham. Nicolas does not present arguments for this doctrine (at least not in any of the writings which have survived). Perhaps because the arguments were well-known, he felt no need to state them.

When we turn to the positive theory of knowledge, we find Nicolas defending the doctrine that whatever appears to exist exists. If there is any certitude concerning things, then what appears to be *is*, and what appears to be true *is true.* The meaning of this is carefully qualified by limiting the appearances in question to the data of external sensation. This doctrine is defended by deducing it from the principle of goodness in the universe, and by showing that the rejection of the doctrine really assumes its truth. For suppose that it is argued: appearances can be accepted provided that (1) the medium between object and sense is suitable, (2) the sense-organs are in good condition, and (3) the distance of the object is neither too great nor too small. Now any argument which renders all sense-experience doubtful removes the possibility of any certainty. But demanding that the above requirements are fulfilled has such an effect. For either we know by sensation that this is so, in which case sensation is after all a trustworthy source of knowledge, or we do not know that it is so by sensa-

[30] O'Donnell, *op.cit.*, p. 296. ". . . if the problem of motion were terminated and it were shown that motion is not distinguished from the movable thing as far as things go concerning what exists extra-mentally, and if it were shown that relations are not distinguished from terms, then it could be universally concluded that it is probable that all things are eternal . . ."

tion, in which case there is no ground for certainty at all. The details of his theory are very elaborate and difficult, but the upshot of his discussion seems to be that sense-certainty is the only basis of natural knowledge. Some passages suggest that he does not believe that we can have absolute certainty about things. For in order to have absolute certainty we should have to be certain that what is evident is true, and this cannot be proved but must be assumed as a premiss. It is possible, he seems to be saying, that what is evidently and clearly perceived is false. If, then, we are to have any certitude concerning natural appearances, we must accept as a premiss that what is evidently and clearly perceived is true.

If we turn our attention to the status of causal knowledge in terms of the principle of the good and the probabilities which result from its adoption, we find a different point of view from the one expressed in the earlier controversy with Bernard of Arezzo. In that controversy, it will be remembered, Nicolas held that neither logic nor experience provides knowledge that there are or can be natural causes. Under the aspect of probable cognition, the situation is altered, and he allows that probabilities can be induced for active powers existing in things. The examples given to support this probability are the experiences we have of ease and difficulty, which attend our activities.

It must be emphasized, however, that the whole positive system offered as probable is defended only as probable and not as true. This was said to be a "foxy excuse" by his accusers at Avignon, and might suggest that it was Nicolas' real intention to assert propositions as true which were inconsistent with the Catholic faith. The historian cannot determine the hidden intentions of men. But it is worthwhile noticing the logic of the situation. The Articles of Paris of 1277 had condemned the doctrine of two truths, i.e., the doctrine that a statement could be demonstrated by natural philosophy and be opposed to the faith. Whether anyone ever openly advocated such a view is doubtful. It is clear that the fourteenth-century philosophers and theologians who favored the substitution of genuine probabilities for pretended demonstrations were not guilty of the error of the double-truth doctrine condemned by the Bishop of Paris. Pièrre de Ceffons, Mirecourt, and Autrecourt are all clear on this point, and were stating merely that falsehood may appear more plausible than truth. If we circumscribe positive law (including ecclesiastical decisions), some theses opposed to Christian dogmas are more probable than those dogmas.

If we turn our view to one of Nicolas' contemporaries we find a somewhat different point of view on some of the questions at issue. John of Mirecourt's opinions were also condemned in 1347. We are limited in our knowledge here to the publications of his two *Apologies* and some questions from his lectures on the *Sentences*. In the sixth question, Mirecourt asks whether any truth can be known *evidently* by a created being. In order to answer the question Mirecourt gives a description of evidence. Evidence is of two sorts: one is the *special* evidence of the first principle (i.e., the principle of contradiction); the other is the *natural* evidence of our natural capacity. (A) Now *special* evidence has the following features. It is evidence by means of which one assents that something is the case without any hesitation, this assent has been so caused that it cannot be withheld, and it is impossible that the assent occur and what is asserted not be true. In other words special evidence involves an assent free from any suspicion or conjecture or opinion. Because it is naturally caused by necessitating causes, it excludes faith since faith involves an act of will. Because it is impossible that the assent of special evidence be false, natural evidence is excluded. (B) Natural evidence is the evidence by which one assents that something is the case without hesitation; it occurs when the assent is naturally caused in such a way that assent cannot be withheld; and, it is impossible that such assent be mistaken if we grant the general influence of God and exclude miracles.

I have paraphrased as literally as possible because almost every word is of importance. In particular, the assent of natural evidence must be *naturally caused*. If God were to bring about someone's assent by causing such a person to believe what is false, the assent in this case would not be *natural*. Whether God would in fact cause belief in a false proposition is not in question here. The only reason for the qualification is the doctrine of divine omnipotence taken in its absolute sense. Thus as long as assent is brought about *naturally* (and this excludes all miracles and all supernaturally induced beliefs), it is impossible that such assent be mistaken.

Mirecourt now derives the following conclusions: (1) An intellectual created being can know with special evidence all propositions which are self-evident (that is, evident from the meanings of their terms) such as "If a man exists, an animal exists," and can know all propositions which can be deduced by a formal consequence from self-evident propositions. By a *formal consequence*, Mirecourt understands a formally valid argument.

2) An intellectual created nature can know with special evidence that something exists and, in particular, it can know that itself exists. For since if this created intellectual being did not exist, it could not doubt; by contraposition, if such a being can doubt that it exists, it follows that it exists. Likewise, if such a being believes that something exists, it follows that something (sc. the doubting being) exists. This is a form of the argument used by St. Augustine to refute the Sceptics. Mirecourt goes on to outline an argument for the existence of God based on the existence of something. If something exists it is either dependent or independent. If it is independent, then God exists for independence is a *description* of God. If it is dependent, it depends on something, and since there cannot be an infinite regression of dependent beings, there must ulti-

mately be an independent being, so that God exists. But since it is not evident that such an infinite regression is impossible, Mirecourt does not accept this argument as conclusive.

3) It can be known with special evidence that any proposition which follows logically from self-evident propositions is evidently and necessarily true. For it is unqualifiedly evident that, if P is evident and if P *implies* Q is also evident, then Q is evident. The exact wording of the text makes Mirecourt's meaning plain: it is impossible that the logical consequence of a self-evident proposition be false.

4) A created intellect is or can be unqualifiedly certain that it understands, cognizes, etc. Even if God could not produce assent or dissent without the aid of secondary causes, it would still be evident to the soul that it knows, derives, senses, lives, etc.

5) This special evidence is limited. By its means no one can know for certain that something other than himself exists. For example, we cannot know that whiteness exists, that a man exists, that two or more things exist, etc. For it is not evident that there is any contradiction involved that something appears to be thus and so when in fact it is not thus and so.

6) No future contingent proposition can be known by this special evidence.

7) By means of *natural* evidence (the second sort of evidence) it can be evident to a created soul that whiteness, blackness, etc. exist, that a man or an ass exists, that there are many things, etc.

8) It can even be known by *natural* evidence that there are truths which are not themselves evident. For an angel knows with complete evidence that God is Triune and the angel also knows that a human being believes that this is true. Thus the angel knows that a proposition is true which is not evident to someone who believes it.

In the first apology, Mirecourt makes his intentions plain. He does not intend to deny any experience or any evidence.

He does not mean to say that *natural* evidence is any more open to question than is the principle of contradiction. He merely wishes to say that the existence of God, of natural causes and effects, and the like cannot be established merely on the basis of logically certifiable propositions.[81] We might on any single occasion be mistaken in perception, but not on many occasions.

I have indicated here the character of the critique of natural knowledge in two of the theologians of the fourteenth century. It must not be supposed that these are isolated instances. The articles of Michalski contain texts of many other theologian-philosophers of the period who argue along similar lines. It must not be supposed that the extreme views of Nicolas of Autrecourt were unchallenged. Thomas of Strasbourg attacks Autrecourt's doctrines in his *Sentence-Commentary*, and we find refutations of Autrecourt in John Buridan's *Questions on Aristotle's Metaphysics* and his *Questions on Aristotle's Physics*, in Albert of Saxony, and others. Still, the criticism of Aristotle's philosophy continues into the fifteenth century.

Pierre d'Ailly, a cardinal of the Church, uses the argument which Nicolas had used to discredit the claim of Aristotle. He goes so far as to say that Autrecourt's condemnation was unjust. He began his *Commentary on the Sentences* around 1375 and continued work on it for twenty-five years. His views derive from Ockham, Autrecourt, Holcot, and other theologians of the fourteenth century. The appeal to probabilities is a characteristic feature of d'Ailly's philosophy.

Although each one of my perceptions could be supernaturally caused, it is improbable that all my perceptions are illusory. The occurrence of miracles would lose all significance if there were no natural causes, and miracles would be morally pointless, unless they were infrequent. Hence I can hold that my sensations reveal a world of objects.

But from the strictly theoretical point of view, we must

---

[81] Stegmüller, *Prima Apologia Johannes de Mirecuria*, loc.cit.

admit that God can do anything by Himself that he accomplishes with secondary causes. Hence it is not evident in the highest degree that something other than myself exists. Assuming the common course of nature, evidence of the existence of objects external to myself is available.

There is a degree of cognition that is infallible. This is derived from the principle of contradiction. Not even God can make us err about this first principle; while He could force me to state a contradiction, He could not make me accept it with understanding. Thus, with this highest grade of evidence, I can know that I exist, understand, desire, etc.

We do not in the present life have an absolute, simple concept of God and hence no direct cognition of God. This is connected with another aspect of human cognition. When we know a self-evident proposition we know the proposition rather than what is signified by the proposition. For example, the following proposition is true and even immediately self-evident: "If truth does not exist, it is true that truth does not exist." But we cannot infer from this, as some of the thirteenth-century Scholastics following Augustine had done, that the Truth (God) exists. The inference, that is, from propositions to things is, in general, unjustified, and, in particular, unjustified in the case of the proof of divine existence.

Although "God exists" is, in itself, necessary and even self-evident to the blessed who know God face to face, it is not evident to us in the present life that this is the case. Therefore, although Anselm was a devoted man, his arguments were sophisticated and fallacious.

One of the most interesting of d'Ailly's critiques is directed against Aristotle's argument for the existence of God taken from motion. D'Ailly points out that a captious debater could argue as follows:

1) It is not unqualifiedly evident that something is moved; movement may be only apparent. (This recalls an argument of Autrecourt.)

2) Even if we grant that an object is in motion, we do not have to grant that it comes from some other object.

3) Granted that all motion is caused from another thing and granting that there is no infinite series of movers we cannot infer a first unmoved mover. For the captious opponent could say that the first mover is unmoved for the present but not absolutely unmovable.

4) We cannot exclude the possibility that there is a circularity of causes and effects, i.e., A causes B, B causes C, and C causes A.

5) We cannot be sure that there is no infinity of essentially ordered causes. For God by His absolute power could create such an infinite series.

6) Moreover, the newness of things cannot be inferred from appearances. (Nicolas of Autrecourt may be the source of this.)

7) The argument that if something exists anew it was produced is not evident.

8) It is very difficult to explain what it means for one thing to be *from* another thing or to be effected or produced by another thing.

From all this it is clear that the doctrine of Aristotle ought to be called opinion rather than knowledge. There are few if any propositions of Aristotle that have been demonstrated. Those who adhere to Aristotle's authority with excessive tenacity are therefore very reprehensible. Pierre d'Ailly allows that an argument for the existence of God is probable and should be accepted as a good argument. (This is Ockham's argument from conservation of being.)

The essentially new feature of fourteenth-century Scholasticism thus appears to be a more critical attitude toward the methods and doctrines derived from ancient sources and used by philosophers and theologians to investigate nature and to defend and rationalize theological commitments. In some cases the critical attitude amounts to a greater degree of caution, but in the more radical instances discussed in this chapter, it amounts to a rejection of substantive doctrine based on a critique of the methods and assumptions ultimately derived from Greek philosophy, in particular from Aristotle.

It would be misleading, however, to leave the impression that the majority of Scholastics in the fourteenth century went as far as did Nicolas of Autrecourt. Certainly very few carried criticism and Scepticism so far. The important fact for the student of the history of thought is that the fundamental weaknesses and the crucial difficulties in the attempt of religious philosophers in the Middle Ages to form a synthesis of philosophy and revelation were discovered by medieval thinkers using the devices of reasoning which had been developed during the medieval period itself. It is not too much to say that the medieval critique of medieval thought was, from the logical point of view, far superior to its repudiation by the Humanists and philosophers of the Renaissance.

CONCLUSION

THE FOREGOING account of some medieval thinkers has at the least the defects of any general treatment of intellectual history. A selection is bound to reflect the limitations of the author's knowledge and the present state of knowledge of the period. Moreover, in leaving out of account the philosophies of lesser figures it sometimes conceals from the reader philosophical investigations of great importance to subsequent development, or it omits philosophical doctrines which have great intrinsic merit. In the present case, the omission of Meister Eckhart or Nicolas of Cusa illustrates one such deficiency, while the failure to discuss Gregory of Rimini or Albert of Saxony illustrates the other. But as there are so many figures in medieval thought whose discussions either influenced the later history of philosophy and theology or were of perennial value, any historical account which does not discuss every known philosopher or theologian in this period will be lacking in some serious respect. A choice was, therefore, inevitable.

As I said at the outset, medieval philosophy was regarded as ancillary to other concerns, particularly to theology, but also to morals and political theory. Hence we have misguided expectations if we hope to find, in the religious philosophers of the Middle Ages, the sort of independent spirit of inquiry which characterizes many but by no means all philosophers during and after the Enlightenment. Their philosophical conclusions were, for the most part, consistent with what they supposed to be revealed truth. It is true that revelation was often so interpreted that consistency with existing science and accepted canons of reasoning was made easier of accomplishment. But there were limits to interpretation of revelation, and when the limits were reached, philosophical investigations were radically affected. In Islam the result appears to have been the eventual termination of genuinely philosophical enquiry. In Christendom, the result was an increase in the variety of possible or probable constructions of the world but also the realization of the limits of demonstrative reasoning in theological and natural knowledge.

Yet it would be a mistake to suppose that the critical tendencies of some of the fourteenth-century philosophers were accepted on all hands. The schools of the followers of Scotus, Thomas Aquinas, Albert the Great, and others continued into modern times, and there are also new developments of Scholastic thought in the Renaissance, for example, the system of Suarez.

What is more, the philosophers of the seventeenth century owe not only their philosophical terminology but also many of their conceptions, arguments, and conclusions to those philosophical theologians of the thirteenth and fourteenth centuries who did not reject the belief that reason and revelation are fundamentally compatible and who believed that some basic truths common to theology and philosophy are capable of strict demonstration. Thus most of the arguments of Descartes, Spinoza, Leibniz, and Locke for the existence of God as well as many of their views about the nature of substance and causality are derived from medieval sources.

In fact, much of what was consciously or inadvertently rejected of medieval thought was more valuable than what was taken over. This is especially true of the gradual disappearance of medieval logic and semantics. The bad effects of this can be seen, for instance, in the discussions of the nature of universal concepts and the views about causal connection. Little of the discussion of these topics in the seventeenth and eighteenth centuries is better and most is worse than what can be found in the fourteenth century.

It would be a mistake also to suppose that the predominantly theological concentration of medieval thought stifled interest in natural scientific matters. There was a constant questioning of specific natural scientific doctrines of Aristotle and other ancient authors. There were some important observations of natural phenomena and, in fact, some discoveries of importance in optics, magnetism, and biology. The main deficiency of medieval scientific activity was the paucity of experiments. But in this connection two things must be kept in mind. Fruitful experiment in physical science requires the existence of mathematical techniques and specialized instruments of observation (e.g., accurate clocks, telescopes, and microscopes), and these were not available until the seventeenth century.

Although there were antiphilosophical tendencies exhibited by religious men in Christendom, Islam, and Judaism from the earliest times, the view that finally prevailed in Christendom was relatively favorable to philosophy and to science. Since the physical world bears the traces of its Creator, a knowledge of the physical world is to be encouraged in order that man perceive the result of the Creator's activity and so be led to a knowledge of the Creator. Moreover, the Aristotelian ideal of knowledge for its own sake was transformed into the religious quest for the knowledge of God. Human knowledge of the physical world is thus a step in the present life toward the promised beatific vision of God.

The intellectual history of the Western world after the Reformation is, in part, a gradual rejection of almost all the characteristic features of medieval culture. The finite closed world of the medievals was replaced by an infinite universe. A prime mover was no longer required in the physical theories of Newton and his successors. Hume and Kant demolished most of natural theology leaving only the teleological argument in a very attenuated form and this was in turn eliminated by the acceptance of the theory of natural selection. The critique of Revelation by Spinoza and his successors brought about another fundamental change. Men were no longer obliged to reconcile revelation with philosophy and science. Nor, to the extent that this critique was accepted, was it possible to retain revelation by allegorical interpretation. More recent developments in philosophy have raised doubts about the very meaningfulness of ancient and medieval philosophical terminology.

It is not for the historian to pronounce final judgments about whether this general rejection of the main features of medieval thought was altogether sound. In some particular cases, the persistence of the problems or, at least, some things like the problems of medieval philosophers suggests that it was not. But, however this may be, an understanding of the history of thought from the fourth to the fifteenth century is indispensable to an understanding of modern philosophy and science. Moreover, while there is no guarantee that past errors will not be repeated in new and improved ways, a knowledge of what earlier philosophers have said may provide some protection against mistakes. History is what men are assumed to have experienced, and to learn from this experience it is necessary to retain and to reexamine it incessantly.

SELECTIVE BIBLIOGRAPHY

CHAPTER 1: Introduction

Armstrong, A. H., *Plotinus*, London 1953.

Clagett, Marshall, *Greek Science in Antiquity*, New York 1955.

Documents of the Christian Church, New York 1947.

Epstein, I., *Judaism*, New York 1959.

Grube, G.M.A., *Plato's Thought*, Boston 1958.

Jeffery, Arthur, *Islam: Mohammed and His Religion*, New York 1958.

Ross, W. D., *Aristotle*, London 1949.

Wolfson, H. A., *Philo*, Cambridge, Mass. 1948.

CHAPTER 2: St. Augustine

Basic Writings of St. Augustine, ed. Whitney J. Oates, New York 1948.

Gilson, E., *The Christian Philosophy of St. Augustine*, New York 1960.

Portalie, E., *A Guide to the Study of St. Augustine*, Chicago 1960.

Works, trans. in *The Fathers of the Church*, New York 1952.

CHAPTER 3: The Mystical Element in Medieval Thought: Pseudo-Dionysius and John Scotus Eriugena

Bett, H., *Johannes Scotus Erigena*, Cambridge 1925.

Cappuyns, M., *Jean Scot Erigène*, Paris 1933.

John Scotus Eriugena, *On the Division of Nature*, Book I, trans. Charleen Schwartz, Annapolis 1940.

John Scotus Eriugena, translation of *De Divisione Naturae*, IV, 7-9 in R. McKeon, *Selections from Medieval Philosophers*, Vol. I, New York 1929.

Pseudo-Dionysius, *On the Divine Names* and the *Mystical Theology*, trans. C. E. Rolt, Society for the Promotion of Christian Knowledge, 1920.

CHAPTER 4: Anselm and the Beginnings of Scholasticism

Anselm, *De Veritate*, trans. in R. McKeon, *Selections from Medieval Philosophers*, Vol. I, New York 1929.

———, *Proslogium*, trans. A. C. Pegis in *The Wisdom of Catholicism*, New York 1949.

———, *Proslogium; Monologium;* etc., trans. Sidney North Deane, LaSalle, Illinois 1903.

Barth, K., *Anselm: Fides Quaerens Intellectum*, New York 1960.

Damian, P., *De Divina Omnipotentia E Altri Opuscoli* (ed. Paolo Brezzi and Bruno Nardi), Florence 1943.

Gilson, E., *Sens et nature de l'argument de saint Anselme*, AHDL, 9 (Paris 1934), 5-51.

CHAPTER 5: Abelard and the Problem of Universals

Abelard, P., *History of Abelard's Adversities*, Toronto 1954.

Cottiaux, J., *La conception de la théologie chez Abélard*, Revue d'histoire ecclésiastique, Louvain 1932.

Gilson, E., *Eloise and Abelard*, Chicago 1951.

McKeon, R., The Glosses of Peter Abelard on Porphyry, *Selections from Medieval Philosophers*, Vol. I, New York 1929.

The Metalogicon of John of Salisbury, tr. D. D. McGarry, Berkeley 1955.

Peter Abelards philosophische Schriften, Münster i. W., 1919 (BGPM, Vol. 21).

Peter Abelards Theologia "Summi boni," etc., Münster i. W., 1939 (BGPM, Vol. 35).

Sikes, J. G., *Peter Abailard*, Cambridge 1932.

CHAPTER 6: Philosophy in the Islamic Middle Ages

de Boer, T. J., *Geschichte der Philosophie im Islam*, Stuttgart 1901.

de Vaux, Carra, *Le penseurs de l'Islam*, Paris 1921-1926.

Fakhry, M., *Islamic Occasionalism*, London 1958.

Hernandez, M. C., *Historia de la filosofia espanõl*, Madrid 1957.

Munk, S., *Mélanges de Philosophie juive et arabe*, Paris 1927.

Pines, S., *Beiträge zur islamischen Atomenlehre*, Berlin 1936.

Rosenthal, E.I.J., *Political Thought in Medieval Islam*, Cambridge 1958.

AL-FARABI:

Alfarabis philosophische Abhandlungen, Leiden 1892.

Alfarabi's Philosophy of Plato and Aristotle, trans. Muhsin Mahdi, Glencoe, Illinois 1962.

AVICENNA (Ibn Sina):

Afnan, S. M., *Avicenna, His Life and Works*, London 1958.

Corbin, H., *Avicenna and the Visionary Recital*, trans. W. P. Trask, New York 1960.

Goichon, A. M., *La Distinction de l'essence et de l'existence d'après Ibn Sina*, Paris 1937.

Horten, M., *Die Metaphysik Avicennas*, Halle 1907.

Ibn Sina, *Le Livre de Science*, 2 Vols., trans. M. Achena and H. Massé, Paris 1955.

————, *Livre des Directives et Remarques*, trans. A. M. Goichon, Paris 1951.

————, *La Metaphysique du Shifâ*, trans. M. Anawati, Quebec 1952.

————, *Psychologie d'Ibn Sînā (Avicenne) d'Après Son Oeuvre Aš-šifâ'*, ed. and trans. Jān Bakoš, Prague 1956.

Rahman, F., *Avicenna's Psychology*, London 1952.

AL-GHAZALI:

Al-Ghazali, *Tahafut, al-Falasifah*, trans. A. Kamali, Lahore 1958.

Watt, W. M., *The Faith and Practice of Al-Ghazali*, London 1953.

IBN RUSHD (Averroes):

Averroes, *On the Harmony of Religion and Philosophy*, trans. G. F. Hourani, London 1961.

————, *Averroes' Tahafut al-Tahafut*, trans. S. Van den Bergh, London 1954.

Gauthier, L., *Ibn Rochd (Averroes)*, Paris 1948.

IBN TOFAIL:

Ibn Tofaïl, *Hayy ibn Yaqdhan, roman philosophique d'Ibn Thofail*, trans. Leon Gauthier, Beirut 1936.
————, *The History of Hayy ibn Yaqzan*, trans. S. Ockley, revised by A. S. Fulton, London 1929.

CHAPTER 7: THE PHILOSOPHY OF THE JEWS IN THE MIDDLE AGES

Altmann, A., and Stern, S., *Isaac Israeli*, London 1959.
Crescas, *Critique of Aristotle*, trans. H. A. Wolfson, Cambridge, Mass. 1929.
Guttmann, J., *Philosophies of Judaism*, New York 1964.
Ibn Gabirol, *Extraits de La Source de Vie*, trans. S. Munk in *Mélanges de Philosophie juive et arabe*, Paris 1927.
————, *The Fountain of Life*, trans. H. E. Wedeck, New York 1962.
————, *La Source de Vie, Livre III*, trans. F. Brunner, Paris 1950.
Husik, I., *A History of Medieval Jewish Philosophy*, New York 1960.
Maimonides, *The Guide of the Perplexed*, trans. S. Pines, Chicago 1963.
————, *Guide to the Perplexed*, trans. M. Friedländer (Dover), New York 1956.
Saadia, *The Book of Beliefs and Opinions*, trans. S. Rosenblatt, New Haven 1948.

CHAPTER 8: PHILOSOPHY IN THIRTEENTH CENTURY CHRISTENDOM

Bacon, R., *Opus Majus*, trans. R. B. Burke, Philadelphia 1928 and in R. McKeon, *Selections from Medieval Philosophers*, New York 1929.
Bochenski, I. M., *A History of Formal Logic*, Notre Dame, Indiana 1961.
Boehner, P., *Medieval Logic*, Chicago 1952.
St. Bonaventure, trans. in R. McKeon, *Selections from Medieval Philosophers*, New York 1929.

St. Bonaventure, *De Reductionum Artrium Ad Theologiam*, trans. E. T. Healy, St. Bonaventure, New York 1955.

――――, *Itinerarium Mentis In Deum*, trans. P. Boehner, St. Bonaventure, New York 1956.

Gilson, E., *The Philosophy of St. Bonaventure*, New York 1938.

Grosseteste, R., translations of three treatises in McKeon, R., *Selections from Medieval Philosophers*, New York 1929.

――――, *On Light*, trans. C. C. Riedl, Milwaukee 1942.

Kneale, W. and M., *The Development of Logic*, Oxford 1962.

Moody, E. A., *Truth and Consequences in Mediaeval Logic*, Amsterdam 1963.

CHAPTER 9: St. Thomas Aquinas

Aquinas, St. Thomas, *Basic Writings of St. Thomas Aquinas*, New York 1945.

――――, *On the Truth of the Catholic Faith (Summa Contra Gentiles)*, Image Books 1956.

Bourke, V., *The Pocket Aquinas*, New York 1960 (a nearly complete bibliography of English translations of Aquinas is to be found in the introduction to this book).

Gilson, E., *The Christian Philosophy of St. Thomas Aquinas*, New York 1956.

CHAPTER 10: Duns Scotus

Bettoni, E., *Duns Scotus: The Basic Principles of His Philosophy*, Washington, D.C. 1961.

Duns Scotus, *De Primo Principio*, trans. E. Roche, St. Bonaventure, New York 1949.

――――, *Philosophical Writings*, trans. A. Wolter, Edinburgh 1962.

Gilson, E., *Jean Duns Scot*, Paris 1952.

CHAPTER 11: William of Ockham

Hochstetter, E., *Studien zur Metaphysik und Erkenntnislehre Wilhelms von Ockham*, Berlin 1927.

Moody, E. A., *The Logic of William of Ockham*, New York 1935.

William of Ockham, *Philosophical Writings*, trans. P. Boehner, Edinburgh 1957.

CHAPTER 12: THE CRITICAL TENDENCIES OF THE
FOURTEENTH CENTURY

Dal Pra, M., *Nicola di Autrecourt*, Milano 1951.
de Gandillac, M. Patronnier, *Usage et valeur des arguments probables Pierre d'Ailly*, AHDL, 8 (Paris 1933).
Lappe, J., *Nikolaus von Autrecourt*, BGPM 1908.
Vignaux, P., *Nicolas d'Autrecourt* in *Dictionnaire de théologie Catholique*, Vol. XI, Paris 1931.
Weinberg, J., *Nicolaus of Autrecourt*, Princeton 1948.

The Abbreviations "BGPM" and "AHDL" refer to Beiträge zur Geschichte der Philosophie der mittelalters, and to Archives d'histoire doctrinale et littéraire du moyen âge.

NAME INDEX

Abelard, St., 60, 70, 72-91, 177, 180
Abrahams, I., 76
Abraham Ibn Daud, 150
Abubacer, cf. Ibn Tofail
Adelard of Bath, 82, 83
Albert, St., cf. Albertus Magnus
Albert of Saxony, 180, 267, 286, 290
Albertus Magnus, 97, 129, 158, 175, 178, 291
Alexander of Aphrodisias, 95, 137
Alexander of Hales, 158
Alfonso, M., 134
Altmann, A., 102, 103, 106, 143, 145, 146, 147
Amalric of Bena, 49
Amaury of Bène, 49
Ambrose, St., 31
Anawati, M., 244
Anaxagoras, 75
Anmonius, 95
Anselm, St., 32, 58, 60-71, 73, 74, 160, 168, 169, 221, 222, 287
Aquinas, St. Thomas, 6, 23, 45, 70, 87, 97, 99, 108, 115, 117, 118, 121, 129, 130, 145, 156, 158, 159, 170, 171, 175, 182-212, 221, 224, 225, 233, 244, 247, 274, 291
'Arabi of Murcia, Ibn Al-, 105
Arberry, A. J., 111
Aristippus, Henricus, 10
Aristotle, 7, 9, 10, 13-21, 24, 35, 37, 60, 72, 80, 84, 86, 87, 90, 91, 94, 95, 99-102, 104, 105, 108, 109, 113, 128-131, 133-137, 139, 150-153, 156-160, 162, 164, 169-172, 174, 176-178, 186-188, 190, 192, 196, 197, 201, 202, 204, 207, 214, 215, 235-239, 243, 247, 249, 252, 255, 264-267, 270, 271, 273, 275, 277, 278, 286, 288, 289, 292
Amstrong, A. H., 128
Arnauld, A., 34

Ashari, Al-, 95, 96
Astralabe, 74
Augustine, St., 6, 8, 23, 30-44, 49, 50, 62, 65, 66, 70, 77, 90, 144, 159, 160, 164, 166, 169, 194, 197, 207, 269, 284, 287
Avempace, cf. Ibn Bajja
Averroes, cf. Ibn Rushd
Avicebron, cf. Ibn Gabirol
Avicenna, cf. Ibn Sina

Bacon, R., 161, 162, 163
Bajja, Ibn, 108, 125-127
Barbarus, Hermolaus, 266
Basil, St., 48, 49, 55
Baudry, L., 241, 248, 254, 258-261, 265
Berkeley, G., 23
Bernard of Arezzo, 272-276, 282
Bernard de Clairvaux, 73, 76, 77
Boas, G., 239
Boehner, P., 78, 85, 250, 252, 258, 265
Boethius, 6, 10, 58, 60, 65, 66, 72, 77, 80, 84, 157, 174, 175, 177, 178, 183, 203, 204, 211
Boethius of Dacia, 172, 173
Boethius of Sweden, cf. Boethius of Dacia
Bonaventure, St., 39, 69, 70, 72, 164-170, 199, 210, 220, 221, 233
Brunner, F., 147
Buridan, J., 267, 286
Burleigh, W., 180

Carame, 114, 117
Carneades, 31
Chalcidius, 10, 76
Charles the Bald, King, 48, 49
Chartres, 39
Chatelain, 171
Chosroës, 94
Chrysippus, 176
Cicero, 30, 75
Clagett, M., 9, 30, 32